Jenny Geddes,

OR

PRESBYTERIANISM

AND ITS GREAT

CONFLICT WITH DESPOTISM.

BY THE

Rev. W. P. BREED, D.D.

PHILADELPHIA:
PRESBYTERIAN BOARD OF PUBLICATION,
No. 821 CHESTNUT STREET.

WESTCOTT & THOMSON,
STEREOTYPERS, PHILADA.

CONTENTS.

I.

II.

III.

IV.

A WORD TO THE READER.

THIS volume, in the aim and intent of the writer, is much more expository than polemical. Its object is to illustrate the character of, and to call attention to, the service rendered to the cause of God and man by the church system to which we hold, and not to attack other sister evangelical denominations. With them we have no quarrel. On the contrary, when we consider how God has blessed them—how many godly ones have lived, laboured and died among them—how many souls have been converted through their instrumentality, and thus the service rendered by them to our common Christianity—we are constrained to bid them God-speed. At the same time holding, as we assuredly do, that our Presbyterian system comes nearest of all to the scriptural standard, to the pattern showed in the mount, and that it is therefore best adapted for the nourishment and defence of the faith, we desire, as far as we may, to lead its adherents to deeper insight into its validity, to higher admiration of its beauty, and to greater enthusiasm in its maintenance and propagation.

It has long been our conviction that one subject upon which the common mass of Presbyterians need information is Presbyterianism—its distinctive character as an ecclesiastical system, and its history. We are persuaded that a more thorough acquaintance with it would tend, not only to awaken the great body of its adherents from a sleepy assent to its validity, but to powerfully confirm them in their allegiance, and even to enkindle them to enthusiastic admiration. The facility with which, now and then, one and another of its children pass into other Christian folds, the easy carelessness with which parents allow their children to be drawn away from the Church of their birth demonstrate a sad ignorance of the system for which their fathers fought and bled and died. Recognizing other denominations as sound in general evangelical faith, they fail to see that outside of all such questions lies the great question of church government, which, when scriptural, is the divinely-appointed conservator of sound doctrine, and when unscriptural tends to impair, and often sadly corrupts it, and very often betrays it to its foes. While a Presbyterian may himself live a holy life in another fold, he has more to do than simply to live and die safely. He is bound to consider the force of his example upon others; bound to lend his influence to the upholding of that external form of church polity which, while it shields orthodoxy in doctrine from destructive assault, best fosters piety in the heart, and trains it up toward its loftiest ideal.

It is greatly to be regretted that as the sweet chestnut always, so ecclesiastical history is almost always, shut up in hirsute burs—the burs of a rigid scientific treatment—putting it out of the reach of all but the highly cultivated, and generally making its perusal by them more a matter of duty than of pleasure. And among the objects for which the Church should devoutly and ardently pray is the raising up of some Prescott, Motley, Macaulay, Bancroft, or Froude, to clothe her history in the winning forms of a fascinating diction and style of handling, and thus furnish her thrilling facts with wings on which to fly into the welcoming doors of the general mind.

In the mean time, we have put forth this very humble effort to group together some of the facts and principles of our Presbyterianism—not to instruct the erudite or to bring forth new treasures from original sources, but, if we may, to awaken some new interest in at least a few minds among the masses of our people in a subject second to few in legitimate claim to their attention and study. Our book opens and closes with the scene at St. Giles, Edinburgh, in which Jenny Geddes and her stool figured so conspicuously. And as this scene exhibits the culmination of a long, sharp conflict between Church and State, we have first drawn an outline of church government as generally accepted by Presbyterians, and of the relations that properly subsist between the Church and the State, at once separating and uniting them; adding also a sketch of Scottish church-history—the story of that memorable conflict in which Presbyterianism fought so manfully the battle of both the Church and the world. With painful consciousness of the imperfection of the work attempted, the writer still hopes that it may prove the seed of some salutary fruit.

PHILADELPHIA, Nov., 1868.

JENNY GEDDES AND HER STOOL.

JENNY GEDDES.

I.

JENNY GEDDES AND HER STOOL.

WRITERS of human annals have been accustomed to divide their subjects into two general classes. The one comprises those which are truly and in themselves in a high sense historic, affecting widely and powerfully the interests of men and nations. The other embraces agencies and events whose significance is too trivial, whose influence is too feeble or plays in too narrow a circle to entitle them to any marked place upon the historic page.

It is evident, however, that events exceedingly minute in themselves may, by the force they borrow from circumstances, the principles they symbolize, the incidents to which they give rise, or the interests they come to affect, emerge into true historic dignity.

Thus history has not disdained to record that in the infancy of the Massachusetts colony, Canonicus, the haughty chief of the Naragansetts, sent to Plymouth a bundle of arrows bound together with the skin of a rattlesnake, and that Governor Bradford filled the skin with powder and shot and sent it back to his Indian majesty. Not that either Indian or arrows, powder or shot, or their exchange was a matter of any moment, but in this case the affair was a declaration of war on the one hand and an acceptance of the challenge on the other—a war which, had it been prosecuted, might have annihilated either an Indian tribe or the infant colony in which lay embosomed a nation and a civilization.

A few words from the lips of a monarch are in themselves no more than the shaking of a leaf in the wind, but spoken in the ear of a foreign ambassador at his court may not only shock the finances of a continent, but may bring nations into hostile and bloody collision.

The advent of a little seed upon the shore of some island in the sea is in itself an event lost in its own insignificance. But if that seed embosom the germ of some nutritious fruit, and, springing up into prolific maturity, in the course of years reproduce its kind until the whole island is supplied with its productions, its landing on those shores comes to be an event of historic magnitude and importance. Its fruit may not only feed thousands of native islanders, but, becoming an article of commerce, enrich them, build them houses, improve their domestic habits, cover their nakedness with comely habiliments and clothe the island in the rich attire of an advanced civilization. Nay, more, it may awaken the cupidity of greedy foreigners, and tempt the navies of distant powers to take forcible possession of those fertile fields, and other powers, jealous of this intrusion, may protest, and follow their protest with armed resistance; and thus out of the bosom of that little seed shall grow events the record of which shall fill many a bloody page of human history.

The personage named upon our title-page was one of so humble a rank in life, of such grade of intellectual power and culture, and of such general insignificance, that the mention of her as a subject of discourse might seem only an excuse for literary trifling. She was the consort of no monarch—the daughter of no queenly or titled mother. She was no cultivated Aspasia, fit to lecture on eloquence in the presence of a Socrates and captivate the heart of a Pericles. Neither was she a Hannah More, nor a Florence Nightingale, nor a brilliant beauty, dazzling the eyes of some royal court. Far from it; and yet, if we mistake not, it will be found that the part she played in life's drama, though of a very humble and uncouth sort, was, if not a prolific cause, at least the symbol and instrument of principles and events second in importance to very few in the course of human history.

Jenny (or Janet) Geddes was a Scotch woman, a native of that land of great minds and heroic champions of Calvinistic orthodoxy. Born perhaps about the close, before or after, of the sixteenth century, toward the middle of the seventeenth she found herself a resident of the city of Edinburgh. No doubt her position in life was very humble—her food and raiment, perhaps of the coarsest kind, procured by the labour of her own hands.

Whether this was her maiden or matrimonial name history does not say. She was certainly poor, for in the great cathedral church of St. Giles there was no place for her in the pew, if indeed these conveniences had yet found place there; so she went to church with her stool in her hand,

and sat upon it in the aisle wherever she could find a convenient and unoccupied spot.

She was evidently a person of decided character, and did her own thinking, at least on certain subjects; and as the sequel will show could, upon occasion, without consultation with her husband, if indeed she were blessed with matrimonial alliance with any one of the rougher sex, do her own acting also, and that with decision and energy. She was a Presbyterian of the orthodox hue, and, familiar with her Bible, she demanded conformity to its teachings in all matters of faith and worship.

It was in the month of July—a month since become so memorable in the history of human freedom—on the twenty-third day of the month, that Jenny emerged from domestic obscurity to historic celebrity and renown. On that day there was a strange ferment throughout Scotland and a wild excitement in the city of Edinburgh. King Charles had resolved to make Presbyterianism give place to Prelacy throughout the realm. A book of canons had been prepared subversive of the whole system of Presbyterian government, and had been enjoined upon the realm by proclamation upon the king's simple prerogative. Following this book came a liturgy as a law of public worship, and a royal edict had commanded its introduction into all the churches of the realm on this memorable Sabbath day. Notice to this effect had been given the Sabbath before, and hence this intense excitement. For the Scottish people knew that if this measure were carried into effect by the authorities, Presbyterianism was virtually in its grave.

As the hour of Sabbath service approached, the streets of Edinburgh were thronged with crowds of people—every bosom throbbing, every eye flaming with excitement. But whither were they directing their steps? Conspicuous from many a point in the city of Edinburgh is a lofty tower, terminating in an open, carved stonework, with arches springing from the four corners and meeting together at the top in the form of a crown. Already more than three centuries were looking down from that tower-top. It rose from the centre of a vast and venerable pile, including the High Church at the eastern end, where Knox so often preached, and within which pile "forty altars" were at one time supported. It was thither mainly the crowds were pressing, and among them Jenny Geddes. Not being overburdened with modesty, she elbowed her way through the crowd to a convenient place, in near proximity to the pulpit, and seated herself on her throne.

The edifice was filled to repletion with titled nobility and the nobler untitled nobility of the Scottish Presbyterian masses. There were present archbishops, bishops, the lords of the session, the magistrates of the city, members of the council, "chief captains and principal men," and Jenny Geddes and her stool.

The excitement was becoming every moment more intense. The minutes dragged themselves along with tormenting tardiness and the suspense was becoming almost breathless.

When the feeling was wrought up to its highest tension the Dean of Edinburgh made his appearance, clad in immaculate surplice, book in hand—the fatal book of the liturgy—the device of English Prelacy for the reform of Scotch Presbytery. The book was opened and the service begun.

The cup was now full, though as yet no one pretended to know, no one dreamed, what form of expression the pent-up indignation of the outraged people would assume. The question was soon decided.

No sooner had the first words of the book,

through the lips of the dean, reached the ear of Jenny, the stern prophetess on her tripod, than a sudden inspiration seized her. In an instant she was on her feet, and her shrill, impassioned voice rang through the arches of the cathedral:

"Villain! dost thou say mass in my lug?" and in another instant her three-legged stool was seen on its way, travelling through the air straight toward the head of the surpliced prayer-reader.

The astounded dean, not anticipating such an argument, dodged it, but the consequences he could not dodge. He had laid his book, as he thought, upon a cushion—the cushion proved a hornet's nest. In an instant the assembly was in the wildest uproar. Hands were clapped; hisses and loud vociferations filled the house, and missiles, such as the hand could reach, filled the air. A sudden rush was made toward the pulpit by the people in one direction, and from the pulpit by the dean in the other.

On the retreat of the dean, the Bishop of Edinburgh took his place in the pulpit, and solemnly commanded the winds and waves to be still, but no calm followed. He was as rudely handled as his brother in oppression, and nothing but a vigorous onset of the magistrates saved his lawn and mitre from the rough hands of Jenny Geddes' soldiery.

At length, the people having been forcibly ejected from the house, the affrighted dean re-entered the pulpit and resumed the service; but the uproar without, the pounding at the doors, showers of stones hurled through the windows, turned the place into a bedlam, drowned the voice of the dean and compelled a suspension of the service.

When the dean and the bishop came out of the church, decked in their prelatical plumes, they were in no small danger of being torn in pieces by the excited, outraged masses, and were followed through the streets with the cries—

"Pull them down! A pope—a pope! Antichrist—antichrist!"

The magistrates managed to keep the peace in the afternoon, but when the performance was over the tumult in the streets was greater than ever. The Earl of Roxborough, returning with the bishop in his carriage, was so pelted with stones and so pressed by the crowd that his life was in danger.

Thus the scene that opened with such pomp and circumstance closed in discomfiture and chagrin. The liturgy, prepared with such care and painstaking, and from which so much was hoped, went up like a rocket and came down as rockets are wont to descend. Here ended the first lesson.

Now, he would be marvellously astray who should suppose that this sudden hurricane at St. Giles was but a passing and unmeaning summer squall. It was in truth the outburst of a national feeling. A mighty ferment at this time pervaded the national mind. Great principles were at stake, and the Scottish masses, well comprehending their nature and the drift of events, were solemnly resolved to vindicate their settled religious convictions in the great controversy at whatever hazard and cost.

When that irregular band of patriots, dressed in Indian attire, marched through the streets of Boston and tossed those tea-chests into the bay, they at the same time virtually tossed British sovereignty overboard; and Jenny Geddes' party at St. Giles signed the death-warrant of civil and ecclesiastical tyranny in both Scotland and England! The storm had been gathering for nearly forty years, and this bursting of the cloud marked a crisis in a great national revolution. It was the first formidable outbreak against the tyranny of the Stuarts, and Jenny Geddes' stool was the first shell sent screaming through the air at those merciless oppressors of the two realms, and the echoes of that shell are reverberating to-day among the hills.

"Protestantism was a revolt against spiritual sovereignties, popes, and much else. Presbyterianism carried out the revolt against earthly sovereignties and despotisms. Protestantism has been called the grand root from which our whole subsequent European history branches out; for the spiritual will always body itself forth in the temporal history of men. The spiritual is the beginning of the temporal. And now, sure enough, the cry is everywhere for liberty, equality, independence, and so forth; instead of kings, ballot-boxes and electoral suffrages."

THE CHURCH.

II.

THE CHURCH.

THE powers that came into collision that day at St. Giles were not merely a mob on the one hand, and heady, imperious ecclesiastics on the other, but deep-lying principles of civil and ecclesiastical authority. That outbreak was but one incident in the protracted war between Church and State—a war which began centuries before, and which is not yet ended. And it has been characterized by a sterner severity, has evoked into play higher and wilder passions, has given occasion for the display of grander heroisms on one hand and more savage tyrannies on the other, than most of the collisions between man and man. We now direct attention to the Church as one of the great parties in the conflict.

"THE CHURCH" embraces the whole body of believers, in all ages of the world. "Christ loved the *Church*, and gave himself for it," Eph. v. 25. "A church" includes, sometimes, a handful of believers, worshiping or living in a single house. "Greet Priscilla and Aquila; likewise the church that is in their house," Rom. xvi. 5, 6. But when we read of "the Church of God which is at Corinth" (1 Cor. i. 2), we are confronted with a body of professed believers, organized under governmental forms, with officers and laws, and through these possessing the unity of a single body. And in writing of *the Church*, we propose simply to direct attention *to the form which church government assumed in apostolic times under the teaching of the Holy Ghost.*

The necessity for government among professed believers in Christ arises from the same sad fact that compels the organization of civil governments among men—namely, human depravity.

True, indeed, the Christian is a new creature. He has been born again of water and of the Spirit. New views, new desires, new principles of action control the mind, and through it the man.

But this change, great as it is in fact and in ultimate consequences, does not, except when it occurs in the moment of death, upon the instant transform man into an angel. It only deposits in the nature a new leaven to contend with old depravities, and gradually, in the hand of the Holy

Ghost, to master and finally expel all that remains of sin and depravity. It lays a basis for new exercises and for a new history. A new life is introduced into the fast-decaying nature, which in its movements calls into new and healthful play all the innate or connate powers of the soul. As the main stream sweeps along in its current the feebler tributaries, so does this new life grapple with and carry along in its heaven-tending sweep all the natural issues of the mental and moral life. But in this effort it meets with stubborn and constant resistance.

Were Christians perfect, a few simple rules would suffice for the preservation of order and the harmonious and effective working of the whole machinery of ecclesiastical life. But the obvious imperfection of all, and the inability of Christians to read their own hearts, much more the hearts of others, open the way for the sure introduction of tares among the wheat—unconverted members to communion-tables, unconverted pastors into pulpits—and hence roots of bitterness are certain to spring forth, needing some efficient power to eradicate them; controversies are generated that can be allayed only by the strong arm of authority.

Hence, if the Church is not to become a mass of decay and confusion, and sink to worse than inefficiency, there is absolute necessity for some effective system of government, to decide upon the qualification of candidates for the pulpit and the communion-table, and then, if need arise, to discipline and eject the unfit and unfaithful.

For want of such government, many a Church, once pure in doctrine and efficient in action, has become first an unsightly deformity, then a fortress and propagandist of soul-destroying heresy, and then an utter ruin. The golden candlestick has been removed out of its place and a darkness more dense than ever has enshrouded the people. And even when the evil has not reached such extremes, in many a noted instance a powerful Church has become divided against itself; gross errors in doctrine nestling side by side with orthodoxy; wickedness and piety dwelling together under the shadow of the same altar.

A striking example of what a Christian Church may become through want of anything like an efficient system of government and discipline, may be seen in the present condition of the Church of England. Of this venerable, and in many respects noble Church, no Christian heart can desire to think, no Christian tongue to speak, in other thoughts and terms than those of respect and affection. She has been too long a main bulwark of Protestantism; her records show too brilliant a list of names respected for talent and distinguished for piety; she has given too noble a band of martyrs to the flames, and has furnished our libraries with too many volumes on sound theology and practical piety, to be lightly treated with disrespect. But even charity that covereth the multitude of sins cannot be blind to, and ought not to be silent respecting, the many flagrant derelictions of even such a Church. With an unexceptionable creed, it is difficult to say what forms of heresy in doctrine, and what style of immoralities in life, both among clergy and people, are not at this day to be found in the bosom of this Church. From what it requires a very keen vision to distinguish from rank Romanism and flagrant Unitarianism, down to rationalistic infidelity, through every grade of error, the darkness is spread. True, pious and learned prelates and clergy of lower rank utter frequent and manly protests. True, many within her bosom grow sick at heart at the sight of evils they cannot stay or expel. But, as with the patient under a hopeless disease, the recuperative power is too weak, and the noble witnesses protest and submit.

The sickening story of Colenso attests her utter impotency for discipline. At a recent meeting of "convocation" a well-known "dean" spoke nearly four hours in the "lower house" upon this case, in which he made these fearful statements: "I might mention several prelates, and many obscure clergymen, who certainly, on some of these matters, hold the same opinion as the Bishop of Natal. I might mention one who has ventured to say that the Pentateuch is not the work of Moses—that the narratives of historical incidents are coloured by the necessary infirmities of the human writers—and that individual is the one who now addresses you!" And then he asked why they did not lay their hands on him.

Now, although much of his language in that speech was somewhat guarded, and some of his expressions are capable of an interpretation that would not shock the Christian sense, yet uttered as they were in defence of such a man, and by one who distinctly avows his own agreement and the agreement of bishops and obscurer clergy with the principles of that man, it can only be understood as the expression for himself, and the imputation to those of whom he speaks, of sentiments so nearly infidel that orthodoxy can give them no other name. But where in that Church is the power to purge itself of these heresies and eject from her bosom those who thus corrupt the faith once delivered to the saints?

The necessity of some well-ordered and efficient government in the Church being manifest, a question of grave importance arises as to its legitimate and wisest form.

On this our appeal must be to the will of the King. The divine will might be signified in one or other of two ways: First, an explicit and complete system might have been laid down, as in the case of the Mosaic constitution, in plain, literal terms, thus forestalling controversy, and binding the Church by formal legal enactments. Or, in the absence of this, the will of the great Head of the Church might appear, as indeed it does appear, in the course actually adopted in the organization of the original society. In the sacred edifice erected by apostolic hands we may assuredly find a safe model for all climes and generations, to depart from which necessitates a clear and valid justification on the part of those who venture upon such departure. The Church most nearly like that of the New Testament, in the rank, functions and names of its officers, is without doubt that which may most safely challenge the scrutinies of reason and conscience.

In our quest for a church model in the New Testament, we may not, however, forget that, from the nature of the case, we shall come upon many customs, agencies and officers necessary during the emergence of the Church from Judaism, and its secure establishment upon its own independent foundations, but destined to pass away when the new empire had made good its claim to existence among men. To displace Judaism on the one hand, and Gentilism on the other, required that, for a time, the Church be clothed with miraculous mastery over the powers of nature, over sicknesses, demons, and even over death itself. But this work once accomplished, these miraculous powers are for ever withdrawn. To ascertain, then, what is now demanded to conform the Church to the New Testament model, we must carefully distinguish between the temporary and permanent, between the preparatory and complete, the scaffolding and the building itself.

Turning our eyes, then, toward that scene of organization, the first and most imposing object that arrests our attention is the Divine Head; the great Master Builder; High Priest, and now only Priest in Zion, and King as well as Priest—"His head and hairs white as snow, his eyes as a flame of fire, his feet like unto fine brass, as if they burned in a furnace, with the seven stars in his right hand, walking in the midst of the golden candlesticks." He was and is the Church's King. His word is law, his dominion absolute. Once on earth, he is now in heaven, ascended thither to a throne, in full sovereignty as Head of the Church, and Head over all things to the Church. He left no successor below. He appointed no visible vicar. Who claims such an office is a usurper—that "wicked," whom "the Lord shall consume with the spirit of his mouth, and shall destroy with the brightness of his coming!"

The government of the Church, then, is in a high and holy sense an absolute monarchy, for Jesus Christ is the Head and Source of all governmental power and authority received by and exercised over men.

Grouped around this sacerdotal Monarch we find a great variety of religious officers, some of whom are appointed merely for the exigencies of the time, not intended to be permanent, and whose offices ceased for ever with the life of the incumbents.

1. Among these are the Twelve Apostles, princes in Zion, according to the number of the tribes of Israel.

The very character of their endowments and the nature of their official functions rendered their office incapable of transmission to successors, except by a perpetual series of miracles. An essential qualification for the apostleship was the ability to testify as eye-witnesses to the resurrectiou of Jesus Christ from the dead, and hence the incumbent must have seen him alive after his resurrection; but this could be the case with none others than those of that one generation without a miraculous revelation of the risen Saviour to each successive candidate for the holy office.

The importance of Christ's resurrection from the dead, as a great fact in the history of redemption, is recognized in many provisions and doctrines of the gospel scheme. To glorify this event the observance of the Sabbath was transferred, not to the day of the week on which Jesus died, but to the day on which he rose from the dead. It was also essential to complete the plan of redemption.

This plan was one complex whole, which could lack no one part without becoming wholly vain. The golden chain that binds the redeemed soul to the throne of God, consisted of seven several links: the incarnation of Christ, his obedient life, his atoning death, his resurrection, his ascension, his session at the right hand of God, and his active intercession there in behalf of those for whom he died. Strike out any one of these links, and the whole chain is a mere rope of sand, leaving our poor bark drifting upon the rocks of sin, condemnation and woe. But our salvation is most intimately connected with the last—the intercession.

For all the rest is vain for us until the Spirit apply to us the purchased redemption. But this Spirit is given in response to Christ's intercession. "He is able to save them to the uttermost that come unto God by him, *seeing he ever liveth to make intercession for us.*" But if he be not raised from the dead, there can be no intercession in heaven and no salvation on earth.

Besides, Christ himself staked all his claims to the Messiahship upon his resurrection.

Over and over again he assured his disciples that he would rise again. Almost his last words to them were these: "After I am risen, I will go before you into Galilee—*there shall ye see me.*" Nor had he merely whispered this assurance in the ears of his friends—he had thundered it in the ears of his foes. And they well remembered it, saying, "We remember that this deceiver said, when he was yet alive, After three days I will rise again." Hence their request for a seal and a guard for his sepulchre; for they saw that even if his body were stolen away by the disciples, and the report go abroad that he had risen, "the last error would be worse than the first."

If, now, though he had been a three years' wonder to the nation, and had uttered many admirable words, yet had he failed to fulfil this oft-repeated assurance, what could his friends say, and how could his foes be brought to believe in him? Had he not risen from the dead, all faith in him would have been for ever buried with him in his own sepulchre.

And all remember Paul's elaborate exposition of the bearing of this great fact upon the whole scheme of salvation: "If Christ be not risen, then is our preaching vain, and your faith is also vain. If Christ be not raised, your faith is vain; ye are yet in your sins. Then they that are fallen asleep in Christ are perished," 1 Cor. xv. 12–19.

Thus the whole evidence of Christianity is embosomed in the one fact of Christ's resurrection from the dead. If, indeed, he rose, then is there one glorious Name given, under heaven, among men, whereby men may be saved; if not, the whole scheme is a vanity and vexation of spirit—nothing more.

Hence this fact was too vitally important to be left to its own authentication. An inspired jury of twelve men must be ordained, who could go to prison and to death as witnesses thereto. And the one fundamental, distinguishing duty of the apostolic office was *to certify the world of this great fact, and to authenticate their appointment to this office by working miracles in the name of the Risen One.* They were to organize churches and oversee the whole new empire; but all their other works were grounded upon this one great duty of witnessing to the resurrection of their Lord.

The word *apostle* means *messenger*, and in this general sense many were called apostles, but none other than the sacred twelve are ever mentioned as *the* Apostles.

And, for the time, the appointed number must

be retained. Hence, when Judas fell, Peter said to the one hundred and twenty, all of whom had seen Jesus after his resurrection, "Of those which have companied with us from the beginning, *must one* be ordained to be WITNESS WITH US, with us *of his resurrection.*" None others could fill the office assigned to the twelve but such as were solemnly ordained thereto. They were to be witnesses on the stand, testifying before all the world to the great culminating, crowning fact in the history of redemption—the resurrection of Christ.

So JESUS named them. "In those last solemn moments," writes the Rev. Albert Barnes, upon this point, "when he was about to leave the world. when the work of atonement was finished, and when he gave the apostles their final commission, he indicated the nature of their labour and the peculiarity of their office in these words: '*Thus it is written, and thus it behooved Christ to suffer, and to rise from the dead on the third day,* and ye are WITNESSES of these things,'" Luke xxiv. 46–48.

This peculiar title and office the apostles expressly challenged for themselves. At Pentecost, Peter, standing with the eleven, charged home the murder of Jesus upon the Jews, and then added:

"This Jesus has God raised up, whereof we all are *witnesses*," Acts ii. 22.

Again, to the Sanhedrim, "Peter and the other apostles" said, "The God of our Fathers raised up Jesus whom ye slew and hanged on a tree. Him hath God exalted to be a Prince and a Saviour, and *we* are *witnesses* of these things."

So essential was it to the unique office of the apostleship to have actually seen Jesus after his resurrection that Paul was fitted therefor by a miraculous exhibition to his eye of the Risen One! And to this he appeals in justification of his claim before the Corinthians: "Am I not an apostle? Have I not *seen* Jesus Christ our Lord?" 1 Cor. ix. 1. "And last of all *he was seen of me*, also, as of one born out of due time," 1 Cor. xv. 8.

Thus, from the very nature of the case, the apostles could have no successors; and who lays claim to such succession must be able to show that by miracle he too has seen Jesus Christ our Lord.

A second marked peculiarity in the office of the apostle is seen in the extent of his sphere of labour. The whole Church was his parish. He might go with his fellow apostles or singly, whithersoever the exigencies of the case required. No province, no city, no presbytery, was exempt from his oversight. Pastors, elders, deacons, if delinquent or erratic, were open to their rebuke.

In this the only claim to succession is that put forth by the triple-crowned tyrant on the banks of the Tiber, the Great Apostle of the Apostasy.

2. Besides the twelve witnesses, our blessed Saviour also appointed, on a certain occasion, seventy others, and sent them forth, two and two, into every city and place whither he himself would come, investing them with miraculous powers, and charging them to preach the gospel of the kingdom, Luke x. 19. These, however, instead of constituting a band of permanent officers, disappear again almost as soon as they appear. The object of their appointment was merely to spread the knowledge of the kingdom more widely than was possible to the twelve.

3. The twelve apostles and the seventy evangelists were the only officers appointed immediately by the Saviour; and they, or at least the former, were appointed as organizers of the Church; but neither the one nor the other formed any part of the permanent organization.

Besides these, in later days, many other officers were employed for the time, but who left no successors. Some of these are named in the twelfth of First Corinthians. After the apostles, *prophets* are mentioned—"men who spake for God as the occasional organs of the Spirit." Then *teachers*—"uninspired men who had received the gift of teaching." After that, *miracles*, or "men endowed with the power of working miracles." Then *gifts of healings*—"persons endowed with the power of healing diseases." *Helps*—"persons qualified to help the officers of the church, probably in the care of the poor and the sick." *Governments*—"those who had authority to rule." And, finally, *diversities of tongues*—"persons having the gift of speaking in foreign tongues."

"On this enumeration," writes Dr. Charles Hodge, "it may be remarked that it is not intended to be exhaustive. Gifts are mentioned in verses eighth and tenth, and elsewhere, which have nothing to correspond with them here.

"Secondly, every office necessarily supposes a corresponding gift. No man could be an apostle without inspiration, nor a healer of diseases without the gift of healing. If any man, therefore, claims to be an apostle, or a prophet, or a worker of miracles, without the corresponding gift, he is a false pretender.

"Thirdly, the fact that an office existed in the

Apostolic Church is no evidence that it was intended to be permanent. In that age there was a plenitude of spiritual manifestations and endowments demanded for the organization and propagation of the Church which is no longer required. The only evidence that an office was intended to be permanent is the continuance of the gifts of which it was the organ, and the command to appoint to the office those who are found to possess the gifts. Had the gift of sight been discontinued, it would avail little that men should call the mouth and nose *eyes*, and demand that they should be recognized as such. This is precisely what the Romanists and others do when they call their bishops apostles, and require men to honour and obey them as though they were."

Later still in the history of the Church we find the title "angel of the Church," as in Rev. i. 20: "The seven stars are the angels of the seven churches."

These words form a part of the glowing introductory vision of the Apocalypse. The Son of man appeared to the Seer of Patmos walking in the midst of the golden candlesticks, and in his right hand, the hand of firmer grasp, seven stars. The candlesticks are the churches and the stars the angels—that is, the officers of those churches. The Son of man, the Sun of Righteousness, the blazing source and centre of all spiritual light, employs these angel-stars as the official human medium through which he pours upon the churches to which they severally minister the light of instruction, example and consolation.

This term, *angel*, is a favorite Scripture title for the *minister of religion*. The prophets are called angels: "Thus spake Haggai, the Lord's angel." So also the priests: "The priest's lips should keep knowledge, for he is the angel of the Lord of Hosts," Mal. ii. 7. And the Jews were accustomed to give this title to the minister who officiated in the service of the synagogue. And the seven epistles in Revelation are addressed to the angels of the churches, to which they severally ministered.

And in these epistles the title is given, not to any one man, but to the collective body of ministerial incumbents in the churches specifically named. Thus, in the epistle to the angel of the Church at Smyrna, we read, "I know *thy* works; fear none of the things which *thou* shalt suffer. Behold, thou angel, the devil shall cast *some of you* into prison, that *ye* may be tried. Be *thou* faithful unto death, and I will give *thee* a crown of life."

The object here addressed, now collectively and now distributively, is the same, for the words specify impending dangers and persecutions, and then consolations to support under them; and we may not accuse the venerable exile of the rhetorical confusion of attempting to administer comfort to one person, or body of men, under affliction, by telling others of consolations in store for them, or them of consolations in store for others.

The first of these epistles is addressed to the angel of the Church at Ephesus. That this angel consisted of no single person may be seen in the account given in the twentieth of Acts of the scene at Miletus: "And from Miletus, Paul sent to Ephesus, and called to him the elders of the Church," and these elders he thus addressed, "Take heed to all the flock of God, over the which the Holy Ghost hath made you *bishops.*" Thus, we have here the collected body of pastoral Ephesian bishops, to which John afterward wrote, styling them the angel of the Church at Ephesus.

And in the fourteenth chapter of this book the aggregate Christian ministry in all the world is called an angel: "And I saw another angel fly in the midst of heaven, having the everlasting gospel to preach *unto every nation, and kindred, and tongue, and people.*"

Thus the whole Christian ministry in the world is the angel of the whole body of professing Christians in the world; and any given number of ministerial brethren, who represent an aggregate of Christian congregations, are, in Scripture language, the angel of that aggregate; and each pastor is the angel of the congregation to which he ministers.

Besides the temporary officers of the Church, appointed and qualified for its organization under the form, there were permanent officers called deacons. An account of the institution of this office is given in the sixth of Acts. The deacon, as will there be seen, was not to be a ruler, but only a distributor of alms to the needy, godly poor.

The Church then was not organized under governmental forms while Christ was yet on earth. The preparations were all made. John the Baptist did his work, and the seventy temporary evangelists finished theirs, and their official character is never mentioned in the New Testament after the resurrection. Up to the time of Christ's death, whereby he "finished transgression and made an end of sin, and made reconciliation for iniquity" by the one great sacrifice, the old Church could not give place to the new. Nor did the disciples and apostles, in their dismay and bewilderment, know what to think or do till the Holy Ghost at Pentecost enlightened their minds and marked out a clear path before them.

In proceeding now to unfold the system of government instituted by the apostles, let it be remarked:

1. That each Church was placed under *permanent rulers.*

The Church, as organized, was not a pure democracy, in which the government was administered by the people in the mass, but a system under which certain rulers, however designated and inducted into office, were invested with the powers and exercised the functions of government.

Dr. John Mason writes: "There are three terms employed in the New Testament to express the authority which is to be exercised in the Christian Church—one meaning *to lead*, another *to stand before, to preside over*, and the third, *to act the part of the shepherd;*" and all the powers thus specified are named as belonging to Church officers. In Heb. xiii. 7, 17, 24, we read: "Remember them which have the rule over you—your rulers"—"*obey* them and submit yourselves. Salute all them that have the rule over you." It is significant that these rulers are spoken of as many, without any hint that the powers of government were ever invested in an individual. The term here employed to signify *rule* is the same as that found in Matt. ii. 6: "Thou Bethlehem in the land of Juda art not the least among the *princes—rulers*—of Juda, for out of thee shall come a *governor—ruler*—that shall *rule* my people Israel."

In 1 Thess. v. 12 it is written: "We beseech you to know them which labour among and are *over you* in the Lord." In the single Church at Thessalonica there were several persons in official position over the brethren. The word here employed means to preside over and govern, as we see in 1 Tim. iii. 4: "A bishop must be one that *ruleth* well his own house."

Again, in 1 Pet. v. 2, 3: "The elders which are among you I exhort; feed, act the shepherd to, govern, control the flock of God which is among you, taking the oversight thereof, acting as bishop over them." And in Acts xx. 17, 38, the elders are commanded to *feed* the flock over which they had been made overseers. This word, act the shepherd, is common in the Greek classics as a designation of the kingly office; kings are called the shepherds of the people. Of David it was said in 2 Sam. v. 2: "Thou shalt *feed,* act the shepherd to my people, and be a *captain* over them."

Of Christ, also, it is said in Matt. ii. 6, "He shall rule—feed—be shepherd to my people." And in Rev. ii. 27, the same word is used, "He shall rule them with a rod of iron."

Thus we see that the several churches were placed under officers who were invested with all the powers necessary for the exercise of a wise and authoritative government and discipline.

2. These rulers were *elders.* "Let the *elders* that rule well be accounted worthy of double honour," 1 Tim. v. 17. "The *elders* which are among you *feed,* rule, govern the flock of God which is among you, taking the oversight thereof, exercising the duties of the bishopric," 1 Pet. v. 1, 3. "From Miletus Paul sent to Ephesus and called the *elders* of the Church and said to them: Take heed to all the flock over the which the Holy Ghost hath made you *bishops,* to feed, rule, govern the Church of God," Acts xx. 17, 28. Thus in the one Church at Ephesus there were

several who filled the office of rulers, and these rulers were *elders*. Paul and Barnabas "ordained elders in every church, or *church by church*," Acts xiv. 23. Having brought the work of organization to a certain degree of maturity in Crete, Paul left Titus, his assistant and companion, there "to set in order the things that were wanting, and ordain *elders* in *every city*," Titus i. 5.

3. As these elders are called rulers and invested with all governmental authority, so in fact *they exercised their powers in the work of discipline and control.*

As Mr. Barnes well says, there were hundreds of churches, yet only two instances are mentioned in which the apostles in any way interfered in cases of discipline. That calls for discipline were very numerous is evident from the fearful defections from the faith mentioned in the Epistle to the Galatians, and from pure morals among the Corinthians. And as each of these churches was organized under an eldership commanded to rule the flock, the work of discipline naturally and necessarily fell to them.

Accordingly, in 2 Thess. iii. 14, Paul charges the Church, "If any man obey not our word by this epistle, note that man and have no company with him." They were to censure him and authoritatively debar him from Christian privileges. This charge being given to the Church as an organized body, must be addressed to those officers whose duty it was to "feed," rule, govern the flock and act the bishops over it.

Again, in the 5th chapter of 1 Cor. an account is given of an instance of gross immorality calling for rigorous discipline—for the infliction of a penalty which consisted in delivering the offender over "to Satan for destruction of the flesh." Now Paul, as an apostle, held by virtue of his office the right to interfere anywhere and at any time in the affairs of any Church. But in the Church at Corinth he felt a peculiar interest as its founder and the instrument in the hands of God of the conversion of many of its members. They were his spiritual children dearly beloved. "For though ye have ten thousand instructors in Christ, ye have not many *fathers*. For in Christ Jesus I have begotten you through the gospel," 1 Cor. iv. 15. Now in our churches cases not unfrequently arise in which discipline by the ordinary methods is impossible. Sometimes the body of the church and the elders are so at variance that any censure by the latter is felt by the former to be the result of prejudice, or the eldership may be so divided as to make an effective decision impossible. In such a case, the presbytery sometimes lays its commands upon the session or eldership, and they are constrained to proceed accordingly. Sometimes, not very unfrequently, the presbytery takes the whole matter into its own hands, and of itself settles the question.

In the case before us, among the Corinthians, from some cause, discipline in the ordinary way was hindered and the offender went unpunished. There were now three legitimate methods in which the apostle might have proceeded in this case:

First, he might have committed the whole matter to Timothy, his travelling companion, and bid him to settle the matter. He sometimes did this: "I besought thee to abide at Ephesus when I went into Macedonia, that thou mightest charge some that they teach no other doctrine," 1 Tim. i. 3. And Timothy was now at Corinth with a commission from the apostle to execute just such tasks as this: "For this cause I have sent unto you Timotheus, my beloved son and faithful in the Lord, who shall bring you into remembrance of my ways which be in Christ, as I teach everywhere in every Church," 1 Cor. iv. 17.

Or, *second*, the apostle might have decided the matter himself by virtue of his plenary authority as an apostle, and sent a formal excommunication of the offender with the bearer of this epistle.

Or, *lastly*, in proper recognition of the dignity and authority of the eldership, he might simply direct them as to the course they were to pursue, and thus reinforced by an apostle's judgment they could control all opposition and carry the matter to a final settlement. Now, in fact, the apostle chose the last course of the three. Leaving Timothy entirely out of view, he directed the Church to take the matter in hand and issue it in the regular way: "For I verily, as absent in body but present in spirit, have judged already as if I were present concerning him that hath so done this deed." To his own mind the proper course was perfectly clear: "In the name of our Lord Jesus Christ, *when ye are gathered together*, and my spirit"—Paul was in spirit among them as a member of their eldership—"with the power of the Lord Jesus Christ to deliver such an one to Satan." Thus, even as an apostle, he yet acted with and through the eldership. The Church obeyed and inflicted the condemnation. The punishment was "inflicted of many," 2 Cor. ii. 6.

The bench of ruling elders performed their task, and the result was, "that the offender was brought to such sorrow that he was likely to be overwhelmed," 2 Cor. ii. 7. And now another act of government was needed. The offender must be restored. But, as Mr. Barnes says, "Even an apostle did not assume the prerogative of saying that he *should* be reinstated in the Church; he did not of his own authority restore him; he placed him before the Church and asked them to do it." "Sufficient to such a man is this punishment, so that contrarywise"—reversing your judgment—"*ye* ought rather to forgive him. Wherefore I *beseech* you that *ye* would confirm your love toward him. To whom ye forgive anything I forgive also." The Church *first*, and then the apostle. He simply confirms *their* sentence.

The only other case of discipline in which the apostles are mentioned as taking part is one alluded to in 1 Tim. i. 20: "Hymeneus and Alexander, whom I have delivered unto Satan, that they may learn not to blaspheme." In giving charge to Timothy, Paul incidentally speaks of this case of discipline in which he, as an apostle, had authoritatively acted.

It is not stated, nor can it be known where this

case of discipline occurred, whether in Macedonia where Paul now was, or during some earlier period when Timothy was with him. All that we can gather is, that it was a case with which Timothy was familiar. We learn from it that there were occasions in which, owing to the inexperience of the elders, or to divisions among them, or to the confusion into which the Church had been thrown by the boldness and recklessness of blasphemers, it was necessary that the apostle exercise directly his undoubted right to inflict the extraordinary penalty of delivering over to Satan. And it may be that in this case also, as in that at Corinth, the apostle, as himself an elder, acted with the other elders and through them.

4. These elders were the *only permanent* officers ordained to *bear rule* in the *Church of the New Testament.*

The Epistle to the Philippians is addressed to "all the saints at Philippi, with the bishops and deacons." The whole Church, including its board of officers, is here addressed, and the only officers are bishops and deacons. The deacons were not rulers, but officers to receive and distribute alms to the poor. In this *one* Church at Philippi were *several* bishops. These bishops were elders. "For this cause I left thee in Crete to ordain *elders* in every city, if any be blameless, for a *bishop* must be blameless." Bishops and elders are the same, and the epistle is addressed to the elders and deacons. And as this Church was organized by Paul himself, we may be sure that it was complete in all its appointments.

And as Jesus, while labouring in the narrow field of Palestine, required not only twelve apostles to be constantly with him for their instruction, but for a time seventy evangelists, to go before him whithersoever *he himself* would come, and whose office ceased when he ceased his travels, so the Apostle Paul, the great Church organizer, with the whole world before him, required and appointed at least two elders, Timothy and Titus, to be his companions in travel, and, when occasion required, to remain behind him and finish work which he had begun.

About the year 53, Paul associated Timothy with him at Lystra, as a "minister" and helper, Acts xix. 22. At the close of this year he was with him at Berea, Acts xvii. 14. When Paul reached Athens he sent word for Timothy to rejoin him there, and to come with all speed, v. 15. At Corinth, Timothy reached his spiritual father, Acts

xviii. 5. The next two years he made a part of the apostle's retinue; was with him when he wrote both Epistles to the Thessalonians, 1 Thess. i. 1; 2 Thess. i. 1, and at the close of that period was sent with Erastus into Macedonia, Acts xix. 22. Three years after he was sent to Corinth, 1 Cor. iv. 17, and the next year had returned, and was with Paul when he wrote his second Epistle to the Church there, 2 Cor. i. 1. He was one of the seven who composed the apostle's train that same year when he left Greece and went into Asia. Thus Timothy acted as "minister" to Paul and did the "work of an evangelist," 2 Tim. iv. 5. Paul "besought him to abide a while at Ephesus" to do a certain work, expecting soon to join him there, and to be diligent in his work "till he come," 1 Tim. i. 3; iii. 14; iv. 13. Timothy had no thought that Ephesus was his home and the special field of his labours, and he remained there only at the earnest request of the apostle. The only instances in which he is known to have been at Ephesus at all, are—first, the time when he was sent thence into Macedonia, Acts xix. 22, and the time when Paul begged him to remain there "till he come," 1 Tim. iv. 13.

Now, as a "minister" to an apostle and an

"evangelist," he was entrusted with tasks that might just as well have been assigned to any other travelling elder. As Paul's representative, during the brief parenthesis of time he spent in this place and that, he could ordain elders, commit the things which he had heard of Paul among many witnesses to faithful men, who should be able to teach others also, put the brethren in remembrance of these things, charge them that they teach no other doctrine, and execute any other service entrusted to him by the apostle, who was constantly inspecting his work, correcting any errors into which he might fall, and setting his seal upon any work done according to the will of the Holy Spirit.

It has been hastily assumed that Paul calls Timothy an apostle in 1 Thess. i. 1; ii. 6, where, after thus opening the Epistle, "Paul and Sylvanus and Timotheus," he says, "*We* might have been burdensome to you as the apostles of Christ." If this were so, it was very different from his mode of speaking in 2 Cor. i. 1, "Paul an APOSTLE, and Timothy" not an apostle, but "*our brother*." And in Col. i. 1, "Paul an *apostle* of Jesus Christ, and Timotheus *our brother*." He does not write, Paul and Timotheus, apostles of

Jesus Christ, though in Phil. i. 1 he does write "Paul and Timotheus, *servants* of Jesus Christ." And in 2 Thess. ii. 1–6, we read, "Ye know that *we* were shamefully entreated at Philippi." But Timothy was not shamefully entreated there. So in 1 Thess. i. Paul writes, when *we* could no longer follow *we* thought to be left in Athens *alone*. We, I Paul alone. And Paul is speaking of himself alone when he says, "We might have been burdensome to you as apostles of Christ, but *we* were gentle among you as a nurse cherisheth her children; wherefore we would not come unto you, even I, Paul, once and again." Thus Timothy *is* called an evangelist, a minister, a brother, but never an apostle in the New Testament.

Timothy, then, was simply an itinerant missionary, and where he was when Paul wrote his second letter to him it is impossible to say. That he was *not* at Ephesus is seen in 2 Tim. iv. 12, where Paul says, "I have sent Tychicus to Ephesus," which he would hardly say to one at Ephesus; for Tychicus, already on his way to Ephesus, would reach it before the letter arrived, if he were not already there. Then Paul says, "Trophimus I left sick at Miletum," and Paul would hardly write all the way from Rome to tell one in Ephesus that he had left another sick only thirty miles off.

Titus was another of these itinerant evangelists. For a while he was left in Crete to set in order the things that were wanting and ordain elders in every city, and in the apostle's name to instruct them and the people in their duties, Titus i. 5. Then when judicious elders had been placed in office these churches were to be left to their control, and Titus was to hasten away elsewhere. "When I shall send Artemus unto thee, or Tychicus, be diligent to come unto me to Nicopolis," Titus iii. 12. Again, we find Paul sending him from Ephesus to Corinth, 2 Cor. xiii. 18; and then leaving Ephesus himself he expected to meet Titus at Troas, in which he was sadly disappointed: "I came to Troas, but had no rest in my spirit because I found not Titus my brother," 2 Cor. ii. 12, 13. So he went on to Macedonia, where Titus rejoined him, 2 Cor. vii. 5, 6. Again Paul sent him to Dalmatia: "Demas hath forsaken me and is departed unto Thessalonica, Titus to Dalmatia," 2 Tim. iv. 10. And should we inquire, as certain persons did, "Who is this Titus?" Paul answers "he is"—not an apostle, but—

"my partner and fellow-helper concerning you," 2 Cor. viii. 23.

Thus Titus, like Timothy, was simply an elder, employed by the apostle to do certain important services here and there, to hasten from place to place, and assist in organizing the churches under a permanent eldership, and to instruct those elders in the duties of their high office.

The elder or presbyter, then, is the only ruling officer in the New Testament Church; and whoever lays claim to any governmental office higher than this or other than this within the Church of Christ, and especially one who challenges authority over elders, must make good his claim by some plain revelation of God given subsequent to apostolic times. The Romish cardinals may elect one of their number to headship in the papacy, and when elected and inducted into office he shall be the vicar, not of Christ, but of the conclave, while in the Church of Christ he is nothing. The present female head of the English Church establishment may nominate or appoint, and by her "license, under her royal signet and sign manual, authorize and empower one to be" a bishop or archbishop, and this officer may be a baron, and, as such, sit in the House of Lords and act as secular legislator, and may hold his courts of various character, but in the Church of Christ he can be at the highest no more than an elder, and, as such, is capable of no other acts than such as pertain to the eldership.

5. This office of the eldership was but the continuation of one that had existed from the earliest period in the Church of God.

It is a well-known fact that the human race, as it radiated in various directions from its ancient home in the East, bore with it those seeds and animals which are most needful for its service and support. Rice, wheat, pulse and the vine; the horse, the ass, sheep, goats and cows, and many other animals, have been, from the first, and still are, the almost inseparable companions of man. The same is largely true also of those words that denote family relations—father, mother, child; of words that designate the various parts of the body; of names of the heavenly bodies, and of those expressive of various bodily acts, as eat, drink, sleep and walk. Through all migrations, through all changes of climate, customs and institutions, however great and diversified they may be, those things which either grow out of the life of a people or are most needful for its well-being cling to man in steady and almost unvarying relationship.

The same is true of those institutions through which the domestic and civil life have been taught from earliest years to express themselves. And thus we see the chosen people of God, while parting with many things during the lapse of ages, and adopting and naturalizing among themselves many new customs and habits, yet, through all migrations, vicissitudes and revolutions, still clinging to the eldership as to a part of its social, tribal and national being.

Even during the residence in Egypt, at first as the adopted children and favorites of the realm, and then as its slaves, under hard bondage in brick and mortar, that people, so far from sinking into anarchical dissolution among themselves, retained, in the venerable eldership, something more than the mere semblance of a regular organization—whether from force of habit or from a half-unconscious assurance that the day would dawn when this institution would come to play an important part in their national life. How far anything like a thorough governmental economy obtained among the enslaved people it is not easy to say. But that the hour for putting on the sandals for the march to the land of promise, freedom and national power found a sort of magistracy in the eldership, is very certain. For out of the burning bush God gave the command to Moses: "Go and gather the *elders* of Israel, and say, The God of your fathers, the God of Abraham, Isaac and Jacob appeared unto me," Ex. iii. 16. Equally certain is it that these elders were and acted as the acknowledged representatives of the people. The command to Moses was: "Thus shalt thou say to the *children of Israel,* Go gather the *elders* of Israel and say *unto them.*" And in Ex. iv. 20–31, "Moses and Aaron went and gathered together all the *elders* of Israel, and Aaron spake all the words which the Lord had spoken unto Moses, and did the signs in the sight of *the people.*" Thus the people were in the elders, and the elders stood and saw and acted for the people.

The seventy elders mentioned in Numbers xi. 25, who acted as assistants to Moses and Aaron, were not then first ordained to office, but merely selected for a special purpose from a body of men already in official position. They are spoken of as "seventy of the elders," Ex. xxiv. 1. In distress and humiliation for the defeat at Ai, Joshua *and the elders* of Israel put dust upon their heads.

And when the hour of victory had come, the *elders* went up with Joshua before the people of Ai, Josh. vii. 6; viii. 10. During the period of the judges, the elders still held their place in the national and local magistracies, and, from their numbers, must have exerted a powerful influence in shaping and controlling affairs. At Succoth, Gideon found and dealt with elder-princes to the number of seventy-seven. And in the last chapter of the book of Judges, we find the eldership of the whole nation in council respecting the interests of one of the tribes. In the book of Samuel repeated mention is made of the elders, now deciding the question of war and peace, 1 Samuel iv. 3, and now taking into their own hands, under God, the momentous matter of a national revolution, transmuting the republic into a monarchy, 1 Sam. viii. Even under the monarchy they still held their place. It was the eldership that adjusted matters with David in Hebron and made him king, 2 Samuel v. 2. And when David, after the insurrection under Absalom and the defeat of the rebel prince, looked again homeward in his exile, he asked, "Why are the *elders* of Judah last to bring back their king?" 2 Samuel xix. 11. The elders filled the place of counsellors and assistants of the king. They accompanied David when he went to bring back the ark from the house of Obed-Edom, 1 Chron. xv. 25.

In Proverbs xxxi. 23, Solomon alludes to the high and honourable place of the eldership, when he writes of the virtuous woman, "Her husband is known in the gate when he sitteth among the *elders* of the land."

The disruption under Rehoboam, which resulted in the overthrow of pure religion among the seceding tribes, spared, however, the eldership. When the imperious Ben-hadad demanded of Ahab the surrender of all his treasures, the king called all the *elders* of the land to consultation, 1 Kings xx. 2–9. And in 2 Kings x. 1 we find Jehu writing letters to *the rulers* of Israel, "*the elders.*"

And the eldership still held its own during the Babylonish exile: "The letter which Jeremiah sent from Jerusalem unto the residue of *the elders* which were carried away captives," Jer. xxix. 1. And in their exile the people consulted Ezekiel through the eldership: "Certain of the elders came to inquire of the Lord, and sat before me."

With the restoration to Palestine the elders

also came with the people. Ezra (x. 8) speaks of the "council of the princes and the elders;" that is, the princes were the elders.

And Jesus found this venerable institution still in existence and operation. When he entered the temple, the chief priests and the *elders of the people* demanded of him, "By what authority doest *thou* these things? and who gave *thee* this authority?" Matt. xxi. 23. And in the crowd that under the lead of Judas invaded the awful privacies of Gethsemane, elders of the people held their place, Matt. xxvi. 47. They were among the accusers of Christ before Pilate, Matt. xxvii. 12, and also among the counsellors that invented the falsehood by which the soldiers were to account for the disappearance of Jesus from the sepulchre, Matt. xxviii. 12.

It was before the elders that Peter made defence for the healing of the impotent man, Acts iv. 8–23. They condemned Stephen, Acts vi. 12. They were chief among the persecutors of Paul, Acts xxiii. 14.

Thus, through the whole course of church history preparatory to the inbringing and establishment of the New Testament system, we discern a twofold principle at work—that of permanence coupled with that of evanescence, the changing with the unchanging; a divine form, clad now in this and now in that, and now in a still different style of apparel. The fundamental doctrine, like its divine Author, is the "same yesterday, to-day and for ever." From the shutting of Eden's door upon the fallen race to the transplanting of the millennial paradise to that of heaven, the plan of salvation is unchangeably the same—justification by faith alone, faith in a substituted, atoning Saviour.

But in its external garb it underwent divers and numerous changes. Now it appears in patriarchal rites, antediluvian and postdiluvian. Now it walks before us in the peculiarities of the Abrahamic and now of the Mosaic scheme. Here we find priest and Levite, and these officiating now in the ambulatory tabernacle and now in the stationary and massive temple. Now the administration is largely autocratical, as under Moses and Joshua, and now more formally republican, as under the judges; and now regal, from Saul to Zedekiah; and then in exile; and then provincial under Medo-Persian rule; and then semi-anarchical from the death of Ezra and Nehemiah to the Romans and the advent.

But through all other changes the eldership

remains the one pillar of cloud by day and fire by night. Moses passes away and Joshua passes away, and judges and kings pass away, and with Malachi the noble, heroic race of the old prophets passes away, and at last priest, Levite, tabernacle and temple, altar and sacrifice, and the holy city itself, all are gone; while the eldership, modified, indeed, as to some peculiarities of function, but the same in all its essential characteristics, still remains, and yet remains, and will remain as the one enduring ruling office of the Church of God on earth till the great angel shall lift his hand and swear that time shall be no longer. And even in heaven, where no altar, sacrifice, priest or Levite appears, the relics and memorials of the eldership are still preserved; and round about the throne are the four living creatures representing the hosts ransomed from the four quarters of the globe, and the four-and-twenty elders, representing the angel of the Church, its ministry and government—twelve ruling elders, and twelve preaching *and* ruling elders, according to the number of the twelve tribes of Israel.*

When, then, we find in the Church one office holding place through so many centuries, and sur-

* On this subject see the *Princeton Review* for Jan., 1847.

viving so many offices that have passed away, we might reasonably take it to be a part of the official framework that was to last to the end, and hence it would awaken no surprise to see the eldership pass from the Church of the Old Testament into that of the New.

The Saviour, in his journeyings in every Jewish town, and the apostles, in very many Gentile communities, found the synagogue. And it was their wont, first of all, within their enclosures to break the glad news of the kingdom: "And when Jesus departed thence he went into their synagogue," Matt. xii. 9. "And when he was come into his own country he taught them in their synagogue," Matt. xiii. 54. So Paul and Barnabas on that first missionary tour, when they reached Salamis, "preached the word of God in the synagogues of the Jews," Acts xiii. 5. At Antioch, in Pisidia, they "went into the synagogue on the Sabbath day," Acts xiii. 14. And so at Iconium, Acts xiv. 1. And so everywhere.

But the leading feature in the government and worship of the synagogue was the eldership, comprising a bench of elders, one of whom, called bishop, overseer or angel, was the presiding officer; and from this eldership appeal lay to the great synagogue at Jerusalem. And when, as was no doubt often the case, the whole or the greater portion of the synagogue were converted under the preaching of an apostle, what more natural than that the synagogue itself, just as it stood, became a Christian church? And when the synagogue in the main clung to the old faith and drove out the Christian converts, what more natural than that they, with the elders that believed, should at once organize a Christian synagogue upon the model with which they were so familiar?

In the words of Archbishop Whately, a distinguished and learned prelate of the Church of England, "It appears probable—I might say, morally certain—that wherever a Jewish synagogue existed that was brought, the whole or the chief part of it, to embrace the gospel, the apostles did not there so much *form* a Christian church as *make an existing* congregation Christian, by introducing the Christian sacraments and worship, and establishing whatever regulations were requisite for the newly-adopted faith; leaving the machinery (if I may so speak) of government unchanged; the rulers of the synagogue, elders and other officers, whether spiritual, ecclesiastical or both, being already provided in the existing institution. And it is likely that several of the earliest Christian churches did originate in this way—that is, that they were converted synagogues, which became Christian churches as soon as the members, or the main part of the membership, acknowledged Jesus as the Messiah.

"The attempt to effect this conversion of a Jewish synagogue into a Christian church seems always to have been made, in the first instance, in every place where there was any opening for it. Even after the call of the idolatrous Gentiles, it appears plainly to have been the practice of the Apostles Paul and Barnabas, when they came into any city where there was a synagogue, to go thither first and deliver their sacred message to the Jews and 'devout (or proselyte) Gentiles;' according to their own expression (Acts xiii. 16), to the 'men of Israel and *those that feared God.*'

"And when they found a church in any of those cities in which (and such were probably a very large majority) there was no Jewish synagogue that received the gospel, it is likely they would still conform in great measure to the same model."

This a point of great importance. For the apostles, at work now upon the permanent organization of the Church, would hardly begin upon one model and then end upon another. They would not form the new converts into organizations which must soon be taken to pieces for reconstruction upon a different plan.

And this emerging of the synagogue into the Christian church, this facile gliding of the ancient eldership into its new relations and clustering of the new converts about them, explains the strange fact that no explicit mention is made of the first organization of the Christian eldership. Of the organization of the apostolic office, and of that of the deacons, we have detailed account, while the *first* mention of the elders finds them already in office and is purely incidental! At the prophecy of Agabus, at Antioch, respecting the dearth in Judea, contributions were promptly raised and sent to *the elders* by the hands of Barnabas and Paul, Acts xi. 28–30. And thus in the mother model church, at Jerusalem, we find elders already in office, without a hint previous or subsequent as to the fact, time or mode of their appointment.

This quiet transition of the old Church into the new, of the synagogue into the Christian congregation, is in harmonious accord with the common course of Divine Providence in both the natural and spiritual kingdoms. Except when absolutely necessary (as in the exodus from Egypt), there is no violence of transition, no precipitation from old into new relationships. In nature the seasons glide quietly the one into the other. The night melts into dawn, and the dawn into day. God is never in a hurry. With him one day is as a thousand years and a thousand years as one day. It was by no thundering edict, no violent convulsion that the old dispensation gave place to the new. They quietly overlapped each other until knitted together—the latter absorbed the former. Christ was careful to attend the great national feasts in the temple, and the last public act of his life was to engraft the Supper upon the Passover. And for many years after, the Christians waited upon God in the temple-service, and Paul sedulously avoided everything that was calculated needlessly to shock the prejudices of Judaism.

"As the Church," writes Neander, "was continually increasing in size, the details of its management also multiplied; the guidance of all its affairs by the apostles could no longer be conveniently combined with the exercise of their peculiar apostolic functions; they also wished, in accordance with the spirit of Christianity, not to govern alone, but preferred that the body of the believers should govern themselves under their guidance. Thus they divided the government of the Church, which hitherto they had exercised alone, with tried men, who formed a *presiding council of elders,* similar to that which was known in the synagogues."

Thus it remains a beautiful illustration of the identity of the Church, from first to last, that the eldership, the permanent, never-changing characteristic element of the former ecclesiastical system, is retained as the sole governmental agency in the latter and the last.

6. These elders are also called *bishops* in the New Testament records.

In the twentieth of the Acts we read that Paul sent from Miletus to Ephesus and called to him the elders of the church and said to them, "Take heed, therefore, to all the flock over the which the Holy Ghost hath made you *overseers*"—*bishops* in the original. So also in Titus, the first chapter, "Ordain elders in every city, if any be blameless—for a *bishop* must be blameless."

So Neander writes: "The name presbyter, which is the same as that of elder, by which this office was first distinguished, was transferred from the Jewish synagogue to the Christian Church. But when the Church extended itself among Hellenistic Gentiles, with this name borrowed from the civil and religious constitution of the Jews, another was joined thereto, which was more allied to the designation of social relations among the Greeks and adapted to point out the official duties connected with the dignity of presbyters. The name *episcopoi*—bishops—denoted overseers over the whole of the Church and its collective concerns, as in Attica those commissioned to organize the states dependent on Athens received the title *episcopoi;* and, in general, it appears to have been a frequent one for denoting a guiding oversight in the public administration. Since, then, the name *episcopos* was no other than a transference of an originally Jewish and Hellenistic designation of office, adapted to the social relations of the Gentiles, it follows that originally both names *related entirely to the same office,* and hence both names are frequently interchanged as perfectly synonymous. Thus Paul addresses the assembled presbyters of the Ephesian Church as episcopoi—bishops; and in 1 Tim. iii. 1 the office is called episcopé—bishopric; and in verse 8 the office of deacon is mentioned as the only existing church office besides. It is certain, therefore, that every church was governed by a union of the elders or overseers *chosen from among themselves,* and we find among them no individual distinguished above the rest who presided as *primus inter pares*—chief among equals—though probably in the age immediately succeeding the apostles" (and what departure from primitive doctrine and polity do we not find in this age?) "the practice was introduced" (yes, *introduced*) of "applying to such an one the name of episcopos—bishop—by way of distinction."

Wickliffe, "the morning star of the Reformation," was for "rejecting *all* human rites; and with regard to the identity of the order of bishops and priests in the apostolic age he was very positive." For in those times he says "the distinct orders of pope, cardinals, bishops, archdeacons and deacons were not invented."

In England, as late as King Edward VI., the Reformers "believed but two orders of churchmen in the Holy Scriptures—namely, bishops and deacons." And the early English Protestant clergy dared not withhold the right hand of fellowship from ministers of foreign churches that had not been episcopally ordained, "there being no dispute about reordination, in order to church preferment, till the latter end of Queen Elizabeth's reign."

In January, 1588, Bancroft, chaplain to the archbishop, in a sermon at Paul's Cross, broached the novelty that "the bishops of England were a distinct order from the priests, and had superiority over them by divine right and directly from God." Whitgift, the learned and zealous Prelatist, said of this new-fangled fancy that "he rather wished than believed it to be true." Dr. John Reynolds, regarded at that time the most learned man in the Church of England, in an answer to this offensive sermon, said: "*All who have for five hundred years last past endeavored the reformation of the Church, have taught that all pastors, whether they be called bishops or priests, are invested with equal authority and power*—as first the Waldenses, next Marsilius Patavianus, then Wickliffe and his scholars; afterward Huss and the Hussites, and, last of all, Luther, Calvin, Brentius, Bullinger and Musculus. Among ourselves we have bishops, the queen's professors of divinity in our universities, and other learned men consenting therein, as Bradford, Lambert, Jewel, Pilkington, etc. But why do I speak of particular persons? *It is the common judgment of the reformed churches* of Helvetia, Savoy, France, Scotland, Germany, Hungary, Poland, the Low Countries, *and our own.*"

Against such pressure of authority has the fancy made its way to acceptance, in one fragment of the Church of Christ outside of Rome, that in apostolic times the name bishop was anything more than another name for presbyter or elder!

This perfect equality among the divinely-appointed rulers in the Church does not hinder, if temporary exigencies require, the appointment by his co-equal brethren of an elder to the special duty of oversight in some one extended field of labour. Even the pure Presbyterianism of Scotland did not hesitate in 1560, on account of the paucity of ministers, to divide the realm into districts, and appoint "one of the Protestant party to take the general charge of religious matters in each, giving them the title of superintendents; but when it was proposed to make the bishop of Galloway superintendent of Galloway, the proposal was rejected, lest the appointment of a bishop should give some colour to the idea that the office was Prelacy under a different name."

7. The question now arises as to the method by which men legitimately find their way into official position in the Church.

To this it may be answered that the whole process is initiated, controlled and concluded by the

Spirit of God: "Feed the flock over which the *Holy Ghost* has made you overseers." In this procedure his first step is to call men by faith and repentance to Christ: "To all that be in Rome *called* to be saints." Out of the body thus called the officers of the Church are to come. Even in the Jewish commonwealth no foreigner could wear the crown; much less in that of Christ may aliens and strangers bear rule. Then, in the heart of some professed and acknowledged citizen of the kingdom, the Spirit works the desire or willingness to fill, sometimes pressing by powerful constraint the candidate to seek admission into this high and holy office: "For, though I preach the gospel, I have nothing to glory of; yea, woe is unto me if I preach not the gospel."

And now the Church—the people—must intervene. The candidate must apply to the Church, or the Church, discerning through the Spirit his evident qualifications, must apply to him. In either case it is the privilege and duty of the Church to utter its voice.

For the Church antecedes the officers. It is her spiritual need that requires official service. The officers are for the Church, and not the Church for the officers. As in the State, government is a mere agency to execute the will of God for the weal of society, so in the Church. And as in the State the inalienable right resides in the people to say who shall do their work and God's in the solemn service of making and executing laws, so even more may the acknowledged citizenship of Christ's kingdom have a deciding voice in the appointment of rulers over them. Christ has ordained offices and incumbents to meet the spiritual necessities of his people, and not that men may enjoy governmental dignities and emoluments. It was to save souls that Christ died: "Christ loved *the Church*, and gave himself for *it*." The Christian, then, not the officer, is the special object of Christ's love—the Christian in or out of official position. An elder-bishop may be lost—a Christian never can.

It accords with the whole drift of ecclesiastical rule, as developed in both the Testaments, that the people, as led by the Spirit of God, shall say who shall bear rule over them. In both the rulers are emphatically styled the "*elders of the people*" (Ex. xix. 17; Matt. xxi. 23).

"Christ," writes Dr. Cunningham, "*has given to the Church* the ministry as well as the oracles and ordinances of God. Rome declares that where there is not a valid ministry, there is not a true Church. Protestantism answers that where there is a true Church, there is, or may be, a valid ministry." And it is the Spirit of God in the hearts of the people that calls a man into actual ecclesiastical position.

As to the scriptural method of procedure in this matter, we are not left without intimation sufficiently clear in the New Testament records.

"Respecting the election to offices in the Church," writes Neander, "it is evident that the first deacons, and the delegates who were appointed by the Church to accompany the apostles, were chosen from the general body, Acts vi; 2 Cor. viii. 19. From these examples we may conclude that a similar mode of procedure was adopted at the appointment of presbyters. But from the fact that Paul committed to his disciples, Timothy and Titus—to whom he assigned the organization of new churches or such as had been injured by corruptions—the appointment, likewise, of presbyters and deacons, and called their attention to the qualifications for such offices, we are by no means justified in concluding that they performed all this alone, without the co-operation of the churches. The manner in which

Paul was accustomed to address himself to the whole Church, and to take into account the co-operation of the whole community, which must be apparent to every one reading his epistles, leads us to expect that where a Church was already established he would admit it is a party in their common concerns. It is possible that the apostle himself, in many cases, as on the founding of a new Church, might think it advisable to nominate the persons best fitted for such offices, and a proposal from such a quarter would naturally carry the greatest weight with it. In the example of the family of Stephanas, at Corinth, we see that those who first undertook office in the Church were members of the family first converted in that city."

The choice of elders by the people is not obscurely intimated in the very word employed to signify their ordination to office, as in the fourteenth of Acts—"when they had ordained elders in every Church." In this passage the pronoun "they" seems to refer only to Paul and Barnabas. But the word translated "ordained" originally signifies to vote by stretching out the hand, and here covers the whole process of designation for and induction into office. Hence the "they" includes, with Paul and his assistants, the people also.

Baptist W. Noel writes upon this point: "According to apostolic precedents, which have the force of law among Christians, the churches elected their ministers; and the appointment of pastors for the churches of Asia Minor by Paul and Barnabas is thus recorded by Luke: '*When they had elected elders for them by the show of hands in every church, and had prayed with fasting, they commended them to the Lord.*' Congregational election having thus been instituted by the apostles, continued for a considerable period in Christian churches. Mosheim, the learned Presbyterian historian, Bingham, the Episcopalian collector of ecclesiastical antiquities, Dean Waddington, Paolo Sarpi, the Roman Catholic historian of the proceedings of the Council of Trent, and Beza, one of the fathers of the Calvinistic Church, Neander, the Lutheran historian of our own days, Bost, the author of the 'History of the Moravian Brethren,' and even Hooker, with his strong anti-popular predilections, all acknowledge this to be the fact. Hence, congregational election became the principle of all the Calvinistic and Presbyterian churches. It was recognized in the Saxon, Helvetic and Belgian

Confessions, and the French churches embodied it in one of their canons of discipline."

The Reformers held "that the ordinary members of the churches or Christian congregations had a right to choose their own pastors and other office-bearers; and that, of course, *a fortiori*, they were fully entitled to prevent any pastor from being intruded upon them without their consent or against their will. This position of the Reformers has been disputed, but I have no hesitation in saying that this is not a question where there is room for *honest* difference of opinion among competent judges."*

Thus there exists in the New Testament Church no ecclesiastical person or body invested with the authority to impose an elder upon a church, or to constrain a church to accept the services of an officer whose qualifications they distrust, or who is to them from any cause unacceptable.

Having now been called, both by the Spirit in his heart and by the same Spirit through the people, still another step awaits the candidate before he can enter upon the functions of the eldership. The work before him is too solemn, pregnant with interests too high and sacred, and with

* Cunningham.

consequences too momentous to be entered upon without significant formalities. He must now be ordained. There must be a solemn convocation of the electors, the people, together with the existing eldership. There must be solemn religious services, prayer and fasting, and laying on of hands of the eldership, and a solemn commendation of the candidate to God and his assisting grace. "And when they had ordained elders in every church, and had prayed with fasting, they commended them to the Lord on whom they believed," Acts xiv. 23.

Thus it was that Timothy, the spiritual child and beloved friend of the Apostle Paul, was ordained. "Neglect not," his spiritual father writes to him—"neglect not the gift that is in thee, which was given thee by prophecy, with *the laying on of the hands of the presbytery*," 1 Tim. iv. 14. Prophecy had foretold his elevation to this office, and the local eldership or presbytery, finding him endowed with the proper qualifications, ordained him. And as the apostles were also elders—"the elders which are among you I exhort, who *am also* an elder," 1 Pet. v. 1—they with their brethren participated in the laying on of hands. So Paul took part in the ordination of Timothy: "Wherefore I put thee in remembrance that thou stir up the gift of God which is in thee by the putting on of my hands," 2 Tim. i. 6. Of what particular persons other than Paul this presbytery was composed we are not told. If other apostles took part in the transaction, they did so as presbyters, as elders, for a *presbytery* can consist only of such. And no ingenuity of criticism, no shrewd hints as to the specific meaning of terms, no suggestions as to what might have been, have ever been able to wrest these passages to any other meaning than that which lies upon their face as a simple, plain record of presbyterial ordination.

8. And now what authority, what powers, has the candidate found in the office into which he has entered?

The original source of all ecclesiastical power is the Saviour alone. Under him all power is in the Church—the mass of the Christian people. But inasmuch as the office-bearers in the Church are the representatives of the people, and, for the purposes of their office, *are* the people, the general authority belonging to the Church is aggregated in the office. Who shall exercise this authority the people are to say; but when the candidate reaches the office, he finds there certain powers, and when he leaves that office he leaves those powers where he found them.

At this point there is a break in the analogy between sacred and secular government. In the latter the people may create or abolish offices, change the whole framework of government; may withdraw powers from one office and transfer them to another. Not so in the Church. No other ecclesiastical office may be created than those designated in the New Testament, and no authority, civil or religious, may either enlarge or contract the powers ordained for such offices. An elder may be called to discharge a great variety of duties, but in all he retains the sole ecclesiastical grade of an elder, and as such can legitimately possess and wield no other powers than those of the eldership.

"The constitution and laws of His kingdom have been fixed by him, and cannot by any human authority be altered, abrogated, or extended. The office-bearers of God's Church are not lords over God's heritage; they have no dominion over man's faith; no jurisdiction over the conscience, but are the mere interpreters of Christ's will, the mere administrators of the laws which he has enacted."

The office of the eldership embraced a twofold function—preaching, and, as has already been shown, ruling also. Both were joined in that of the teaching-elder, while the ruling-elder as such never officially dispensed the Word and sacraments.

The duty of the preaching-elder is pointed out in Titus i. 5, 9:

"For this cause I left thee in Crete, that thou shouldst set in order the things that are wanting and ordain elders in every city, holding fast the faithful word as he hath been taught, that he may be able *by sound doctrine* both to exhort and convince the gainsayers."

Sometimes these duties are mentioned together, as in 1 Tim. v. 17: "Let the elders that *rule* well be counted worthy of double honour, *especially* they who *labour in word and in doctrine.*"

"It is surely abundantly evident in Scripture that pastors have a power of ruling—of exercising a certain ministerial authority in administering, according to Christ's word, the ordinary, necessary business of his Church, and we have irrefragable evidence in Paul's address to the Presbytery of Ephesus that he contemplated no *other* provision for the government of the Church, and the prevention of schism and heresy, than the presbyters or bishops faithfully discharging the *duties of their office,* in ruling as well as preaching" (*Cunningham*).

This power is involved in the very idea of the eldership. The elders of the people are the people's representatives and act for them in Christ's name. These elders of the Church are, for governing purposes, within their legitimate sphere, the Church itself. Their official acts are the acts of the Church for which they act.

When the parochial eldership receives a candidate to the communion-table, in accordance with the laws of Christ, it is the Church that issues the decree of admission. And the act of a single such eldership, in many cases, binds the whole Church of Christ; for in and through them, by his Spirit, Christ himself is acting. If, on proper grounds, this eldership admits one to the communion-table, it admits him to membership in the Church of Christ, and no particular church, with evidence of this admission and without evidence that he has proved himself unworthy of his position, may, without gross wrong, forbid that one a place at the Supper of the Lord.

And, as has already been made apparent, this

eldership is invested with all needful authority and powers of discipline within its sphere. For, as no individual or body of officers is gifted with insight into the heart, it is impossible to guard against the introduction of the unworthy—wolves in sheep's clothing—or of some who have mistaken a sudden glow of religious feeling for true inborn piety. Then, even the truly good may, under temptation, be led astray in word, deed or doctrine. And these evils unchecked would devour and destroy the Church. Hence, to meet exigencies that may arise through human imperfection and sin, and to quell disorders, the parochial presbytery is authorized and bound to vigilant watchfulness, to reprove, rebuke, exhort, to try, censure and expel, according as the case may require.

The fundamental law for the exercise of such authority is laid down by our Saviour himself: "Moreover, if thy brother trespass against thee, go and tell him of his fault between thee and him alone; if he shall hear thee, thou hast gained thy brother. But if he will not hear thee, then take with thee one or two more, that in the mouth of two or three witnesses every word may be established. And if he shall neglect to hear them, tell it to *the Church;* but if he shall neglect to hear the Church, let him be unto thee as an heathen man and a publican," Matt. xviii. 15–17.

"In regard to this passage it may be remarked, first, that it is to be presumed that the Saviour *designed* to embody the principles of discipline here so that they might be applied in all ages of the world, and so that this in all circumstances would be an adequate direction. There is not anywhere in the New Testament a more formal direction given on the subject of discipline, and it can hardly be presumed that on such an occasion the Saviour would have omitted what he designed should be an essential and *permanent* principle. Second, the apostles had been chosen and ordained before that direction was given (Matt. x.), and if he had designed that they alone should have the power of administering discipline, it is unaccountable that there is no intimation whatever that so important a function was conferred on them. The direction 'tell it to the Church' is not one which would be understood as referring to the apostles as being in fact 'the Church.' It is a direction which would be naturally understood as referring to the assembly of the faithful" (*Barnes*).

Thus we have a single congregation under the

oversight and control of a single eldership; but not far away, on all sides, are others like them. Is it the will of Christ that these bodies shall remain in isolation from one another, each pursuing its own course, itself the only interpreter of Christ's laws for itself, and thus, through the diversity of views incident to human nature, working confusion and frequent collision? Far from it. God never made an anarchy; in his domains order and harmonious adjustment of inferior to superior reign everywhere in nature, and not less so in the Church of Christ. Christ's coat is seamless; Christ's body is one, and his Church is that body. It is a kingdom, with careful subjection of inferior to superior authority; and all these churches are bound to realize the great principle of constitutional unity inherent in his Church. If the will of the great King were not hindered by human imperfection, all the particular congregations in the widest empires would be found joined together, not only in harmonious alliance, but under subordination to one great supervising, controlling power.

How necessary such union is, is seen in the simple fact that, except in cases that very rarely occur, no individual congregation can so much as become organized under a parochial eldership without the interposition of the eldership above them. No congregation, no one man, may ordain another to the high office of the pastorate; hence a number of churches within convenient reach are by nature, as it were, and by New Testament law, associated in subordination to the aggregate eldership of the body; and these ten, twenty, or thirty elders in convocation, according to the original and true idea of the eldership, are, for governing purposes, the Church they represent. They together constitute the *presbytery* spoken of by Paul in 1 Tim. iv. 14.

And as presbyteries and councils may err at all times, and especially in their insight into character, and as men are often deceived with regard to themselves, it follows that unworthy men will sometimes find way into the eldership and become heresiarchs, teaching doctrines of devils, and, as wolves, devour the flock they were ordained to feed. Hence, the power to admit to office for the good of the flock involves the power to oversee and watch those once admitted, and to censure and eject from office those who betray their trust.

And to this higher eldership is committed the watchful oversight of the aggregate of churches which they represent. They must hold pastors and churches to their duty—may, in accordance with the laws of Christ, lay commands upon them, and see that those commands are obeyed, or constrain delinquents to show good cause for disobedience—may inspect the records of their proceedings, and approve or censure. If a congregation fall into divisions or corruptions which the parochial eldership, either through indifference or inability, fails to reprove and rectify, then the whole duty passes legitimately into the hands of the superior eldership. Thus the powers inherent in a lesser also inhere in the larger presbytery, and what a parochial presbytery may do in a congregation the superior presbytery may do, if occasion call, in any or all the congregations within its bounds.

But a Church may include thousands of congregations spread over a wide territory, making it impracticable for any one presbytery to meet and exercise proper supervision over all. Hence, presbyteries must be multiplied; new centres of ecclesiastical authority must be located, and contiguous presbyteries, each invested with like authority, overspread the land.

But what about the relation of these presbyteries to one another? May they exist severally in independent isolation? Does church government begin in order and end in anarchy? By no means; the Church, however large, is still one body, and its inherent unity must still find embodied expression. This is done either by the constitution of an eldership or presbytery, which shall embrace the whole body of existing rulers in the Church; or, if this be impracticable, each presbytery may appoint a given number of its members to assemble at specified times, and thus form the great presbytery—"the angel" of the whole Church. And the fact that this body is a body of delegates, and not the actual aggregate of rulers in the Church, implies no modification of its powers as a true presbytery, for even the parochial presbytery is also a representative body standing for the church it represents. And the presbytery next higher is also a representative body, embracing only a part of the actual congregational elderships within its bounds. And it is the essential idea and spirit of the representative eldership that it stands for, and for purposes of government *is*, the Church it represents, whether that eldership be that of a single congregation or that of a wide provincial Church.

We have already seen that in apostolic times individual churches were organized by the ordination of elders in each one; and we have also seen these churches organized under presbyteries, ordaining to office and administering discipline. Let us now glance at the records of the FIRST GENERAL PRESBYTERY assembled at Jerusalem.

The inspired account of this presbytery, as found in Acts xv., well illustrates and confirms the principle that the office-bearers of a given church are, as such, invested with authority to decide judicially "any disputes that may arise about the affairs of the church—to be the ordinary interpreters and administrators of Christ's laws for the government of his house."

Some questions had arisen at Antioch respecting the relations of the old dispensation to the new—as to how far certain of its laws were binding on converts, whether from Judaism or from among the Gentiles. These questions were of general interest to the Church, inasmuch as Jews were scattered far and wide among the Gentiles, and their synagogues interspersed all over the civilized world among heathen temples. As the decision of these questions was to bind the whole Church, the apostles themselves judged it expedient that the voice of the whole Church be heard in the decision.

Accordingly, it was determined that "Paul and

Barnabas, and certain others of them, should go up to Jerusalem unto the apostles *and elders* about this question."

This reference to Jerusalem is somewhat remarkable; for already judgment had been given upon the question by an inspired apostle, and one of no secondary rank, and his judgment had the concurrence of his missionary companion Barnabas. It seems strange, therefore, that the Christians of Antioch should for one moment have withheld their acquiescence. But doubtless this thing was of the Lord. The time was coming when the ministry of the apostles would end, and they would pass away, leaving no successors behind; and as, after their departure, questions of moment would arise which only the Church in council could decide, it was of the highest importance that some precedent should be set under apostolic sanction that might serve as a guide in this branch of church government. For this reason, therefore, among others, Divine providence ordained the formal reference of this matter to the Great Presbytery sitting within the bounds of the mother Church at Jerusalem.

In due time we find the council assembled in solemn convocation. It consisted of apostles and elders; for, after the formal reception of the commissioners from Antioch, "the Church and the apostles and elders" coming together to receive them and hear the "things that God had done with them" (v. 4)—AFTER this—"the apostles the *elders* came together for to consider the matter" (v. 6). None others, then, than apostles and elders were formal, legitimate members of this body; for the decrees there issued are explicitly said to have been "ordained of the *apostles* and *elders* which were at Jerusalem."

In this council there was "much disputation;" then Peter made an address; then Paul and Barnabas declared "what miracles and wonders God had wrought among the Gentiles by them." Then James, who may have acted as moderator of the convocation, probably having been elected thereto by his brethren, summed up the matter and gave his judgment, introducing it with the words, "Wherefore my sentence is." "My sentence is"—literally, "I judge" (as in the Rhemish version; Wicliff—*I deem*). A common formula, by which the members of the Greek assemblies introduced the expression of their individual opinion, as appears from its repeated occurrence in Thucydides, with which may be compared the corresponding Latin phrase, *sic censeo*, of frequent use in Cicero's orations (*Dr. Addison Alexander*).

This view of the matter was so evidently just and judicious that it was accepted by the council, and embodied in a decree which was binding on all the churches. The tone of authority in this decree is very manifest: "It seemeth good to the Holy Ghost and to us to lay no greater burden than these necessary things." And in the missionary tour that followed, Paul delivered to the churches the decrees ordained of the *apostles and elders* at Jerusalem, "for to keep;" that is, to observe with strict obedience. Thus we see that, first, the question was referred by the Church at Antioch to the "*apostles and elders*" at Jerusalem, Acts xv. 2. And then that the "*apostles and elders* came together to consider the matter," v. 6. And, finally, that the decrees are explicitly said to have been ordained of the "*apostles and elders*," xvi. 4. Thus this council was composed exclusively of office-bearers.

But who were actually and formally represented in this first presbytery? We answer, the *whole Church*. The Church of Jerusalem was formally represented by its elders, and the apostles, being elders by virtue of their apostolic office, represented all the churches. Thus this was in reality a council of the whole Church.

It is noticeable, also, that the people attended and manifested great interest in the proceedings of the body: "Then all the multitude kept silence and gave audience to Barnabas and Paul," xv. 12. And they expressed their satisfaction with the result; and this fact is mentioned in the wording of the decree as an additional evidence that the Spirit of God brooded over and led their deliberations to the conclusion reached. The people may have been invited to take active part in the deliberations, though this is not affirmed.

But the narrative may suggest that this point has been too much overlooked in later times. Why might it not conduce to wisdom in ecclesiastical decisions to invite laymen of acknowledged experience and piety, especially when difficult questions arise, to be present in the presbyteries, larger or smaller, and give their views and advice, without joining in the decision? It is difficult to see how any harm could arise, and very easy to see how, sometimes, great good might accrue from such a course.

In 1641, the General Assembly of the Church of Scotland sent a letter to their Presbyterian brethren in England, who had asked their opinion in regard to the congregational scheme of church government, which contained the following passage: "Not only the solemn execution of ecclesiastical power and authority, but the whole exercise and acts thereof, do properly belong unto the officers of the Kirk; *yet* so that in matters of chiefest importance the tacit consent of the congregation be had before their decrees and sentences receive final execution." Henderson says: "Nothing useth to be done by the lesser or greater presbytery in ordering the public worship, in censuring of delinquents, or bringing them to public repentance, but according to the settled order of the Church, and with express or tacit consent of the congregation." Gillespie writes: "It is objected by the Independents that what concerneth all ought to be done with the consent of all. *We hold the same;* but the consent of all is one thing and the exercise of jurisdiction by all another thing." And in commenting upon the council of Jerusalem, he says: "The apostles and elders met, sat and voiced apart from the whole Church, and they alone judged and decreed. In the mean while, were matters made known to the whole Church and done with the consent of all. The brethren are mentioned (along with the apostles and elders) because it was done with their knowledge, consent and applause. "These were the views," writes Dr. Cunningham, from whom we are quoting, "entertained upon this subject by the men to whom we are indebted for the standards of our Church, who held that they were sanctioned by the inspired narrative of the council of Jerusalem, while they held also that neither this nor any other portion of the New Testament warranted or required the ascription to the people of any higher place or standing than this in the ordinary administration of ecclesiastical affairs."

Thus the presbyters in session, acting as the rulers of the Church, are for governing purposes the Church they represent, whether that body be smaller or larger, or the largest of all.

"The radical principles of Presbyterian Church government and discipline are, that the several different congregations of believers, taken collectively, constitute one Church of Christ, called emphatically *the Church;* that a larger part of *the Church*, or *a representation* of it, should govern a smaller, or determine matters of controversy which arise therein; that in like manner *a representation* of the whole should govern and determine in regard to *every part* and to all the parts united—that is, *a majority shall govern*—and consequently that appeals may be carried from lower to higher judicatories, till they finally be decided by the voice of *the whole Church*" (*Presbyterian Form of Government*, p. 425).

In this extract the Great Presbytery, including the aggregate of its ruling eldership, or, what is the same thing, their legitimate representatives, is for purposes of government and discipline, *the Church*. And the necessity for such a governing body, such an "angel of the Church," is involved in the actual and necessary unity of the Church, and in the *inherent right* of every member of the Church to have, if occasion calls, the voice of his Church, the voice of the Christian body to which he belongs, upon questions that lie between him and his opposers. It is his Christian birth-right to be defended against wrong by the angel of his Church. And this Church, this angel, is not this or that congregation, this or that presbytery, this or that synod, for these are but fragments of the Church, not its whole. The Church therefore, which is his ultimate protector from wrong or his ultimate censurer in wrong, is the Great Presbytery, the General Assembly.

It was the *right* of the Christians of Antioch to have a decision of the questions that agitated the congregation from the lips of the Church in session at Jerusalem. This Church thus assembled shall "receive and issue all appeals and references which may be regularly brought before them from the inferior judicatories. They shall review the records of every synod"—which in its sphere has already reviewed the records of every presbytery within its bounds, and which presbyteries have reviewed the records of every congregation severally within their bounds—"and approve or censure them; they shall give their advice and instruction in all cases submitted to them in conformity with the constitution of the Church; and they shall constitute the bond of union, peace, correspondence and mutual confidence among all our churches."

To this Assembly also *belongs*—belongs by inherent right, as the Church—"the power of deciding all controversies respecting doctrine and discipline; of reproving, warning, or bearing testimony against error in doctrine or immorality in practice in *any church, presbytery* or *synod;* of erecting new synods when it may be judged necessary; of superintending the concerns of *the whole Church;* of corresponding with foreign churches on such terms as may be agreed upon by the Assembly and the corresponding body; of suppressing schismatical contentions and disputations; and, in general, of recommending and attempting reformation of manners and the promotion of charity, truth and holiness through *all the churches under their care*" (*Form of Government*, p. 426).

Such, according to the New Testament, is the only legitimate form of church government—a government by an eldership—of a single congregation by its eldership—a government of a cluster of congregations with their several elderships by the aggregate eldership of the cluster—and a supreme government over all by the whole body of the eldership assembled either in mass or by representation.

9. This apostolic form of church government seems to have resisted both the encroachments of corruption and the violence of bloody persecution through the ages from the earliest times in the valleys of Piedmont. There the faithful Waldenses clung, as they even yet cling, to all the essential principles of Presbyterianism.

"As early as the sixteenth century," writes Dr. Smythe, "the Waldensian polity was precisely what it is now. Every church had its consistory; every consistory and pastor was subject to the synod, and it was composed of all the pastors with elders. Over this synod one of the ministers was chosen by his brethren, and without any second ordination presided. This presiding minister was called *then*, as he is called *now*, MODERATOR. He was required, in accordance with the plan of the early Scottish Church, to visit different parishes and to ordain—*only in conjunction with other ministers.* But he was in all things responsible to the synod by which he had been appointed to office."

And Milner (chap. iii. vol. ii.) quotes the following from a book concerning their pastors: "The pastors meet together once every year to settle our affairs in a general synod. The money given us by the people is carried to the said general synod, and is there received by the elders."

10. It is also peculiarly gratifying to Presbyterians to note the fact that the Reformers, "when they broke from the shackles of Romanism, almost with one consent adopted the fundamental principles of presbyterian polity. To this the Church of England constituted the sole exception; for in England, while sound evangelical principles were

working like a mighty leaven among the masses of the people, the formal disseverance from Rome was much more a political than a religious movement. Henry VIII., hampered and tormented by the duplicities and tergiversations of the Pope in the matter of the divorce, was gradually led to see that the prerogatives of his crown as then understood, and also the rights of his subjects, were invaded on all sides by the papacy; and, advancing from step to step, he ended by substituting himself in the place of the pope as head of the English Church.

Afterward, when the new system had taken form, and the need was felt for some defender of its validity, one was found in the learned, eloquent, "judicious" Hooker, whose work on "Ecclesiastical Polity" very naturally received the commendation of Pope Clement VIII. as one in which there were "such seeds of eternity as will continue till the last fire shall devour all learning."

In the famous fourth and fifth propositions of that work he maintains that "the Church, like all other societies, is invested with the power of making laws for its well-being, and that where Scripture is silent human authority may interpose."

Now, while these propositions are capable of

being employed either in behalf of Papacy, Prelacy or Presbyterianism, yet as used by their author they imply certain very explicit and thoroughly groundless assumptions.

It is therein assumed that the Scripture is *silent* on those points of church government in dispute between Prelacy and Presbyterianism. Nay it embodies in explicit statements the whole process of church organization under and government by the eldership. It is also assumed that *the Church* ordained the fundamental laws of the English ecclesiastical establishment. The Church! Was Henry VIII., with his ministers—was the imperious Elizabeth, with her courtiers and statesmen—in any sense *the Church?* Was even the mass of the *clergy* of England for many a long day even in membership with the Church of Christ? At the "Reformation" in England the old Romish clergy were not even dispossessed of their places, but, constrained by the rigours of authority, they hypocritically submitted in form while at heart they were as thoroughly Romish as ever.

The truth is, as has been well stated, that the forms of the English Establishment "originated with royal pleasure; they have changed as the will of our princes have changed; they have been settled by acts of Parliament; formed illegally; corrupted by pensions and overawed by prerogative; and they constitute part of the statute law of the land."

Leaving out, then, the English Establishment, all the churches of the Reformation were essentially Presbyterian in their principles and form.

As to "the mother of the Reformed" churches at Geneva, Mosheim writes: Calvin "introduced into the republic of Geneva, and endeavoured to introduce into all the Reformed churches throughout Europe, that form of ecclesiastical government which is called presbyterian, from its neither admitting the institution of bishops nor of any subordination among the clergy. He established at Geneva a consistory composed of ruling elders, partly pastors and partly laymen, and invested this ecclesiastical body with a high degree of authority. He also convened synods, composed of the ruling elders of different churches, and in these had laws enacted for the regulation of all matters of a religious nature."

How thoroughly Presbyterian was the Church of Scotland, shaped under its great leader, Knox, is known to all. And the Church of Scotland was identical in principles and form with that of

Protestant France; "and no authority," writes Dr. Hodge, "is more frequently quoted by Scotch writers than the *Ratio Disciplinæ* of the French churches."

The French provincial synods were obliged to furnish their deputies to the national synod with a commission in these terms: "We promise, before God, to submit ourselves unto all that shall be concluded and determined in your holy assembly; to obey and execute it to the utmost of our power, being persuaded that God will preside among you and lead you by his Holy Spirit into all truth and equity by the rule of his word."

Between the French churches and those of Holland there was the fullest accord both in doctrine and discipline.

The bishops in Denmark and Sweden constitute but "a slight deviation from the general uniformity of the Reformed churches as a whole," for they derived their ordination from Luther and his fellow-presbyters, and thus "resembled very much the present bishops of the Methodist Church, who derive their authority from John Wesley and two other presbyters, through Dr. Coke, whom Wesley and his associates appointed a bishop. The superintendents of other Lutheran churches are not regarded as holding a distinct, higher office, superior to that of presbyters, and investing them simply as holding that office with jurisdiction over ordinary pastors, but merely as presbyters raised by the common consent of their brethren to a certain very limited control for the sake of order. The doctrine of Presbytery as opposed to Prelacy was not only held by Luther and his associates, but was distinctly declared in the articles of Smalcald, which is one of the symbolical books of the Lutheran Church. There it is set forth that all the functions of church government belong equally of right to all who preside over churches, whether called pastors, presbyters or bishops" (*Dr. Cunningham*).

Thus, at the Reformation, the Church, by almost unanimous consent, flew back, as a child from the wilderness, to its mother's bosom—to primitive New Testament Presbyterianism.

11. Let us now add that *Presbyterianism is essentially a system of representative republicanism.* This is a matter of some considerable practical importance, for sacred and secular governments powerfully influence each other.

"Every religion," writes De Tocqueville, "is to be found in juxtaposition to a political opinion which is connected with it by affinity. If the human mind be left to follow its bent, it will regulate the temporal and spiritual institutions of society upon one principle."

Dr. McCrie, as quoted by Dr. Smythe, also writes: "Who that has duly reflected on the subject can be ignorant that forms of government exert a mighty influence, both directly and indirectly, upon the habits and sentiments of the people—to preserve the spirit and perpetuate the enjoyment of liberty, promote education, virtue and religion?"

Hallam says that "it was imputed to the Puritan faction, with more or less of truth, that not content with the subversion of Episcopacy, and of the whole ecclesiastical polity established in the kingdom, they maintained principles that would *essentially affect civil institutions.* They claimed to their ecclesiastical assemblies the right of determining 'all matters wherein breach of charity may be, and all matters of doctrine and manners, so far as appertaineth to the conscience.' They took away the temporal right of patronage to churches, leaving *the choice of ministers to general suffrage.*"

Thus governments, sacred and secular, directly

and powerfully influence each other, and, other things being equal, that Church possesses at least one decided advantage over all others whose principles of government are most in harmony with those of the nation.

A spiritual monarchy or aristocracy might exist and flourish in a republic; and a spiritual republic may hold its own and even reach high efficiency in a monarchy. But it is evident at a glance—and history abundantly proves that—in either case collisions are often inevitable, and such harmony as is needed for complete prosperity impossible.

Such, indeed, is the influence of governmental principles and forms upon citizen or subject that he cannot escape modifications of even his modes of thought—modifications sure to find expression in his actions. Under regal governments the common enterprises of industrial and commercial life are apt to be conducted in a monarchical style, and under a free republic these shape themselves into republican forms. In Great Britain, aristocracy forces itself into the whole being of social life; while in the United States, not only the most important but the most trivial matters are conducted by means of republican machinery and devices—elections, constitutions and by-laws. So powerful is this influence that in our country all denominations of Christians, whether thoroughly democratic or highly aristocratic in their essential principles, are constrained to adopt devices to bring themselves more or less into harmony with representative republicanism. Independents have their councils, which are in some degree representative bodies, and in some instances these councils are becoming so large and unwieldy that many of the wiser minds among them are sighing for a reduction of the size of these bodies by the formal adoption of the principle of delegation. The Episcopal Church, yielding to this influence, has been constrained to admit the laity to a place in their governing councils; and for the adoption of this principle among our Episcopal Methodist brethren the cry has long been growing louder and louder, and the pressure of public opinion in that direction heavier and heavier. If, then, it be found that Presbyterianism is by nature and divine law in thorough harmony with the universally accepted principles of civil government among us, it gains thereby a prestige of no little practical value; and a way is opened for its high enthronement in the thinking republican mind of the nation. And that Presbyterianism is truly representative republican in its principles, spirit and form, few will venture to deny.

1. A fundamental doctrine of the republican system declares that *the body of the people are, under God, the source and fountain of all the powers exercised in the government of the State.* Man, by nature invested with "dominion over the creatures," is, however, invested by nature with no civil dominion over his brother sovereign. Government among men is replete with a high dignity and majesty, its authority extending to the property, the person, and even the life of the citizen, and in exercising the functions of the magistracy man is invested with a godlike sovereignty. As such, he is a scrutinizing eye, overseeing the conduct, searching out even the motives of men; and as judge also he gives verdict for or against them, and, in the latter case, as executioner, he inflicts censure and penalty. Summoning men to his bar, he separateth them one from another—setting the sheep at his right hand and the goats at his left—and crowns the one class with benediction and scourges the other with condemnation. He is God's minister, sent for "the punishment of evil-doers and for the praise of them that do well."

And the earthly source of these high prerogatives is the mass of the citizenship.

That this is true of the Presbyterian system has already been shown. It maintains that God has given into the hands of the Church as a body the whole magistracy that is to govern in his name, and all ecclesiastical power is exercised under God in the name of the Christian brotherhood, who are kings as well as priests unto God. It utterly disallows the doctrine that ecclesiastical authority is given primarily to the clergy—that these constitute a ruling order set between God and men, authoritatively to interpret for them the Word of God, and for them to say what form of church government shall prevail over them and what law shall bind and guide them.

And while maintaining this doctrine with reference to the brotherhood within, it is even more emphatic in its repudiation of all right to governmental interference from the State without. If the clergy may not lord it, of intrinsic right, over one another or over the people, neither may any external authorities lord it over either laity or clergy. If there is one principle that stands out in pre-eminent relief in the conduct of Presbyterianism in Scotland, it is that of the inherent right of the Church to govern itself without let, hindrance or interference from the State. In the long and bloody war with the State under the Stuarts, while English Prelacy courted, Presbyterianism denounced and repudiated all State dictation and control. It would allow neither king nor parliament either to give it laws or even to convoke the General Assembly, or even, when it could help it, to determine the time, place or frequency of its meetings, much less to have one word to say as to the constituency of the assembly. Again and again it repudiated assemblies which had been controlled and corrupted by State agency and influence, and pronounced all their acts null and void. It told the king to his face that he was neither monarch over nor ruler in, but only a member and subject of, the Church. It scouted the fancy of James, as expressed in his "Basilicon Doron" and "Free Law of Free Monarchy," that one chief function of secular royalty was to govern the Church.

In our own country it was Presbyterianism chiefly that compelled the State to leave the Church in its native independence. "Presbyterianism first proclaimed this doctrine on American shores. It was opposed by Episcopacy in efforts to establish this doctrine in Virginia. And its universal establishment in our country and in the Constitution was the result of the movement made by Presbyterians" (*Smythe*).

The subject of Church and State alliance was long under discussion before the Virginia Assembly, and the measure was first long delayed, and then finally defeated, by the persistent opposition of Presbyterians, in which the Baptists also lent efficient aid, through memorials, protests and protracted and able discussions. And the happy working of the free-church system in that then powerful and influential commonwealth secured its general adoption in the nation. Thus in the Presbyterian Church the doctrine is fundamental that the powers of government inhere in the body of the people, to the exclusion alike of State dictation and interference, and of individual or class prescription.

2. But if these rights belong to the people, it is for them to say *under what particular form they are to be exercised.*

For Presbyterianism necessarily involves governmental machinery—a constitutional framework—as the medium through which the prescribing forces shall reach the subject masses. It knows nothing either of autocracy on the one hand or democracy on the other—nothing of mere arbitrary will. Presbyterianism is neither a one-headed nor a many-headed despot. It is in its very nature a constitutional government, and it is for the native possessors of all governmental authority, the body of the people, to say what particular form the constitution shall assume.

In the civil republic, God, speaking through the people, their social nature and necessities, their reason, judgment and sense of right and wrong, ordains the constitutional medium—all the needful framework and machinery of government. Likewise in Presbyterianism, God, through the apostles, laid down a certain definite governmental system, ordained certain offices to be filled, specified the qualifications of official incumbents, gave these incumbents their proper titles, prescribed the modes of their designation for and induction into office, and the powers to be exercised by them. But while it recognizes the fact that all this lies in the Word of God, in the inspired records of early Church history, it disallows the right of either the State or the clergy as such, or any other persons or bodies of men, authoritatively to interpret these oracles for the people. They alone are they who, with such light as may be given them, are to settle this question under God, and responsible alone to him for the wisdom and righteousness of their decisions. If the people tested the oral teachings of the apostles and resorted daily to the Scriptures to see whether these things were so, as we see in Acts xvii. 11, if even the utterance of an angel from heaven were to be subject to a similar test on the part of the people, as we see in Gal. i. 8, so also are the records of apostolic teachings upon this great subject of church government to come to the same test, and to be interpreted by the common Christian conscience and reason under the illuminating influences of the indwelling Spirit of God. Thus in all genuine reformations the believing people are summoned forth to utter their voice. King Hezekiah ventured but a short way in his work as a reformer without consultation with the princes and the congregation; and when it was proposed to repeat the passover and hold it yet other seven days, the approval of the whole assembly of the people was sought and obtained (2 Chron. xxx. 2–23). And on the Continent and in Scotland, in later days, it was the voice and power of the reformed and reforming people that toppled over the bulwarks of the Papacy and brought deliverance to the world; while in England alone the government took the work into its own hands, and with what result none are ignorant. There, as a zealous advocate of Anglican ecclesiasticism writes, "The people never were consulted in the matter; no popular assembly was held; nothing was put to vote. Their consent was never asked; in all probability it would not have been given, for the great bulk of the people were too ignorant to understand it and naturally disinclined to change their opinions. So also in the catechism, the Church teaches her children to obey their spiritual pastors and masters" (*F. W. Faber*, quoted by *Smythe*).

But Presbyterianism asserts the right and duty of the people to determine, among other things, the constitutional system under and through which the ecclesiastical powers shall go forth from their appointed possessors upon the subjects of government.

True, as has been already said, the fundamental principles of church government are laid down in the word of God, and any deviation from these involves error and entails evil. But no less are the foundation-principles of civil government set forth in the same inspired record, and only by adherence to these can civilization and social happiness be fully realized. But in both the one case and the other these principles are to be ascertained by, and brought into action through, the sanction of the aggregate civil or ecclesiastical citizenship—responsible in this only to their God. If they err, the sin and folly is theirs, and there is no authority on earth to constrain them to amend their conclusions and conduct.

In either case, also, this power to frame constitutions is hedged about with limitations which may not safely be passed. Human constitutions for the government of men are merely the media through which divinely-given principles go into action, and whenever they obstruct the free operation of these principles they are abnormal and illegitimate, and bring human wills into collision with the divine. Presbyteries, larger or smaller, possess certain inherent rights and powers, derived neither from courts superior nor courts inferior, but only through the people from the great Head; and no constitution of human devising may thwart their action or set them aside. Within certain limits man may ordain rules for the government of the family—children may be coerced to a course of education—parents may be punished for cruelty to children—but an edict from the legislature subjecting parents to the dominion of their children would be in itself null and void, as conflicting with fundamental laws of divine ordination. And when any provision in the constitution of any Church conflicts with the laws laid down by the great King for the government of the Church, with the essential rights and duties of the presbytery, larger or smaller, such provision is a usurpation, a folly and a crime, and no one is bound to its outcarrying. But within the divinely-prescribed limits of legitimate human enactment, the people alone as such, without leave asked of the State without or Church dignitaries and authorities within, are to say what particular shape church government shall assume. And this doctrine is an essential element in the presbyterial system.

3. Since, then, the governing authority resides with the people, and they, under God and guided by his law, are to declare what particular offices are to exist, it follows that *only by their voice can any incumbent find his way into official position.*

It is so in civil, it is so in ecclesiastical governments. In either, birth-right dominion over men is a solecism and an absurdity, excepting only in case of clear, express appointment of God, which appointment within the Church is claimed by none, and within the State is now claimed only to be scornfully disallowed by the enlightened common sense of mankind. No man or woman is born with the divine right to fill any office of civil or ecclesiastical government without the consent of the governed. Each Christian congregation is composed of "kings unto God," and no human authority exists, out of its own bosom, to assign to it an officer of any grade or character without its own call and choice. If a man is to fill the office of deacon, to "serve tables," to dispense the charities of the Church to the needy saints, the voice of the Spirit says to the people, "Look *ye* out among you men of honest report, full of the Holy Ghost and wisdom," to be appointed by the laying on of hands and with prayer, "over this business." The people must choose the candidate (Acts vi. 5). If one is to fill the office of ruling-elder, he must, by his obvious fitness for the position, attract the attention of his coequal brethren, and be chosen thereto by their suffrages in public assembly. And only after such election can he be ordained and installed into office. And if one is to fill the pastorate of a particular church, the laws of Presbyterianism demand that he be first elected thereto by the free choice of those whom he is to feed and help in governing. The assignment of a pastor to a congregation by any authority outside of its family circle, either in opposition to their wishes or without their formal consent, is an act of usurpation. Loudly and often has the oppressed Church of Scotland complained and protested against the tyrannies of the patronage system, which is wont to assert its right, and too frequently with success, to intrude its creatures into the pulpit against the will of the pews. And the assignment by a conference or a bishop, or any other person or body of men, of an incumbent to the pastoral office—the people to whom he is to minister not having fixed upon him as the pastor of its free choice—is unscriptural, unrepublican and unpresbyterian; and a people that submits to such a system is, in so far forth, an unrepublican community. In so doing they yield up one of the fundamental and most sacred rights of God's heritage, and give over to others the discharge of one of their most important and sacred duties. The free choice by the people of those who are to rule them is, then, another of the fundamental principles of the Presbyterian republic.

4. Another principle of republicanism, ecclesiastical and secular, demands that *citizens from the various ranks of society shall actually bear rule in the government.* The citizenship in the State embraces a vast variety of interests—industrial, commercial and professional—and in the Church, with the pastorate and eldership, all classes and conditions of people; and to secure impartiality in making and executing laws, these various elements must have place as far as possible in the governing bodies. Only in a legislature thus constituted is there any reasonable security against the iniquities and disasters of class-legislation, security for a harmonizing of, or at least a satisfactory compromise between, the countless and often conflicting interests of the civil or ecclesiastical family. In a free republican legislature we find the farmer, the artist, the mechanic, the merchant, the physician, the banker, the lawyer, and members of whatever avocation that forms a controlling interest in the community.

This principle of republicanism is repudiated by any system that allows an autocracy or aristocracy to prevail in its scheme of church government. In whatever church the pastor rules the congregation, or one body of clergy of itself rules either the congregation or any other body of the clergy, other principles prevail than those of republicanism And as the people become enlightened, and come to see on the one hand their own rights, and on the other the evils which such a system is almost sure to entail, they will challenge their right to a personal share in the functions of government; and as germs imbedded in the Christian heart are sure to find way for ultimate development, so the people are predestinated to attain in all Christian churches an actual share in the governmental administration.

The growth of a gaudy, pompous ritualism in the Church of England is fast opening the eyes of the wise to the evils of the unrepublican exclusion of the laity from actual power. A vigorous writer in a late number of the *London Review* says of this ritualistic question: "We view it as a warfare that must seriously affect the welfare of the land. It is not a question between Geneva and Rome, but whether the laity of the United Kingdom are to submit to the tyranny of priest-craft, to surrender to the clergyman of each parish the power to dictate to them what they are to believe, and to what they are to conform in the ceremonial of their public and private acts of devotion. In the claims of this ritualistic party we recognize deliberate and very powerful efforts to subject the thought of the day, the free religious liberty of the laymen, to the dictation of a body of men in whom there is to be found none of the antecedents of a life which could prove them trained for the use of such despotic spiritual power, nor anything in the act of their ordination, in their appointment to their respective spheres of duty, which for one moment would justify their parishioners in becoming thus subject to them."

Loud complaints are heard of that "autocracy of incumbents of parishes which makes each to reign with no rival near his throne—a total abnegation of the laity of the Church of England, comprising a large portion of the higher middle class, as well as the great majority of the gentry and nobility, and subjecting them to the will of rector or vicar."

Even the *London Times* talks of the necessity of taking a "leaf from Presbyterianism." Lord Sandon, addressing a recent "High Church Congress," speaking of the "priestly feeling" that is nurtured by this autocracy in the rule over a congregation, says that it leads to the establishment "of another master in every household, and ends in raising up a human artificial barrier between man and his God."

Among our Methodist brethren, whose zeal, piety and success are the admiration of all, this question of lay participation in the government of the Church has been for a long time producing profound agitation, and it is a question which must ultimately be decided in favour of the laity, and until then their form of government remains, in this respect at least, unrepublican.

Presbyterianism, however, finds this among its elementary principles. It disallows the right of any one man or any one class to govern alone any one body of the spiritual citizenship. No one pastor may govern alone any one congregation. Each particular governing body, whether it be the session or presbytery, or synod, or General Assembly, embosoms a body of the laity with the clergy. In them, too, may be found the various elements of society represented. There you shall see the mechanic side by side with the reverend professor in the theological seminary, the merchant sitting with his pastor. In most of these bodies the laity actually are, and in all of them they may be, in considerable majority. The session should always comprise a plurality of ruling elders, and in most cases includes three or six or even twelve. In presbyteries and synods they are very likely to be in majority. It is not unfrequently the case that one pastor acts as "stated supply" to two, three, or even four several organized churches, and while all those churches are represented in presbytery by a single pastor, they each send a ruling elder. The same is true of the General Assembly. The first General Assembly of the Church of Scotland, numbering forty members, contained but six ministers. Thus presbyterial governing bodies embrace all that variety of view and interest that characterizes the subject society for which it legislates. In Presbyterianism, therefore, there is no such thing as either an individual or a body of Christians under exclusive clerical control.

And as these ruling bodies are invested also with a judicial character, having authority to receive accusations or appeals, and to try and discipline offenders, our judiciary is both elective and popularly constituted, and a defendant before one of these courts is sure to find among his judges some of his brethren in social rank. If condemned by the session, he may appeal to presbytery, and if dissatisfied with the decision here, he may appeal to synod; and if still dissatisfied his, appeal lies once more to the General Assembly. Thus the humblest member of the Presbyterian Church is secured in the enjoyment of his rights and shielded from injury and oppression by the guardianship of the whole Church.

It thus appears that under our system the people shape the constitution of their spiritual commonwealth, elect their legislative and judicial officers, and form a constituent element in their governing assemblies. This surely is sufficiently republican.

5. *The perfect equality in rank and authority among the rulers* in the spiritual commonwealth is another feature of Presbyterian republicanism.

For the civil republic no inspired system of government is laid down, and hençe it remains with the people to say what offices shall exist and what powers shall inhere in these and those; but the records of the Church, to which the people are bound to adhere in setting up the machinery of spiritual government, allow but one single office—namely, the eldership—and no authority exists on earth for the creation of any other; and all the incumbents in that office are as rulers on a level of entire equality.

Parity among the clergy, as such, is a prime article of the Presbyterian system. By whatever name a minister of the gospel may be called, he is simply and only an elder. His character may outshine that of many, his talents may exalt him to princely dominion in the world of thought, in eloquence he may be an Apollos, in logic a Paul, and in erudition he may surpass all his brethren, but withal he is an elder, and nothing more. Exalted service may be assigned to him, he may fill the office of spiritual superintendent over a large territorial district, or that of moderator in a larger or smaller presbytery, or that of preceptor in a theological chair, yet his sole scriptural title is that of presbyter or elder, and his only rank that of the eldership, in which he is the equal of any other in all the clerical brotherhood.

Besides this, as members of governing assemblies the ruling elders are the coequals of those who preach and administer the sacraments as well as rule. In discussing, in voting and in eligibility to office in these bodies, each ruling elder is the full equal of any other member.

Dr. Charles Hodge, in his tract upon the question "What is Presbyterianism?" writes: "As to matters of doctrine and the great office of teaching, they"—the ruling elders—"have an equal voice with the clergy in the formation and adoption of all symbols of faith. It is not competent for the clergy to frame and authoritatively to set forth a creed to be embraced by the Church, and to be made a condition of either ministerial or Christian communion, without the consent of the people. Such creeds profess to express the mind of the Church. But the ministry are not the Church. So, too, in the election of preachers of the Word, in judging of their fitness for the sacred office, in deciding whether they shall be ordained, in judging them when arraigned for heresy, the people 'have in fact an equal vote with the clergy.'

"The same is true as to the *jus liturgicum*, as it is called, of the Church. The ministry cannot frame a ritual, or liturgy, or directory for public worship, and enjoin its use on the people to whom they preach. And in the exercise of the power of the keys, in opening and shutting the door of communion with the Church, the people"—through their elders—"have a decisive voice."

Indeed, in all the acts of each governing assembly the ruling elders are in every sense the co-equals of their brethren in the ministry.

And it merits consideration whether our common

practice, as frequently and fully as it ought, illustrates and verifies this portion of our Presbyterian theory. It too rarely occurs in our ecclesiastical assemblies that a ruling elder is chosen to act even in a clerkship, and almost never to occupy the moderator's chair, although not unfrequently there are sitting in the body elders endowed with peculiar qualifications for such positions, and who, by virtue of their rank, are as fully entitled to them as their clerical brethren. A practical recognition of the rank, dignities and rights of these rulers would enlarge their sphere of usefulness, increase their interest in the proceedings of these bodies, secure a larger attendance on their part, and thus considerably reinforce the active energy and talent of the Church. Thus, according to the principles of Presbyterianism, our rulers all stand on the same level of rank, dignity and power.

6. Again, in our ecclesiastical republic the *voice of the majority* is the *voice of the government.*

A representative body is, for the purposes to which it is appointed, the body which it represents. The national government is the people, and in and through that government the people make and execute laws and form treaties with foreign powers. But owing to the necessary diversity of knowledge, views and interests, entire unanimity in most cases cannot be expected. Even a jury of twelve men rarely come to such unanimity except by compromise; the feebler must yield to the stronger, and many of the convictions in the jury-box are given up in the jury-room. If, then, we are to wait for entire unanimity in a governing assembly, we must, in many instances, wait for ever; the wheels of government must stop and anarchy ensue. Unless, then, republicanism is to give way to despotism, the principle becomes a necessity that the majority of a body is the body itself, and its voice is the law. The majority of a session is the session—of a presbytery is the presbytery—and so on through the whole series. And in our General Assembly, composed of coequal ministers and ruling elders, the voice of the majority is the law of the Church. A note, already quoted, under the article in our Form of Government entitled "The General Assembly," says: "The radical principles of Presbyterian church government are, 'that a larger part of the Church, or a representation of it, should govern a smaller; that, in like manner, a representation of the whole should govern and determine in regard to every part and to all the parts united;

that is, a *majority shall govern.*'" What is true of the whole is true of each several part—the majority is the body. No house of clergy either governs by itself, or sits apart with a negative upon the doings of the laity. All sit together as equals, discuss on equal terms, any member possessing the inherent right to offer any proposition for the consideration of the body; all vote together, and the vote of the majority is the decision of the question.

But while the majority rules, the rights of the minority are carefully guarded. The sacred right of private judgment is fully recognized, and each one is allowed to appeal for defence directly to the word of God. "The Supreme Judge," saith our Confession of Faith, "by whom all controversies of religion are to be determined, and all decrees of councils, opinions of ancient writers, doctrines of men and private spirits are to be examined, and in whose sentence we are to rest, can be *no other* but the Holy Ghost speaking in the Scriptures."

In judicial processes, "Nothing ought to be considered by any judicatory as an offence, or admitted as matter of accusation, which cannot be proved to be such *from Scripture*, or from the regulations or practices of the Church *founded on Scripture,* and which does not involve those evils which discipline is intended to prevent."

Thus each private member of the commonwealth, if aggrieved by any action of any judicatory, and any defendant in any court, may fall back upon the Holy Word, and if he can there make good his case, the very constitution of his Church compels his rulers and judges to modify their action accordingly. Hence the power of ecclesiastical officers over the people is one of reason and scriptural interpretation, and not of mere official authority.

7. Under a republican form of government it is obvious that *the great body of the constituency are first and last in the thoughts of the legislators.* Legislative enactments are framed for their sakes and go forth in their name and by their authority. The people have only to call with united voice for the passage of some new law or the abrogation of an old one, and their voice is sure to be heard, or, if not, the obstinate servants will be dismissed and their places filled by others. Under such a system, class-legislation, which, where it prevails, tramples upon the rights of the people, destroys their prosperity, and

fills whole provinces with poverty and misery, is impossible.

So also in an ecclesiastical republic, the people are the Church, and are the body for whom the government is bound to legislate. The people are the human source of power, the framers of the government, the electors to office, the creators of legislators; and these creatures of the people must act for the people. There can be, therefore, no legislation for the clergy as against the laity, for without the consent of the laity the clergy can make no law; nor for the laity as against the clergy, for without the clergy the laity can pass no enactment. And as clergy and laity, combined, are the people—the Church—of necessity the people are first and last in the minds of the government. And if a body, like the General Assembly, composed of commissioners from the presbyteries, offend in a given instance the generality of the Church, the latter will see to it that other commissioners, whose views are in fuller accord with its own, shall in a subsequent assembly rectify the doings of its predecessor. And if a presbytery err, its members, mingling with the people, will be sure to hear their rebukes and remonstrances, and at another meeting a new delegation of elders will help them to retrace their steps and amend the offensive enactments. Thus, in the very constitution of Presbyterianism, the people possess all possible security against partial and unjust legislation.

In looking now over the Presbyterian system as a whole, we find it to be made up of an ascending series of lesser and larger republics, all, however, so interlocked together as to constitute one comprehensive whole—a true ecclesiastical *unum e pluribus.* A single congregation, with its pastor and ruling eldership, elected by and acting for and in the name of the people, forms a distinct republic—then the presbytery and synod and General Assembly, each composed of like materials and constructed after the same pattern, another republic—the whole blended into one by the interpenetration of the same general membership by the ascent of appeals from the lower to the higher, and on to the highest; review and control descending from the higher to the lower, and thus from the highest to the lowest; many members, warmed with the common life-blood propelled through them by one heart, moved to action by the common will acting through media called into existence in accordance with New Testament law, by the united mind and combined wisdom of the whole. In this scheme there is a realization of the highest unity in combination with an ever-varying diversity—of the fullest liberty in alliance with the most efficient legal authority. If, therefore, there is republicanism in all its beauty anywhere, it is found in sçriptural Presbyterianism.

8. It remains to add that the republicanism of the Presbyterian system is recognized by writers of every class, acknowledged by impartial historians, claimed as a glory by its friends, imputed as a crime by its foes.

Neander, in a note on the second chapter of his "Planting and Training," etc., writes:

"It is most probable that although all presbyters were called rulers of the synagogue, yet one who acted as president was distinguished by the title of ruler of the synagogue, as *primus inter pares*. In evidence of this, compare Luke viii. 41–49 with Mark v. 22. This is important in reference to the later relation of bishops and presbyters. The analogy to the Jewish synagogue allows us to conclude that at the head of the first Church at Jerusalem a general deliberative college was placed from the beginning—a notion favoured by comparison with the college of apostles; and in the Acts a plurality of presbyters always appears next in rank to the apostles, as *representatives* of the Church at Jerusalem. If any one is disposed to maintain that each of these presbyters presided over a smaller part of the Church at its special meetings, still it must thereby be established that, notwithstanding these divided meetings, the Church formed a whole, over which this deliberative college of presbyters presided, and therefore the form of government *was still republican.*"

"Each individual church," writes Mosheim, "assumed to itself the form and rights of a little distinct *republic* or *commonwealth;* and with regard to its internal concerns was wholly regulated by a code of laws that, if they did not originate with, had at least received the sanction of, the people constituting such church.

"At length the churches of a province became associated, much after the manner of "*confederate republics*, held conventions in which the common interest was provided for; so that the Christian community may be said, thenceforward, to have resembled one large commonwealth, made up, like those of Holland and Switzerland, of many minor republics."

Bancroft writes: "Calvinism is gradual republicanism. In Geneva, a republic on the confines of France, Italy and Germany, Calvin, appealing to the people for support, continued the career of enfranchisement by planting the institutions which nursed the minds of Rousseau, Necker and De Stael. The political character of Calvinism, which, with one consent and with instinctive judgment, the *monarchs* of that day *feared as republicanism,* and which Charles I. declared a religion unfit for a gentleman, is expressed in a single word—*predestination.*"

What historians assert, Presbyterians claim. "Our system of polity," writes Dr. Smythe, quoting from Dr. Rice, "was drawn up at a time when the general principles of government and the great subject of human rights and privileges were more thoroughly and anxiously discussed than at any other period since the settlement of this country. It was during the time when the sages of America were employed in framing the Federal Constitution. And the men who drew up this form of government were, many of them at least, men deeply versed in civil and ecclesiastical history. Perhaps this may, in some measure, account for the striking similarity which occurs in the fundamental principles of our polity and the form of government adopted by the United States. Like that form of government, our polity is neither monarchical nor democratical, but a democratic republic."

"Hence, the more decidedly a man is a Presbyterian the more decidedly is he a republican. So much is this the case, that some Christians of this society, fully believing that Presbytery is *de jure divino*, consider this as decisive evidence that republicanism is of divine institution, and are persuaded that they should grievously sin against God by acknowledging any other form of civil government."

Alexander Henderson writes: "Here is a superiority without tyranny, for no minister has a papal or monarchical jurisdiction over his own flock, far less over other pastors and over all the congregations of a large diocese. Here is parity without confusion and disorder, for the pastors are in order before elders, and elders before deacons; every particular church is subordinate to a presbytery, the presbytery to the synod, and the synod to the National Assembly. Here is subjection without slavery, for the people are subject to the pastors and assemblies; yet there is no assembly wherein every particular church hath not interest and power, nor is there anything done but they are—if not actually, yet virtually—called to consent unto it."

And what Presbyterians claim is charged upon them by their foes.

Dr. Peter Heylin, chaplain to those graceless creatures, Charles I. and Charles II., wrote a work under the following imposing title: "Ærius Redivivus; or, the History of the Presbyterians, containing the Beginnings, Progresse and Successes of that Active Sect—their oppositions to Monarchical and Episcopal Government," etc., etc. And the volume that thus begins ends as follows: "Thus have we seen the dangerous Doctrines and Positions, the Secret Plots and open Practices; the Sacrileges, Spoils and Rapines; the Tumults, Murthers and Seditions; the horrid Treasons and Rebellions which have been raised by the Presbyterians in most parts of Christendom for one hundred years and upward, which having been seen," etc., etc.

Hallam writes: "The discontented party set up their own platform of government by synods and classes agreeably to the Presbyterian model established in Scotland. Though Elizabeth, from policy, abetted the Scottish clergy in their attacks upon the civil administration, this connection itself had probably given her such insight into their temper, as well as their influence, that *she must have shuddered* at the thought of seeing a *republican* assembly substituted for those faithful satraps, her bishops, so ready to do her bidding."

Macaulay speaks of the Scottish preachers as those "who had inherited the *republican* opinions and the unconquerable spirit of Knox."

"Calvin," says Bishop Horsley, quoted by Smythe, "was unquestionably in theory a republican. So wedded was he to this notion that he endeavoured to fashion the government of all the Protestant churches upon republican principles; and his persevering zeal in that attempt was followed, upon the whole, with wide and mischievous success."

Bishop Hughes writes: "Though it is my privilege to regard the authority exercised by the General Assembly as usurpation, still I must say, with every man acquainted with the mode in which it is organized, that for the purposes of popular and political government, *its structure is little inferior* to that of Congress itself. In any emergency that may arise the General Assembly can produce a uniformity among its adherents to the farthest boundaries of the land. It acts on the principle of a radiating centre, and is WITHOUT AN EQUAL OR A RIVAL among the other denominations of the country."

King James, with characteristic coarseness, exclaimed at the Hampton Court Conference: "You are aiming at a Scot's Presbytery, which agrees with monarchy as well as God with the devil."

Charles I. no less cordially detested it. "Show me," he demanded, "any precedent wherever presbyterial government and regal were together without perpetual rebellions. And it cannot be otherwise, for the ground of their doctrine is anti-monarchical. I will say, without hyperbole, that there was not a wiser man since Solomon than he who said, No bishop no king." He said he looked upon Episcopacy as a stronger support of monarchical power than even the army.

Dean Swift, that *ornament* of the English Church, has added his testimony. Speaking of those who took refuge in Geneva from persecution in England, he says: "When they returned, they were grown so fond of the government and religion of the place they had left that they used all possible endeavours to introduce *both* into our country. From hence they proceeded to quarrel with the *kingly* government, because the city of Geneva, to which their fathers had flown for refuge, was a commonwealth, or government of the people."

The poet Dryden, too, more famed for poetry than for piety, wrote:

> "So *Presbytery* and its pestilential zeal
> *Can flourish only in a commonweal.*"

And how thoroughly Presbyterianism has maintained its republican character in America let history show. On this point we are still indebted to Dr. Smythe's able work, "Ecclesiastical Republicanism."

In 1767, an appeal was issued in New York on behalf of the Church of England in America, in which we read: "Episcopacy and monarchy are in their frame and constitution best suited to each other. Episcopacy can never thrive in a republic, nor republican principles in an Episcopal Church. He that prefers monarchy in the State is more likely to approve Episcopacy in the Church. It may reasonably be expected that those in authority will support and assist the Church in America, if from no other motives, yet from a regard to the State, with which it has so friendly an alliance."

A year before the Declaration of Independence, the Synod of New York declared themselves in favour of the struggle for liberty, and during the war their zeal exposed .them to special cruelty on the part of the British soldiery. "They were the first to recognize the Declaration when made, and materially aided in the passage of that noble act."

Bancroft writes, in his seventh volume:

"A similar spirit of independence prevailed in the highlands which hold the head springs of the Yadkin and the Catawba. The region was peopled chiefly by the Presbyterians of Scotch-Irish descent, *who brought to the New World the creed,* the spirit of resistance and the courage of the Covenanters.

"The people of the county of Mecklenburg had carefully observed the progress of the controversy with Britain, and during the winter political meetings had been repeatedly held in Charlotte. That town had been chosen for the seat of the Presbyterian college, which the legislature of North Carolina had chartered, but which the king had disallowed, and it was the centre of the culture of that part of the province."

When the crisis came, a representative committee was appointed and met in Charlotte. "No minutes of the committee are known to exist, but the result of their deliberations, framed with superior skill and precision of language and calm comprehensiveness, remains as the monument of their wisdom and courage. Of the delegates to that memorable assembly, the name of Ephraim Brevard should be remembered with honour by his countrymen. Trained in the college at Princeton, ripened among the brave Presbyterians of Middle Carolina, he digested the system which was then adopted, and which formed in effect a declaration of independence, as well as a complete system of government. 'All laws and commissions confirmed by or derived from the king or parliament are annulled and vacated; the provincial congress of each province, under direction of the great continental congress, is invested with all legislative and executive powers.'"

A wise and judicious system of government was then prepared. The resolves were made binding on all, and the militia companies ordered to provide themselves with arms to maintain them.

"Before the month of May, 1775, had come to an end, the resolutions were signed by Ephraim Brevard, as clerk of the committee, and were adopted by the people with the determined enthusiasm which springs from the combined influence of the love of liberty and of religion. Thus was Mecklenburg county in North Carolina separated from the British empire."

And through the whole momentous struggle Presbyterianism displayed the same ardent, determined, patriotic spirit. To quote the eloquent words of the writer's late beloved friend and former pastor, *Dr. John M. Krebs*—words that it was our lot to hear when uttered from the pulpit—"When the Declaration of Independence was under debate in the Continental Congress, doubts and forebodings were whispered through the hall. The houses hesitated, wavered, and for a while the liberty and slavery of the nation appeared to hang in an even scale. It was then an aged patriarch arose, a venerable and stately form, his head white with the frost of years. Every eye went to him with the quickness of thought, and remained with the fixedness of the polar star. He cast on the assembly a look of inexpressible interest and unconquerable determination, while on his visage the hue of age was lost in the flush of a burning patriotism that fired his cheek. 'There is,' said he, 'a tide in the affairs of men, a nick of time. We perceive it now before us. To hesitate is to consent to our own slavery. That noble instrument upon your table, which ensures immortality to its author, should be subscribed this very morning by every pen in the house. He that will not respond to its accents, and strain every nerve to carry into effect its provisions, is unworthy of the name of freeman. For my own part, of property I have some, of reputation more. That reputation is staked, that property is *pledged* on the issue of this contest. And although these gray hairs must soon descend into the sepulchre, I would infinitely rather they should descend there by the hands of the executioner than desert at this crisis the sacred cause of my country.'

"Who was it that uttered this memorable speech—potent in turning the scales of the nation's destiny, and worthy to be preserved in the same imperishable record in which is registered the not more eloquent speech ascribed to John Adams on the same sublime occasion? It was John Witherspoon, at that day the most distinguished Presbyterian minister west of the Atlantic ocean, the father of the Presbyterian Church in the United States."

Dr. Smythe writes: "We have collected from high authority the following facts: The battles of the Cowpens, of King's Mountain, and also the severe skirmish known as Huck's Defeat, are among the most celebrated in this State, as giving a turning-point to the contest of the Revolution. General Morgan, who commanded at the Cowpens, was a Presbyterian elder. General Pickens, who made all the arrangements for the battle, was also a Presbyterian elder. And nearly all under their command were Presbyterians. In the battle of King's Mountain, Colonel Campbell, Colonel James Williams, Colonel Cleaveland, Colonel Shelby, and Colonel Servier were all Presbyterian elders, and the body of their troops were collected from Presbyterian settlements. At Huck's Defeat, in York, Colonel Bratton and Major Dickson were both elders in the Presbyterian Church. Major Samuel Morrow, who was with Colonel Sumpter in four engagements, and at King's Mountain, Blackstock's and other battles, was for about fifty years a ruling elder in the Presbyterian Church."

"A Presbyterian loyalist," says Mr. William B. Reed, himself an Episcopalian, "was a thing unheard of. Patriotic clergymen of the Established Church were exceptions to the general conduct. The debt of gratitude which independent

America owes to the dissenting clergy and laity can never be paid."

Our Church, then, in form and spirit is thoroughly republican, and the whole tendency of our system is to imbue its clergy and members with republican feeling and sympathy; and in this it is more thoroughly in harmony with the civil republicanism of our government and nation than any other ecclesiastical system that exists under the shadow of our national banner.

CHURCH AND STATE.

III.

CHURCH AND STATE.

WHATEVER society has the right to exist has therein the right to institute and carry out such system of government over its membership as is essential to its continued existence. But if anything on earth has such right, the Church of Christ has; this right based on the will of God. It is by his express command, through his own agency, that it comes into being. It asks no leave of human governments to be. It springs up as the flowers do in the meadows, in lands where civil governments are, and whatever their form, and where they are not, in America and Britain, among the Indians in the forest, in China and Hindostan. It not only asks no leave of civil governments to be, but grows up under their eyes and despite their opposition. No poor sapling on the cold, thin-soiled mountain-side ever struggled more toilsomely and persistently for life than has the

Church, in many a land under the frown, wrath and merciless persecution of secular governments. When its infant King entered the world, Herod trembled, and all Jerusalem with him. But Herod's trembling soon gave place to energetic malice, and he sent his soldiers to kill the royal babe in his mother's arms. From that hour, for many a weary, bloody century, the Church grew, in spite of governmental frowns and violence, until it became a mighty power. The blood of its martyrs proved a prolific seed, and the ashes of martyr-fires, as they were blown upon the people, made them Christians. The Neros and Domitians lent all their imperial power in vain to overcome the power of the gospel and stay the march of faith and repentance.

And this Church possesses, direct from God, the right to institute and carry out its own system of government. This right lies in its own bosom. No secular government may say what form that government shall assume—may modify any one of its laws—may interpose between it and the execution of any one of its sentences against offenders—may make any law that shall, by its operation, interfere with the operation of the legitimate laws of the Church. If it do, the

Church is bound to protest against and disregard such enactments.

But the question as to the legitimate relations subsisting between these two styles of government—the secular and the ecclesiastical—as to how they can coexist among the same people, and just where their boundaries meet and limit each other, is one that has evoked boundless, and sometimes passionate, discussion—has employed the ablest pens, and is even yet far from having found final and generally-accepted solution. How can two several governments within the same territories, operating upon the same persons, yet each entirely independent of the other, coexist without collision? And, in fact, in very few countries have they ever so existed for any considerable length of time. Each has at one time or another encroached upon and attained melancholy ascendency over its neighbour. The conflict between them began very early, and the history of the Church of Scotland is hardly more than a continued succession of such conflicts.

But whenever they do occur, the difficulty has arisen, not from essential antagonism between them, but from some abnormal action on the part of the one or the other. How, indeed, is it possible for them, when acting each within its own legitimate sphere, to come in any way or degree into conflict. God is the Author of both. He has ordained them. And how could he who is infinite in wisdom and who has so wonderfully adjusted the wheels of all nature in their unjarring harmonies; the planetary and stellar systems working with such undeviating accuracy; the oxygen and carbon in our atmosphere, the great predominance of one destroying human, and of the other vegetable life, yet, though ever changing conditions, after six thousand years retaining just their originally-appointed proportions; the light, too, just adapted to the eye and the eye to the light,—how could the Master of all these harmonies make a mistake in the simpler matter of adjusting these powers of Church and State?

Yet the history of the antagonisms between, and alternate encroachments of, civil and ecclesiastical governments fills many a sadly instructive page in the annals of the world.

Nero was the first Roman emperor who enacted laws against the Christians, and these laws were directed against them not as an obnoxious governmental power, but as the professors of a faith that scorned all acknowledgment of the heathen-ism of the empire. In this he was followed by Diocletian and other emperors down to Constantine.

By this time, however, the primitive government of the Church had undergone an entire transformation, and church authority, in the hands of bishops invested with almost regal dignities, had become a power to be either courted or brought under subjection. The first encroachments of the one upon the authority of the other came from the State, and from the time of Constantine "the supreme civil powers, professing to feel an obligation to exert their civil authority for the welfare of the Church and the good of religion," frequently interfered "to a large extent in religious, theological and ecclesiastical matters, professedly in discharge of this obligation."

Constantine himself, though he made no great alterations in the government of the Church, and allowed it to remain, as it had hitherto been, a distinct body politic separate from the State, yet assumed supremacy over it, and exercised to some extent a right to give its government such shape as seemed to him conducive to the general good.

Successive emperors assumed the right to convoke ecclesiastical councils, to preside over them, to appoint judges to decide religious controversies and to settle difficulties arising between bishops and the people. They often determined matters of a purely ecclesiastical nature.

In the mean time, however, without knowing it, they were fostering a power that should one day set its foot upon the necks of kings and claim supreme jurisdiction in matters civil as well as sacred.

The bishop of Rome, through a course of gradual aggrandizement, came at length into possession of vast powers, and began to arrogate to himself the spiritual sovereignty of the whole Church. To make Constantinople another Rome, *her* bishop must claim and receive dignity and authority at least not inferior to that of the latter. Accordingly, the Council of Constantinople, at the end of the fourth century, by formal canon, elevated the bishop of that city into supremacy over those of Alexandria and Antioch—a supremacy soon extended over all Asia, Thrace and Pontus. With these new dignities came new emoluments. Thus for secular ends the civil power played off bishop against bishop, until, by the middle of the fifth century, these dignitaries were "monarchs without disguise."

At length the Roman Empire fell. The barbarian deluge swept all civil power to ruin. All the bonds of society were broken, and a dismal anarchy set in. But the Church did not fall. After the fashion of the times, she converted these barbarians and subdued them to her spiritual sway. And now all eyes turned toward Church dignitaries as the only tower in the sea of confusion. In numerous instances they were appealed to to settle controversies in civil matters, and the idea of supreme dominion in State affairs soon sprang into mind and grew to an early and vigorous maturity.

The man to realize this idea soon appeared in the person of Hildebrand. Of obscure parentage, in 1073 he was elected to the Papal chair and assumed the name of Gregory VII.

Hildebrand was a man of uncommon genius, whose ambition in forming the most arduous projects was equalled by his dexterity in bringing them into execution. Sagacious, crafty and intrepid, nothing could escape his penetration, defeat his stratagems or daunt his courage; haughty and arrogant beyond all measure, obstinate, impetuous and intractable. He looked up to the summit of universal empire with a wishful eye, and laboured up the steep ascent with uninterrupted ardour and invincible perseverance. Void of all principle, and destitute of every pious and virtuous feeling, he suffered little restraint in his audacious pursuits from the dictates of religion or the remonstrances of conscience.

His first aim was to make the see of Rome absolute mistress of the universal Church. This accomplished, he secured the independence of the affairs of the Church from all secular control; and this accomplished, he conceived, and to a large extent effected, the subjection of civil government to the control of the Church—that is, to the Romish pope. In the execution of this last scheme he encountered opposition—formidable, indeed, but only in the end to come off conqueror. Henry IV., Emperor of Germany, a child of licentiousness and ambition, whose approbation Gregory had sought and obtained, by a special and flattering embassage, as the seal of his election to the papacy, afterward indignantly resisted the efforts of the latter to withdraw the officials of the Church from secular sway, and, assembling a diet of the empire at Worms, deposed his antagonist from the papal throne. Gregory, however, neither dismayed by danger nor to be deterred from executing his purpose by whatever opposition, rather rejoiced at the opportunity thus offered of realizing before all the world by a splendid example his grand scheme of universal sovereignty. He accordingly convoked a council at the Lateran palace, solemnly excommunicated Henry, and in the name of St. Peter declared him deposed from the thrones of Germany and Italy, and all his subjects released from their allegiance. Thus the vassal changed place with his master. Henry's subjects, ripe for revolution, willingly accepted their new condition, and a diet was convoked to elect a new emperor. This brought the proud monarch to his knees in sackcloth and ashes. Crossing the Alps with his wife and child, Henry arrived at the pope's residence and begged for an interview. The proud priest would not condescend to look upon his victim till the latter laid aside the insignia of royalty, clad himself in a coarse woollen garment as a penitent, and in this guise had stood barefoot for three days from morning till night in the open court and in the depth of winter. Then, humbly confessing, the wretched monarch was absolved of excommunication, but his restoration to the throne was referred to the diet of the empire.

Thus we are introduced to the *Romish view* of the *legitimate relations subsisting* between *ecclesias-*

ical and *civil government.* Romanism maintains that the civil authorities are as such subordinate to ecclesiastical domination. This view is based upon the lofty character of the objects to which ecclesiastical government is directed. On this ground civil rulers are bound to adjust all those acts which bear upon religious persons and institutions to the laws of the Church. "The popish doctrine," writes Principal Cunningham, "makes the civil ruler a mere tool or servant of the Church, and represents him as implicitly bound to carry out the Church's objects, to execute her sentences, and to make everything subservient to the accomplishment of her designs."

Thus the pope is represented by some Romish writers as "lord paramount of the world," and "invested with supreme power in temporal things;" while others "ascribe to him but an indirect authority in these matters, to be exercised *in ordine ad spiritualia,* which, as he is the judge of when and how far the interests of religion may require him to interfere in secular matters, is just giving him as much of temporal power as he may find it convenient to claim or may be able to enforce."

Further, according to this system, church officers,

in all matters affecting their personal and secular interests, are and ought to be exempt from civil jurisdiction. In whatever land they live, and under whatever form of government, they are subjects first and completely of the Church as represented by its head, the Papal monarch. Whether worthy of pains and penalties for any alleged offence, it is for the ecclesiastical not for the secular courts to decide. Thus the pope in his assumed jurisdiction is omnipotent among his widely-scattered subjects, and every act of the civil government that interferes with this jurisdiction is an offence against God.

In the opposite extreme from this view is that commonly called *Erastian*. Erastus, whose name has become associated with the governmental theory elaborated from views first distinctly pronounced by, though not wholly originating with him, was a native of Switzerland, a physician and a man of erudition. Joining the Reformers, and indignant alike at the exorbitant claims of Romanism and at some of the principles admitted by the Protestants of his time, he went to the opposite extreme, and resolved all the disciplinary powers of the Church into the will of the State. The system which grew out of the principles he advocated seems to be based in part upon exaggerated views of unity in the State, and in part upon a misapprehension of the proper functions of the body politic. This latter is apprehended as an organization so compact and of such close interdependence of organs as to necessitate a single supreme head over all—an ultimate authority to which *all* questions in controversy might be referred for decision. Without a head the body politic is a monster; and with two heads, the one spiritual and the other secular, it is hardly less monstrous. A separate jurisdiction allowed in the State, but uncontrolled by the State, results in the much-dreaded *imperium in imperio*, placing the subject at once under two several and possibly at times opposing jurisdictions, obedience to one subjecting him to penalties from the other.

When, therefore, the question comes up for decision as to which of the great interests of society, the sacred or the secular, shall hold the sceptre, while Romanism gives it to the former as in every sense the higher and more solemn, Erastianism prefers the latter, under the impression that civil government is legitimately entrusted with control over *all* that concerns the well-being of the State.

Mr. Mill, indeed, has affirmed that the well-being of the governed, collectively and individually, is the object of government. But from his extremely low views of spiritual affairs he undoubtedly ignores them altogether, and by the "well-being of society" refers to it in its purely secular aspects. But if he would intimate that all things that conduce to man's well-being are matters for direct control by the State, religion must come first and foremost in the list, and complete Erastianism results.

Lord Macaulay has more explicitly declared that government is designed to protect persons and property; to compel the citizen to satisfy his wants by industry rather than by rapine; to compel him to settle his differences with his neighbour by arbitration rather than by the strong arm; and to direct the whole force of the nation as that of one man against any other society that may threaten with injury.

But while asserting, with all earnestness, the duty of every man in or out of authority to be a religious man, and as such to use all his influence to favour religion as bearing more weightily upon the weal of the citizen for time and eternity than all others combined, yet it can never be conceded that religion, either in its doctrine or government, is at all under the control of the secular power. But according to Erastianism the object of civil government is the citizen, and *all* that concerns man as such. But religion seriously concerns him, and hence religion must be under its control. Religion shapes the whole course of human conduct, and human conduct is one of the direct objects of governmental control, and hence religion must come under its sway. Church censures and discipline directly, and sometimes powerfully, invade the happiness of the citizen, and hence they must be under the efficient oversight and control of the magistrate. While, therefore, church officers may teach and exhort, they may not inflict censure, or, if they do, it may only be as agents and instruments of the civil government.

Erastianism need not deny that the Church is a society within a society; it may admit that this society possesses authority of a certain degree or kind not derived directly from the State; but yet, as the State is supreme, such authority is to be exercised under its eye and within the limits it prescribes, and from all decisions of the church judicatories appeal must lie to the secular power.

The State may, if it please, and when its constitution allows, employ the ecclesiastical power for the benefit of the citizen and the good of society; and it may see fit, as is the case in England. There, among the matters submitted to the jurisdiction of the bishops are the questions respecting wills, marriage and divorce, though they commonly reassign these questions to the State by appointing secular men to examine and decide upon them according to certain established rules. And even over these courts and officers, the civil government maintains a careful superintendence, explaining the laws which concern the extent of their jurisdiction, keeping them within the limits of that jurisdiction, and, if they exceed those limits, issuing prohibitions to restrain them, or summoning to answer for their conduct before the civil courts.

Thus the English Church from the beginning has been thoroughly Erastian. It is the creature and slave of the State. Baptist W. Noel, long under its dominion, in his powerful work on the "Union of Church and State," has drawn a vivid and terrible picture of the rigours and corrupting influence of the State in that Establishment. "Ever since the union of the Church of England with its imperious and profligate head, Henry VIII., who burned alive the friends of the pope and the followers of Zwingli, the State in England, with scarcely the exception of one brief interval, has been steadily opposed to evangelical religion. Queen Mary, though a bigoted Catholic, continued to be the legal head of the Church of England."

The main links that connect the Anglican Church with the State, the Acts of Supremacy and Uniformity, "establish the subordination" of the Church, "*abrogating all jurisdiction and legislative power of ecclesiastical rulers except under authority of the Crown, and prohibiting all changes of rites and discipline without the approbation of the Parliament.*"

Over the clergy Queen Elizabeth ruled with despotic sway. On a question between the bishop of Ely and Cox, this pious queen wrote to the latter: "Proud prelate, you know what you were before I made you what you are. If you do not immediately comply with my request, by ——, I will unfrock you! ELIZABETH."

"She suspended Fletcher, bishop of London, for marrying; and Aylmer having preached against female vanity in dress, she said if he held more discourse on such matters she would fit him for heaven."

Noel shows, by ample quotation from the laws

of the realm, that the State "claims and exercises the right of superintendence over the churches—that bishops and pastors have no manner of spiritual jurisdiction within the churches but from the Crown, which may delegate its authority to ecclesiastical lawyers—that no minister may impeach the royal supremacy in spiritual things under pain of excommunication—that the State determines the settlement of pastors within the establishment, its doctrines and worship, its discipline and government."

And what is this State that thus lords it over God's heritage? It embraces the Crown, the House of Lords and the Commons, the great majority of whom are men not even Christians, and they may all be infidels, and still retain their legal jurisdiction over the Established Church! And that Church has become what it now is by "acts of Parliament formed illegally, corrupted by pensions and overawed by prerogative."

The disastrous effects of Church alliance with the State are powerfully exhibited.

The bishop walks into a palace with a salary of five thousand pounds per annum. He becomes a peer of the realm. He becomes invested with a vast amount of patronage. The archbishops and bishops of England and Wales have together 1248 benefices in their gift, besides other church preferment. And while this wealth and association with worldly rulers tends powerfully to corrupt and secularize, this patronage depresses the clergy into a degrading servility of temper, and works in the prelate a haughty, overbearing spirit. And while the lower clergy cringe before him, he cringes in turn to the ministers of the Crown.

Upon the pastor the effects of this union are no less deleterious. It makes him entirely independent of support by the people, and thus encourages him in indolence. "And, indeed," asks Noel, "is there more than one rector out of ten who preaches, catechises, visits the sick or instructs from house to house?" It makes him secure of his office, though his character may be ever so subversive of piety among his people—though he be "ignorant, idle, a sportsman, a card-player, gluttonous, proud and quarrelsome. Bound under solemn and repeated oaths to maintain the *whole system* of the Establishment, and bribed thereto by a prospective palace and five thousand pounds a year, he must refrain from attacking such notorious and enormous evils as the introduction of irreligious youths into the ministry, the complete fusion of the Church and the world at the Lord's table, the almost total neglect of church discipline, the errors of the articles of the Prayer Book, and many, many others."

If the bishop refuses to induct a candidate presented by the patron, which patron may be and often is an utterly irreligious man, the law lays its hand upon him, and scarcely any presentee is rejected, and the pulpits are full of unconverted men.

Under this system the Church has become "a confused mass of believers and unbelievers, allowing strangers to impose upon them multitudes of ungodly pastors, who bring a spiritual blight upon them. Upon the masses of the working class, the myriads of fashion and the whole army of scientific and literary men, Anglican Christians make scarcely any impression, while a latent and widespread infidelity is making unchecked ravages among them."

He thus concludes his review of this system: "The union of the churches with the State is doomed. Condemned by reason and religion, by Scripture and experience, how can it be allowed to injure the nation much longer? Its State salaries, its supremacy, its patronage, its compulsion of payments for the support of religion are condemned by both the precedents and precepts of the word of God. It excludes the gospel from thousands of parishes, perpetuates corruptions of doctrine, hinders all spiritual discipline, desecrates the ordinances of Christ, confounds the Church and the world, foments schism, tempts ministers to become politicians, embarrasses successive governments, maintains one chief element of revolution in the country, renders the reformation of the Anglican churches almost hopeless, hinders the progress of the Gospel throughout the kingdom, and strengthens all the corrupt Papal establishments of Europe."

Such, then, is genuine Erastianism in its character and results. While Romanism subjects the State to the Church, Erastianism subjects the Church to the State, making the former a component and subordinate part of the latter. And these evils seem to be necessarily involved in a formal governmental alliance of the Church with the State. This, indeed, many of our Scotch brethren most earnestly deny; and while they plead with all zeal for such an alliance, they with equal zeal and warm indignation repudiate and denounce Erastianism. Dr. Chalmers, Dr. Cunningham, and other noble champions of the truth, contend for the utter independence of the Church of all State control, and for the kingship of Christ as sole monarch of the Church; and, while formally admitting that the Church for centuries, not only without State patronage, but in opposition to its persecuting intolerance, fully and nobly accomplished the great ends of its existence—while constantly conceding that, with very few if any exceptions, such alliances have resulted in more evil than good, that in many noted instances the Church in such condition has been induced to consent to civil interference in ecclesiastical affairs fearfully damaging to the cause of truth and righteousness, Dr. Cunningham distinctly declaring, "I am not sure that any Protestant established Church has ever wholly escaped sin and degradation by such alliance, except the Scottish Church at the second Reformation"—acknowledging that even in Scotland, under the Revolution settlement, the fundamental principles of the Church were overturned by secular influence, "so that it became impossible for a man who had scriptural views of what a Church of Christ is, and what are the principles by which its affairs ought to be regulated to remain in connection with it"—yet, with all this, they are fully persuaded that the State, as such, not only lawfully may, but is under solemn obligation to, use its power directly in behalf of the Church, and employ its resources to maintain her ministers and promote her interests. That magistrates, like all other men, should in *all* their conduct be governed by Christian principles, and seek to further the cause of religion, is admitted by all; but when the State consents, out of the national purse, to support, in whole or in part, the ministers and institutions of religion, it is very difficult to convince her of the impropriety of a share in the shaping of the institutions and in the appointment and control of the ministers she thus supports; and on this the State has in fact always insisted, and, as the bitter experience of the Church of Scotland shows, insisted not in vain. If the State pays the salaries of the ministers, she will claim, and not without reason, to share largely in determining who shall receive of her munificence; and she will also claim a large share in determining controversies arising among them. And this results in practical Erastianism of a higher or lower grade. And while the example of the Church in her best, purest and most efficient days, for centuries in succession, stands on record, and with the extended experience of the Church in the

United States in view, it will be very difficult to convince American Christians that "a condition of entire separation from the State and entire dependence upon the contributions of the people" is not only a perfectly lawful and honourable condition for the Church to occupy, but also, in view especially of the fact that governmental union of Church and State has invariably resulted in serious damage to the former, that it is not the only system consistent with the will of God and the welfare of religion. Only thus can the Church keep the ark of God from contamination by men who have neither love for her doctrines nor regard for her purity.

The *third* theory as to the proper relations between the Church and State is that prevalent in our republic.

This involves their coexistence side by side, yet each in complete independence of the other. They are twin sisters of the same parent, neither possessing any dominion over the other.

That civil government exists by ordinance of God, and is by him clothed with authority to reach the end designed in its ordination, few will deny.

No less true is it that the Church exists by virtue of the forthputting of divine power upon human hearts, and it also is invested directly from heaven with authority of a certain kind over its membership.

Equally manifest is it that from the necessity of the case relations of a very intimate character subsist between them. They are children of the same Father. Their subjects are the same persons. These persons, also, are directly affected in their spiritual interests by the character and conduct of the secular government, and in their secular interests by the control and decisions of the spiritual government.

Thus over the two grand departments of human interest, the sacred and the secular, God has ordered two several agencies—the Church, the custodian of religious truth, and the instructor of men therein; and the State, for the protection of men in their rights, and for the restraint and punishment of those who invade the rights of others. The specific duties allotted to the one are entirely distinct from those allotted to the other, though both contribute to the common weal. Like sunshine and shower, the one is not the other, yet both concur in bringing on the harvest.

The Church is not the State, and the State is not the Church, yet they may, and one day will, both comprehend precisely the same elementary constituents. Every member of the Church may be a citizen, and every citizen may be a member of the Church.

Yet they may not invade each other's given spheres of service. The Church cannot annul even an iniquitous enactment of the State, though she may and must protest against it, and through the steady operation of her hallowed instrumentalities strive so to reach the public mind and heart as to bring about the much-needed reform. The State may not formally annul any decree of the Church, even one consigning heretics and atheists to the flames, but she may and ought to see to it that such a law remain a dead letter on the ecclesiastical statute-book.

The Rev. Dr. E. P. Humphrey thus concisely and clearly expounds the practical relations subsisting between the two styles of government, spiritual and civil:

"1. The Church and State are, both of them, ordinances of God.

"2. The province of each is separate and distinct. The Church exists for the salvation of sinners; the State, for the temporal welfare of its citizens. The Church ought not to be predominant over the State, which is pure Papacy; nor subordinate to the State, which is Erastianism; nor simply tolerated by the State, which is semi-Erastianism; but wholly independent of the State, which is the American theory.

"3. Subjects which are purely *secular* in their nature belong exclusively to the State. Questions of the tariff, of banks, income taxes, suffrage, the army and navy, and the like, fall under the sole jurisdiction of the State, and any attempt on the part of the Church to determine them ought to be resisted. So, also, subjects which are purely *spiritual* belong exclusively to the Church. Questions of revealed religion, such as the doctrine of the Trinity and the Atonement, the mode of worship, the sacraments, and the way of Church government, and the like, fall under the jurisdiction of the Church, and any attempt of the State to meddle with them ought to be rebuked. But there are subjects which may be called *mixed*, being in some of their aspects secular and in other aspects religious. Here the rule is obvious. In mixed cases all those aspects which are secular belong to the State, and must be determined by the civil tribunal; all those aspects which are spiritual belong to the Church, and must be turned over to the ecclesiastical courts."

When, therefore, the several spheres of action and specific duties of Church and State are understood, there is neither need of nor room for collision; and that this theoretic harmony is practicable also, is evident from the happy working of the voluntary system in our republic.

Such, then, being the proper relations respectively of Church and State, each independent of the other's control, yet, as twin ordinances of God, closely bound together, each contributing in its own way and measure to the common weal, it is obvious that they should, in every practicable way, lend each other a helping hand in their several spheres. And such is, indeed, largely the case in the United States.

The State not only carefully withholds her hands from imposing unnecessary burdens upon the Church, but in many ways recognizes Christianity as a fundamental principle in the nation. Her magistrates enter office with their hand upon the Bible and by solemn appeal to its God. She appoints chaplains for the legislature and for the army and navy. The Continental Congress, by formal resolution, encouraged the circulation of the Holy Scriptures. These Scriptures are largely read in her public schools. Her laws largely protect the holy Sabbath from desecrations. She throws open her hospitals and asylums to the ministers of religion, and often in negotiation with heathen powers she has secured access for the gospel to heathen millions.

But whatever is done by the State in behalf of the Church is, many times over, repaid in services rendered by the Church in return.

If the State protects the Church, the latter prays for the State. The God of nations, who dashes them in pieces like a potter's vessel or assigns to them a long career of honour and glory, is a prayer-hearing God, and many a time in the history of the nation have her prayers been worth more to the State than an army of fifty thousand men.

In the republic, reverence for law is her very life, and a general spirit of lawlessness her ruin. But to the prevalence of such a spirit she is peculiarly exposed. In lands where the laws come down from a sovereignty acknowledged as of divine right and armed with despotic power, the masses are easily schooled to the spirit of submission. But when law alone is sovereign, and this law the work of legislators created by the people; when laws are made and unmade at the will of the people and by men whose conduct they constantly scrutinize, and whose character they feel themselves possessed, as it were, of a divine right to abuse and malign, law and government are likely to share in the contempt which is so often—and often so wickedly—visited upon the magistracy. But here the Church steps in, and in millions of ears proclaims her doctrine, that government is an ordinance of God—that its ministers are God's ministers as truly as was Moses or Joshua—and thus she reclothes the government with that mantle of majesty torn from her shoulders by the hands of an irreverent democracy. And at all times when popular passions have overflowed in actual or threatened violence, her voice has been on the side of law and order. Always has she proclaimed the duty of rendering unto Cæsar the things that are Cæsar's. And in times of peculiar peril, when the State is threatened with disintegration and utter overthrow; when doctrines are uttered and maintained at the bayonet's point and the cannon's mouth which are as unscriptural as they are ruinous, and whose general prevalence would operate like the suspension of the law of gravitation in nature, dispersing all things in wildest confusion; and when, further, the Church sees in this threatened dissolution the crippling if not the destruction of all her great agencies for benevolent operations in domestic and foreign fields, every holy instinct of her nature impels her, and every solemn obligation binds her, to lift up her voice like a trumpet and ply all her energies in rebuke of the ominous error, and in encouragement and support of the imperilled government ordained of God for the nation's good and for his own glory.

Besides, as population increases and wealth becomes extreme on the one hand and poverty on the other, in spite of whatever opposition it may be in the power of the State to offer, vice will increase; and just as surely as unchecked disease brings death to the patient, so surely will vice, when it reaches a certain point, bring death to the republic, plunging into anarchy or locking up in the prison-house of despotism. And the balm for this chronic tendency, the medicament for this festering sore, is in the Church, and in her alone—in her divine laws, with their awful sanctions, in her great ideas of God, the judgment, eternity and retribution. These ideas are brought into contact with the public mind through the pulpit, the city and other missionaries, mission and other Sabbath-schools; and the service the Church thus renders to the cause of virtue no arithmetic can possibly compute.

Complaint is sometimes made at the exemption of church property from taxation, on the ground that what is lost to the revenues in this way must be made up by the citizens in another, and this involves, to a certain extent, the support of the Church by the State. But there is another side to this question. The Church, through her influence over men, is constantly bestowing upon the State those who most truly and purely fill her various offices. Besides this, she turns from the ways of vice multitudes who else would become murderers, robbers and house-burners, and thus relieves the State of many of her worst enemies, and from the taxation needed for their arrest, trial and support in prison. In a word, let the State seriously burden the Church in her work of purifying the very fountains of society, and she will have to quadruple her taxation even to exist at all.

Coarse complaint is also made by foreign brawlers of the protection afforded to preserve the Sabbath from overthrow. But, if the State wishes to tie a millstone about her own neck, let her seriously cripple the energies of the Church, and if she wishes seriously to cripple her energies, let her lend her aid to the overthrow of the holy Sabbath day.

Thus, at all times and under all circumstances, while carefully refraining from interference with each other's functions—the Church never tampering with the duties of the State and never pandering to the passions of a political partisanship, the State never laying unholy hands upon the ark of God—they should still sympathize with and lend their influence in furthering the prosperity of each other, and thus work harmoniously together for the public weal.

THE CONFLICT.

IV.

THE CONFLICT.

HAVING at the outset introduced the reader to the revolutionary outburst at St. Giles, that first great explosion of the pent-up antagonisms between Presbyterianism on the one hand and despotism on the other, and having sketched an outline of legitimate ecclesiastical government, and the proper relations between it and the State, we will now trace the rise and progress of that fierce conflict in which Presbyterianism fought with despotism and conquered, and then point out some of the fruits of the victory. But let us introduce the war by an inspection of the battle-field.

THE BATTLE-FIELD.

Immediately after the close of the apostolic age corruptions in doctrine and practice, which had long before shown a vicious impatience with the constraints of primitive zeal and piety, set in with a tide that soon buried almost the whole Church in a deluge that arose higher than fifteen cubits above the tops of the mountains.

The great awakening in the sixteenth century found Scotland a field where the beast shook his many heads, brandished his horns and stamped his iron feet without let or hindrance. Remote from the great centres and highways of civilization, the public mind and manners were hardly reached by those forces that played in more favoured lands to soften and subdue and prepare for the coming of the white horse and his rider (Rev. vi. 2). The public character wore, therefore, a peculiar sternness of feature, and retained not a few traces of a hardly-waning barbarism. This condition of things was prolonged by the anarchical confusion of civil affairs. In other countries the system of feudal anarchy, which forbade anything like national unity, leaving the king little more than a powerful baron among scores of others, some of them at times more powerful than himself, impatient of control, following the monarch when they pleased, and deserting his armies upon any freak and at every pique, had yielded to an ever-growing centralization of power, and anarchy had passed reluctantly but surely into the fixed forms of rigid despotism, with its standing armies at the bidding of one vigorous will. But in Scotland the only law was that of confusion, the only unity that of fragmentary disunion. The kings were a "feeble folk" in the midst of their haughty nobles, who each avenged his own wrongs in his own way, and in so doing perpetrated other wrongs sure to bring down sooner or later like wild vengeance from the strong arms and towering passions of the injured. In all the fields and mountains the dove of peace found no resting-place for the sole of her foot. Wars in the deep interior, wars in her mountain gorges, and, more than all, wars almost incessant on the southern border, fierce forays, slaughtering and burning and rapine—these were the scenes that nourished barbarism and frighted civilization away.

And yet all this was anything but a low animal savageism. In the bosom of this rugged mine lay the most precious jewels of valour, endurance, heroism and genius, that, once brought into the forms and under the holy restraints and constraints of evangelical faith, would issue in Knoxes, Melvilles, Hendersons, Chalmers, Duffs, Guthries and Cunninghams.

Macaulay has drawn this picture of that people: "They were singularly turbulent and ungovernable.

They had butchered their First James in his bed-chamber; had repeatedly arrayed themselves in arms against the Second; had slain James the Third on the field of battle; their dissensions had broken the heart of James the Fifth, etc. He adds, that they deposed and imprisoned Mary and led her son captive, and "their temper was rude and intractable as ever."

But now the question arises, What had Romanism done, during the long centuries, and what was it now doing, to infuse the mild, heavenly charities of the gospel into the hearts and minds of this rude, martial, heroic, half civilized nation?

The answer is found in the following words of Dr. McCrie, in his able Life of John Knox:

"The corruptions by which the Christian religion was universally disfigured had grown to a greater height in Scotland than in any other nation within the pale of the Western Church. Superstition and religious imposture, in their grossest forms, gained an easy admission among a rude and ignorant people. By means of these the clergy *attained to an exorbitant* degree of opulence and power; which were accompanied, as they always have been, with the corruption of their order and of the whole system of religion.

"The full half of the wealth of the nation belonged to the clergy, and the greater part of this was in the hands of a few individuals, who had the command of the whole body. Avarice, ambition and the love of secular pomp reigned among the superior orders. Bishops and abbots rivalled the first nobility in magnificence and preceded them in honours; they were privy councillors and lords of session, as well as of Parliament, and had long engrossed the principal offices of State. A vacant bishopric or abbey called forth powerful competitors, who contended for it as for a principality or petty kingdom; it was obtained by similar arts, and not unfrequently taken possession of by the same weapons. Inferior benefices were often put up for sale, or bestowed on the illiterate and unworthy minions of courtiers—on dice-players, strolling bards and the bastards of bishops. Pluralities were multiplied without bounds, and benifices, given in commendam, were kept vacant during the life of the commendator—nay, sometimes during several lives, so that extensive parishes were frequently deprived for a long course of years of all religious service. The bishops never, on any occasion, condescended to preach; indeed, I scarcely recollect an instance of it mentioned in history from the erection of the regular Scottish Episcopacy down to the era of the Reformation.

"The lives of the clergy, exempted from secular jurisdiction and corrupted by wealth and idleness, were become a scandal to religion and an outrage on decency; while they professed chastity and prohibited, under the severest penalties, any of the ecclesiastical order from contracting lawful wedlock, the bishops set an example of the most shameless profligacy before the inferior clergy; avowedly kept their harlots, provided their natural sons with benefices, and gave their daughters in marriage to the sons of the nobility and principal gentry, many of whom were so mean as to contaminate the blood of their families by such base alliances for the sake of the rich dowries which they brought.

"Through the blind devotion and munificence of princes and nobles, monasteries, those nurseries of superstition and idleness, had greatly multiplied in the nation; and though they had universally degenerated, and were notoriously become the haunts of lewdness and debauchery, it was deemed impious and sacrilegious to reduce their number, abridge their privileges or alienate their funds. The kingdom swarmed with ignorant, idle, luxurious monks, who, like locusts, devoured the fruits of the earth and filled the air with pestilential infection.

"The ignorance of the clergy respecting religion was as gross as the dissoluteness of their morals. Even bishops were not ashamed to confess that they were unacquainted with the canon of their faith, and had never read any part of the sacred Scriptures, except what they met with in their missals. The religious service was mumbled over in a dead language, which many of the priests did not understand and some of them could scarcely read; and the greatest care was taken to prevent even catechisms, composed and approved by the clergy, from coming into the hands of the laity.

"Scotland, from her local situation, had been less exposed to disturbance from the encroaching ambition, the vexatious exactions and fulminating anathemas of the Vatican court than the countries in the immediate vicinity of Rome. But from the same cause it was more easy for the domestic clergy to keep upon the minds of the people that excessive veneration for the Holy See which could not be long felt by those who had an opportunity of witnessing its vices and worldly politics. The burdens which attended a state of dependence upon a remote foreign jurisdiction were severely felt. The most important causes of a civil nature, which the ecclesiastical courts had contrived to bring within their jurisdiction, were frequently carried to Rome. Large sums of money were annually exported out of the kingdom for the confirmation of benefices, the conducting of appeals and many other purposes, in exchange for which were received leaden bulls, woollen palls, wooden images, old bones and similar articles of precious consecrated mummery.

"Of the doctrines of Christianity almost nothing remained but the name. Instead of being directed to offer up their adorations to one God, the people were taught to divide them among an innumerable company of inferior deities. A plurality of mediators shared the honour of procuring the divine favour with 'the one Mediator between God and man;' and more petitions were presented to the Virgin Mary and other saints than to 'Him whom the Father heareth always.' The sacrifice of the mass was represented as procuring forgiveness of sins to the living and the dead; and the consciences of men were withdrawn from faith in the merits of their Saviour to a delusive reliance upon priestly absolutions, papal pardons and voluntary penances.

Instead of being instructed to demonstrate the sincerity of their faith and repentance by forsaking their sins, and testifying their love to God and man by practising the duties of morality and observing the ordinances of worship authorized by Scripture, they were taught that if they regularly said their *aves* and their *credos*, confessed themselves to a priest, punctually paid their tithes and church-offerings, purchased a mass, went in pilgrimage to the shrine of some celebrated saint, refrained from flesh on Fridays, or performed some other prescribed act of bodily mortification, their salvation was infallibly secured in due time; while those who were so rich or so pious as to build a chapel or an altar, and to endow it for the support of a priest, to perform masses, obits and dirges, procured a relaxation of the pains of purgatory for themselves or their relations in proportion to the extent of their liberality. It is difficult for us to conceive how empty and ridiculous those harangues were which the monks delivered for sermons. Legendary tales concerning the founder of some religious order, his wonderful sanctity, the miracles which he performed, his combats with the devil, his watchings, fastings, flagellations, the virtues of holy water, chrism, crossing and exorcism, the horrors of purgatory and the numbers released from it by the intercession of some powerful saint,—these, with low jests, table-talk and fireside scandal, formed the favourite topics of the preachers, and were served up to the people instead of the pure, salutary and sublime doctrines of the Bible.

"The beds of the dying were besieged and their last moments distracted by avaricious priests, who laboured to extort bequests to themselves or to the Church. Not satisfied with exacting tithes from the living, a demand was made upon the dead. No sooner had the poor husbandman breathed his last than the rapacious vicar came and carried off his corpse-present, which he repeated as often as death visited the family. Ecclesiastical censures were fulminated against those who were reluctant in making these payments, or who should themselves be disobedient to the clergy; and for a little money they were prostituted on the most trifling occasions. Divine service was neglected; and, except on festival-days, the churches in many parts of the country were no longer employed for sacred purposes, but served as sanctuaries for malefactors, places of traffic or resorts for pastime.

"Persecution and the suppression of free inquiry were the only weapons by which its interested supporters were able to defend this system of corruption and imposture. Every avenue by which truth might enter was carefully guarded. Learning was branded as the parent of heresy. The most frightful pictures were drawn of those who had separated from the Romish Church, and held up before the eyes of the people to deter them from imitating their example. If any person who had attained a degree of illumination amid the general darkness began to hint dissatisfaction with the conduct of the churchmen and to propose the correction of abuses, he was immediately stigmatized as a heretic, and, if he did not secure his safety by flight, was immured in a dungeon or committed to the flames. And when at last, in spite of all precautions, the light which was shining around did break in and spread through the nation, the clergy prepared the most desperate and bloody measures for its extinction."

Thus much had Romanism done, and this was the style of its present doing to civilize and Christianize the genius, the manners of Scotland. And into such a scene was Presbyterian Protestantism about to enter, to scourge out the desecrators that made merchandise of souls, overturn the tables of the money-changers and the seats of them that sold doves, and transform the whole den of thieves into a house of prayer.

THE INVASION.

Had Scotland been shut up from invading influence from abroad, and shut in under the sole tuition of the Spirit, there can be little doubt either that the Reformation would sooner or later have raised its banner within her bounds, or that in reconstructing religious doctrine and worship on the ruins of rejected Popery she would, as did nearly the whole reforming Church, have spontaneously reverted to a true scriptural Presbyterianism. As it was, however, most of the influences that crossed the border and survived the crossing were Presbyterian. In the middle of the fourteenth century, Wickliffe, who, as we have seen, was very positive "as to the identity of the order of priests and bishops in the apostolic age," was shining as the morning star of the Reformation, and the penetrative power of the truth was remarkably illustrated in the reach and force of his beams. "The more this subject is investigated," writes Dr. McCrie in his Life of Melville, "the more clearly am I persuaded that the opinions of Wickliffe had a powerful and extensive influence upon the Reformation. Even in Scotland they contributed greatly to predispose the minds of men to the Protestant doctrine." And here, as elsewhere within the realm of Popery, Protestantism was compelled to track its early way in fire and blood.

About the beginning of the fifteenth century, John Resby, a disciple of Wickliffe, crossed from England to Scotland, repeating the teachings of his master, and soon found his way into the flames. Twenty-five years later, Paul Craw, a Bohemian and a disciple of Huss, whose views had been largely shaped by perusal of the writings of Wickliffe, entered the Scottish arena, and, for the crime of preaching Christ, was sent after Resby to a martyr's grave. And lest winged words from his dying lips should reach the ears of spectators and evoke forbidden thoughts and emotions, he was burned with a brass ball thrust into his mouth. In these desultory but bloody conflicts between the infant Reformation and the giant Papacy a century rolled away.

By this time the contest had become warmer, and had begun to assume more formidable proportions. Inroads were more frequent, and neither attack nor resistance less resolute. The leaven of God working in other nations was feeling its way through Scottish minds and hearts. Protestant writings crept into the kingdom, and stole from hand to hand. Men read and thought, and longed and prayed, and those who found a way taught in secret and trained up a numerous soldiery for the war. Argus-eyed Rome could not fail at length to discern the approach of danger, and in 1525 it induced the Parliament to enact a prohibition against the importation of religious books, and against all public "disputations about the heresies of Luther, except it be to the confusion thereof, and that by clerks in the schools alone."

Ere long the kingdom was startled by the discovery that the new heresy was penetrating even into royal blood. In 1528, Patrick Hamilton, a "youth of royal lineage, and not less distinguished by high mental endowments," came back from his communings with Luther and Melancthon on the Continent, and began to preach the things that he had seen and heard. His high social position, his elegance of manners, his eloquence and holy zeal gave him easy and powerful access to the popular heart, and filled his foes with indignation. Among the eyes fixed upon him were those of James Beaton, archbishop of St. Andrews, who, during the minority of James V., ruled the State, while he, largely also, ruled the Church. A little fearful of both the young king's sympathy and the popularity of Hamilton, he managed first to despatch the former on a pilgrimage to the shrine of St. Dothess, and then to decoy the latter, under certain pretences, to St. Andrew's. There he brought him before a council that condemned him to death. To give force and validity to the sentence, he induced every person of note within reach to sign it, and on the last day of February, 1528, Hamilton was bound to the stake. Removing his outer garments, he gave them to his faithful servant, saying, "This stuff will not help me in the fire, and will profit thee. After this you will receive no more good from me, but the example of my death, which I pray thee keep in mind; for albeit it be bitter to the flesh and fearful in man's judgment, yet it is the entrance into eternal life, which none shall possess that denies Christ Jesus before this wicked generation." An explosion of gunpowder, though scorching the victim, refused to light the pile; but fire was procured, and the victory was won! Romanism remained master of the field.

But from every drop of that doubly-ennobled blood there arose a voice of thunder, preaching the blessed "evangel," and every spark of that consuming fire set another heart on fire with truth. The report of that martyrdom spread through the kingdom and put into a multitude of mouths the questions: "For what was Hamilton burned? What is that secret power that can make men welcome so awful a death and turn even horrid martyrdom into singing joy?" The blood of the martyrs proved the seed of the Church. Even some of the friars began to question and speak words that savoured of the new heresy. The archbishop, alarmed and irritated at the discovery that his silencing flames proved only a rousing trumpet, threatened to repeat the so far worse than futile experiment upon others; when one who heard him remarked, "If your reverence will burn any more, you had better do it in a cellar, for the smoke of Hamilton hath infected as many as it blew upon."

But the holy man preferred the open canopy of heaven for his pious work, and here and there the smoke was soon seen curling up to heaven, telling that other "god-souls" preferred a martyr's death to an apostate life. In August, 1534, two more were sent to heaven in the martyr's fiery chariot.

And in February, 1538, five more were burned "in one huge pile," on Castle Hill, Edinburgh. A little later, two more wrote their testimony in fire and blood at Glasgow. One of them, a young man, at first shrunk from the flames, but recovering spirit, he fell on his knees, gave thanks to God, and, rising, exclaimed: "Now I defy death! Do what you please—I praise God I am ready!" Even the archbishop quailed before this scene, but was driven through to the bloody end by his murderous attendants.

The next year the archbishop went to the bar of God to give account of these murders to Him who said, "Inasmuch as ye have done it unto one of the *least* of these my brethren, ye have done it unto ME." He was succeeded by his nephew, Cardinal David Beaton. Able, cunning, shamelessly licentious, implacable, unmerciful, utterly unscrupulous, hesitating at no measures to reach his ends, he was a legitimate son of the papacy and the pope's right arm, and the truth's and the nation's scourge for many a dreary year. He took an early opportunity to certify the world as to what the Reformation might expect at his hands, by burning in effigy Sir John Borthwick, who had fled to England.

THE VICTIM AND HIS VICTOR.

In December, 1542, James V. passed to his grave from a life filled with struggles with his turbulent nobility, leaving a kingdom distracted with disorder, and a daughter, the wretched Mary, queen of Scots, then seven days old; and, in spite of a document forged by the cardinal appointing himself with others to govern the realm, James Hamilton, earl of Arran, in a meeting of nobles was appointed regent.

The cardinal's popularity was not increased by the discovery, soon after the king's death, of a list of some hundreds of persons who were to have been denounced as heretics and their property confiscated.

For a time, Arran favoured the Reformation, and in 1542 an act of Parliament declared it lawful that the Scriptures be read by all the people in their native tongue, and the holy, mighty Book was soon found in almost every person's hands, to the indignation and chagrin of the pious cardinal. But Arran, being a weak and fickle man, soon fell under the power of Beaton, who was thus enabled to rule the realm almost as effectually as if he had been regent in name. And now, with the reins of government well in hand, he began to crack his merciless whip over the bleeding back of the Reformation.

At Perth five men and one woman were brought before him; the men were hanged and the woman drowned. The poor creature had refused to invoke the Virgin during the pains of child-birth. She first looked on while her husband was slain, exhorting him to constancy, and was then dragged to a pool, and removing her babe from her breast, passed into the cold waters, and thence to the banks of the river that flows out from the throne of God and the Lamb. Departing thence, the cardinal made a wide circuit of blood through the realm, taking with him the submissive Arran to witness and sanction his zeal for the Lord.

Tired at length in the chase after meaner game, he fixed his eye upon *George Wishart*, brother of the laird of Pittarow. Having been banished for teaching the Greek language, he had returned to do even a worse thing—to preach Jesus. Crowds hung on his eloquent words and melted under his fervent appeals. Mild, gentle, patient as the beloved disciple, he displayed a character of surpassing loveliness. Driven from point to point, he preached now on the hillside, now by the wayside, now in the open fields. Beaton first sent a pious priest to stab him, but Wishart caught the assassin's arm and the dagger fell to the ground. Again, a cunning message came, begging him to visit a dying man, and armed men waylaid him to take him dead or alive. Then the Earl of Bothwell was sent to capture him, and the martyr was secured and lodged in the fatal sea-tower at St. Andrew's, an ancient seaport forty miles northeast from Edinburgh. The victim was at last in hand. The ceremonies of trial were soon despatched, and the regent was requested to finish up the work. He being induced to hesitate, Beaton attended to it himself. A "pile and a gallows were prepared under the windows of the castle," where the cardinal might feast his eyes on the welcome spectacle. Wishart was then led to the stake, his hands bound behind his back, a rope about his neck, a chain about his waist and bags of gunpowder fastened to various parts of his body. Lest a rescue should be attempted, the cannon of the castle were loaded and trained upon the spot of execution. At the stake, Wishart kneeled down and prayed, saying, three times, "O thou Saviour of the world, have mercy on me! Father of heaven, I commend my spirit into thy holy hands." His executioner asking his pardon, he kissed him, saying, "Lo, here is a token that I forgive thee: my heart, do thine office." The trumpet sounded, the match was applied, the gunpowder exploded, and yet the victim lived. "This fire," said he, "torments my body, but no way abates my spirit." Then looking up to the cardinal, the spirit of prophecy came upon him, and he said, "He who in such state feeds upon my torments within a few days shall be hanged out at the same window, to be seen with as much ignominy as he now leaneth there in pride;" and soon after he joined the general assembly on high.

But while one may succeed in damming up a stream for a time, the ever-gathering waters will at length assert their mastery over man and sweep obstructors and obstructions together away. And the stream that Beaton was hindering flowed out from the eternal decrees of God. Hence his every victory was a defeat, his every victim a victor. A profound indignation was stirred by the murder of Wishart, and the chill of its shadows set Beaton at work upon the fortifications of his castle. But what cares destiny for mortared piles!

The night of the 28th of May, Beaton spent with his mistress, and as she left one gate in the morning the workmen entered at another, and with them five or six men, who, sauntering to the porter's lodge, inquired for Beaton. One of these was William Kirkaldy, of Grange, and with him Peter Carmichael, James Melville, John Lesley, brother to the Earl of Rothes, and Norman Lesley, son of the same. Making their way to the cardinal's apartment they found the doors closed and barricaded within.

"Open the door!" rang through the halls.

"Who calls?" asked the cardinal. "Will you spare my life, if I open the door?"

"Perhaps."

"Nay, swear that you will—swear by God's wounds."

"That which was said is unsaid."

Fire was now procured, and at the crackling of the flames and intrusion of the smoke a boy within opened the door, and in stalked the avengers. The wretch sank back in his chair, exclaiming:

"I am a priest—I am a priest: ye will not slay me?"

Lesley and Carmichael then each stabbed him.

But Melville, now coming forward, and pushing the others aside, said:

"This work and judgment of God, although it be secret, yet ought to be done with greater gravity."

Then, putting his sword to Beaton's throat, he said:

"Repent thee of thy wicked life, but especially of the shedding of the blood of that instrument of God, Mr. George Wishart, which, albeit the flames of fire consumed before men, yet cries it with a vengeance upon thee, and we from God are sent to revenge it. I protest that neither hatred of thy person, nor love of thy riches, nor fear of any trouble thou couldst have done me in particular, moved or move me to strike thee, but only because thou hast been and remainest an obstinate enemy to Christ Jesus and his Holy Evangel." He then thrust him through, the wretched man exclaiming, "I am a priest—I am a priest! Fie, fie!—all is gone!"

They then carried his body to the same window whence he had gazed upon the burning Wishart, and hung it out before the gaze of the crowd below.

Thus was the earth rid of one of the multitude of treacherous, malicious, grossly licentious and mercilessly cruel ecclesiastics with which Romanism has cursed it.

Soon after, a party of gentlemen who favoured the Reformation took possession of the castle and resisted a siege conducted by the regent, and compelled the besiegers to make terms with them. About the beginning of April JOHN KNOX entered the castle.

JOHN KNOX.

Carlyle, in his own way, speaks much truth respecting great men, in his discourse of their "manner of appearance in our world's business—how they have shaped themselves in the world's history, what ideas men formed of them, what work they did. For, as I take it, universal history—the history of what man has accomplished in this world—is, at the bottom, the history of great men who have worked here. They were the leaders of men, these great ones; the modellers, patterns, and, in a wide sense, creators, of whatsoever the general mass of men contrived to do or attain." Machiavelli has said that the world is made up of three orders of men—those who perceive with their own powers, those who perceive when matters are explained to them, and those who do not perceive at all. The first of these are the truly great men. They are, as it were, the concentration of the times in which they live. Certain great principles are at work in the general mind, waiting to be embodied in a creed, or in a maxim, or in a trumpet-call to action. That something is at work, that something needs to be done, all know, but just what, none can say. But here or there is a man endowed with certain gifts and with certain susceptibilities, on whom, as on a delicately-strung harp, these principles play and strike out the tune of the hour; and, when once the key-note is given, the multitudes recognize it as just what they have been waiting for, and at once join in responsive chorus. Thus great men are the heart and become the mouth of the age. And the natural and intense admiration of men for genius and bravery greatly increase at once the power and responsibility of these great leaders of their kind. The Creator endows these men with their gifts, and, when he will, he leaves them largely to the counsel of their own will to determine the side they will take in the great war between right and wrong; and here we have Beatons, Loyolas and Alvas, and there a Cromwell, a William the Silent, a Washington. And, when he will, he at once creates, endows and appoints these leaders to office among men; and then we have here a Moses or a David, and there a Luther and a Knox. Knox was at once a child and father of the Reformation in Scotland. Richly endowed with mental power and with keen insight both of men and of the nature of the service to which God was then calling him and his country, he was a true son of Issachar, with understanding of the times to know what Israel ought to do. His also was that bravery that could dare whatever duty bade.

It was, we suppose, a happy circumstance for mankind, though the source of many temporary woes to Scotland, that the throne took the lead in the opposition to the Reformation. Had it been otherwise, had the crisis found the crown solicited by inducements to rid itself of subjection to Rome and to take the whole of reform into its own hands, the result might have been a reproduction in Scotland of another Church of England—a strange conglomerate of popery and protestations, error and truth, with a "Calvinistic creed, a Romish liturgy and an Arminian clergy;" and Scottish Church history might have told the tale of other Henries and Elizabeths.

But God had ordained otherwise; and as the

Reformation found its chief enemies on and near the throne, its clear-headed, resolute-hearted Christian leaders were compelled to subject the prerogatives of royalty to a searching investigation, a rigid, manly scrutiny. If the monarch was absolute by divine right, it would be very difficult to find any other place for Christ within the realm than such as might be assigned him by the will of the reigning king—that king not unfrequently a chief favourite of Satan. But if the kingly prerogative was indeed hedged about by natural and easily defined limitations, it behooved those who contested this point with royalty to find out and exhibit those limitations, that all parties, seeing the truth, might fight in its light, and having learned, might with good conscience and hearty will assert and maintain their respective rights and discharge their several duties.

These limits of jurisdiction soon showed themselves to the eagle eye of Knox. If there ever was a true man among men Knox was he. Hume, of course, abuses him. Hallam speaks of his "sanguinary spirit." Nor can any one claim for him a courtly delicacy and refinement of manners without making him an exception to the whole character of the age in which he lived. Modes of conduct and styles of utterance had not yet parted with barbaric rust, not yet learned the elegances of the modern courtier. Luther and Henry VIII. spoke of each other in the coarsest terms, and the latter dignified one woman whom he made his wife and the nation's queen with the elegant title of "great Flemish mare." The indecent speech of George Buchanan to the Countess of Mar, who caressed young King James after a severe flogging by the former, is probably a fair specimen of the colloquial refinement of those times. Queen Elizabeth, as is well known, could upon occasion give vent to her anger in true sailor-like profanity. It is hardly, therefore, to be wondered at if Knox, a son of yet unpolished Scotland, should have been somewhat less courtly in speech and manners than a modern princess—should have used at times very plain and emphatic language, and have called a wicked and adulterous queen a "Jezebel," and have said to her that "Samuel feared not to slay Agag, the fat and delicate king of Amalek—neither spared Elias Jezebel's false prophets and Baal's priests, though King Ahab was present. Phineas was no magistrate, yet feared not to strike Cozbi and Zimri in the very act of fornication. And so, madam, your grace may see that others than chief magistrates may lawfully inflict punishment on such crimes as are condemned by the law of God."

Yet, if he told the truth in plain terms, he did it in a good cause; and for the whole drift of his influence and character of his service among men he merits the admiration and gratitude of mankind. Carlyle writes: "This that Knox did for this nation we may really call a resurrection as from death. The *people* began to *live;* they needed first of all to do that at what cost and costs soever. Scotch literature and thought, Scotch industry, James Watt, David Hume, Walter Scott, Robert Burns—I find Knox and the Reformation acting in the heart's core of every one of these persons and phenomena.

"It seems hard measure that this Scottish man now, after three hundred years, should have to plead like a culprit before the world; intrinsically, for having been in such a way as it was then possible to be the bravest of all Scotchmen. Had he been a poor half-and-half, he could have crouched into a corner like so many others; Scotland had not been delivered, and Knox had been without blame. He is the one Scotchman to whom of all others his country and the world owe a debt. He has to plead that Scotland would forgive him for having been worth to it any million 'unblameable' Scotchmen that need no forgiveness. He bared his breast to battle, had to row in French galleys, wander forlorn in exile, in clouds and storms, was censured, shot at through his windows, had a right sore fighting life; if this world were his recompense he had made but a bad venture of it. I cannot apologize for Knox. To him it is very indifferent, these two hundred and fifty years or more, what men say of him. But we, having got above all those details of his battle and living now in clearness on the fruits of his victory—we, for our own sakes, ought to look through the rumours and controversies enveloping the man into the man himself, and understand and honour his real character.

"This post of prophet to his nation was not of his seeking. Knox had lived forty years quietly obscure. He was the son of poor parents—had lived as tutor in gentlemen's families, preaching when any one wished to hear his doctrine—not fancying himself capable of more—when one day a small body of Reformers, besieged in St. Andrew's Castle, the preacher said suddenly, 'There ought to be other preachers; all men who had a priest's heart and gift ought now to speak, which gifts and heart one of their own number—John Knox the name of him—had.' Poor Knox was obliged to stand up; he attempted to reply, burst into tears and ran out."

"The school of Knox," writes Hallam, "if so we may call the early Presbyterian ministers of Scotland, was full of men breathing their master's spirit, acute in disputation, eloquent in discourse, learned beyond what their successors have been and intensely zealous in the cause of Reformation. Their system of local and general assemblies infused, *together with the forms of a republic*, its energy and impatience of external control, combined with the concentration and unity of purpose that belongs to the most vigorous government."

Of this man Froude writes, in his impartial, learned and elegant volumes:

"John Knox became the representative of all that was best in Scotland. He was no narrow fanatic, who, in a world in which God's grace was equally visible in a thousand creeds, could see truth and goodness nowhere but in his own formula. He was a large, noble, generous man, with a shrewd perception of actual fact, who found himself face to face with a system of hideous iniquity.

He believed himself a prophet with a direct commission from heaven to overthrow it."

Again he writes: "Such was Knox, the greatest of living Scotchmen. The full measure of Knox's greatness no man in his day could estimate. It is as we look back over that stormy time and weigh the actors in it one against the other that he stands out in his full proportions. No grander figure can be found in the entire history of the Reformation in this island. Cromwell and Burghley rank beside him for the work which they effected, but as politicians and statesmen they had to labour with instruments which they soiled their hands in touching. In priority, in uprightness, in courage, truth and stainless honour, the Regent Murray and our English Latimer were perhaps his equals; but Murray was intellectually far below him, and the sphere of Latimer's influence was on a smaller scale. The time has come when English history may do justice to one but for whom the Reformation would have been overthrown among ourselves; for the spirit which Knox created saved Scotland; and if Scotland had been Catholic again, neither the wisdom of Elizabeth's ministers, nor the teaching of her bishops, nor her own chicaneries would have preserved

England from revolution. His was the voice that taught the peasant of the Lothians that he was a free man, the equal in the sight of God with the proudest peer or prelate that had trampled on his forefathers. He was the one antagonist whom Mary Stuart could not soften nor Maitland deceive. He it was that raised the poor commons of his country into a stern, rugged people, who might be hard, narrow, superstitious and fanatical, but who, nevertheless, were men whom neither king, noble nor priest could force to submit again to tyranny. And his reward has been the ingratitude of those who should most have done honour to his memory."

We have seen that after the slaying of Beaton, Knox entered the castle of St. Andrew. His preaching there adding fuel to the fires of the Reformation, his foes secured a French army, took the town, and in flagrant violation of treaty stipulations, but in strict conformity with Romish morality, made Knox a galley-slave. England now resenting the union between France and Scotland, and the treachery of the regent, invaded the country, conquered a peace and procured the liberation of Knox. Thus delivered from the hands of his persecutors, he went first to England and then to the Continent, and remained mostly at Geneva until the year 1555.

In 1554 Arran was succeeded in the regency by a French woman, Mary of Lorraine, daughter of the Duke of Guise, widow of Henry V. of Scotland, and mother of Mary, Queen of Scots. This woman was "at once fearless and cunning," and the "fatal link that bound Scotland to France and the papacy."

In 1555 Knox returned to Scotland and set out on a preaching tour through the realm, everywhere throwing firebrands into the stubble-heaps of withering Romanism. Bent on staying the conflagration, the priesthood summoned Knox to appear before them at Blackfriar's Church, Edinburgh. He obeyed the summons, accompanied by several gentlemen, and at his appearance the court dissolved. Knox then preached openly and powerfully in the city, and soon after yielded to the solicitations of his former flock at Geneva and returned to them for a season. As soon as he was known to be beyond reach, the summons was repeated, and Knox not appearing was burnt in effigy by his heroic persecutors.

Mary of Guise, the queen-regent, now tried her hand in quelling the Reformation, and summoned the Protestant preachers before the council on the old charge of stirring up sedition—for with despotism, civil and ecclesiastical, it is always seditious to speak and act as a freeman. But such crowds accompanied the ministers to the place of trial that, like the witch of Endor, the queen-regent found that she had evoked an apparition in whose presence her cheek turned pale and her nerves were paralyzed. To allay this apparition a proclamation was issued remanding the crowds to the borders; but instead of obeying the proclamation the people pushed their way boldly, perhaps rudely, into the very council-chamber where the queen sat surrounded by her bishops; and Chalmers of Gadgirth, speaking for the rest, said, "Madam, we know that this proclamation is a device of the bishops and of that bastard (the primate of St. Andrew's) that stands beside you. We avow to God that ere we yield we will make a day of it. These idle drones oppress us and our tenants; they trouble our preachers and would murder them and us. Shall we suffer this any longer? No, madam, it shall not be!" And at once every man put on his steel bonnet, when persecution apologized with a falsehood, and the heroic men went home in triumph.

ORGANIZATION.

Principles can act with their legitimate concentrated force only through organized forms; and as royalty and Romanism were organized and armed, it behooved the Reformation no longer to trust to desultory impulse and individual action, but to consolidate its forces and construct an organism through which it might speak and act with efficiency and power.

The first formal step in this direction was taken December 3, 1557. The country seething with excitement, Knox in exile, the foe burning with the spirit of persecution and revenge, it became evident to the dullest apprehension that unless something was done, and that promptly, nothing would remain but submission and annihilation. Accordingly, the Protestant lords and gentry assembled at Edinburgh. The spirit that animated these men may be gathered from the speech cited above of Chalmers of Gadgirth and the conduct of his steel-bonneted companions. And, being assembled, resolved to defend their principles at "what cost or costs soever," they formed and subscribed this bond:

"We, perceiving how Satan, in his members, the anti-Christs of our time, cruelly doth rage, seeking to downthrow and destroy the evangel of Christ and his congregation, ought, according to our bounden duty, to strive in our Master's cause even unto death, being certain of victory in him—the which, our duty being well considered, we do promise before the majesty of God and his congregation that we, by his grace, shall with all diligence continually apply our whole power, substance and our very lives, to maintain, set forward and establish the most blessed word of God and his congregation, and shall labour at our possibility to have faithful ministers purely and truly to minister Christ's evangel and sacraments to his people. We shall maintain them, nourish them and defend them, the whole congregation of Christ and every member thereof, at our whole power, and wairing (expending) of our lives against Satan and all wicked power that does intend tyranny and trouble against the aforesaid congregation. Unto the which holy word and congregation we do join us, and also do renounce and forsake the congregation of Satan, with all the superstitious abominations and idolatry thereof; and moreover shall declare ourselves manifestly enemies thereto by this our faithful promise before God, testified to his congregation by our subscription at these presents. At

Edinburgh, the third day of December, 1557 years. God called to witness."

In reading this document we find that the principles, thoughts, and even forms of expression, in our celebrated Declaration of Independence are not so thoroughly original as we have fancied. Scotch Presbyterianism anticipated Jefferson more than two hundred years.

This declaration and bond was signed by the earls of Argyle, Glencairn and Morton, Archibald lord of Lorn, John Erskine of Dern, and a great number of other distinguished men, who thenceforth were called LORDS OF THE CONGREGATION.

This step toward organization was known as "THE FIRST COVENANT."

The Romish protest against the *covenant* took the usual form—*martyrdom.* The victim was an aged priest named Walter Mill, on whom Beaton the cardinal had in former days sought to lay his bloody hands. Discovered now by a spy, he was brought to St. Andrew's; and though he defended his course with marked ability, he was condemned to the stake. But no one could be found to act as executioner of the old man, and the archbishop was compelled to employ one of his own domestics. From the midst of the flames the aged martyr said,

"As for me, I am fourscore and two years old, and cannot live long by course of nature; but a hundred better shall arise out of the ashes of my bones. I trust in God I shall be the last that shall suffer death in Scotland for this cause."

It was now the turn of the Covenanters to speak, and while the people of St. Andrew's raised a great pile of stones upon the spot hallowed by the death of Mill, the lords of the congregation complained to the queen-regent of the conduct of the bishops, and the preachers blew the gospel trumpet till its sounds reverberated from all the hills over all the plains.

THE APPARITION.

Mary of Guise was now deep in a scheme for the overthrow of the Reformation; and her programme, to the writing of which she was helped by the skill and cunning of all papal Europe, embraced the following items: a league between Scotland, France and Spain; the settling of the Scottish crown upon a child of the papacy, Francis, the dauphin of France and husband of Mary, "Queen of Scots;" the invasion of England; the dethronement of Elizabeth and the transfer of her crown to some popish head. By consummate skill and duplicity, concealing on the one hand and revealing on the other what would further her scheme, she succeeded in inducing the too unwary *lords of the congregation* to consent to the union of the crowns of Scotland and France.

But an essential part of the plan was full possession of Scotland, and to the completion of this work she now addressed her energies. By proclamation she had forbidden any person to preach or administer the sacraments without authority from her bishops, and a secret treaty existed between her and her clergy, by which they had engaged to raise a large sum of money to enable her to raise and maintain the military forces needed for her purposes. With an army now in hand she entered upon her work. Paul Matthew, John Christison, William Harlow and John Willock were cited to stand trial before the Justiciary Court at Stirling on the 10th of May, 1559, for disregarding her proclamation, teaching heresy and exciting sedition.

To a deputation of Protestants, remonstrating against such violence, she answered:

"Maugre their hearts and all that would take part with them, these ministers shall be banished Scotland, though they preached as soundly as ever St. Paul did."

They reminded her of her pledge, to which she answered:

"It becomes not subjects to burden their princes with their promises farther than they pleased to keep them."

But the time had gone by when Scotchmen could brook, even in princes, a morality so shameless or despotism so insolent; and they replied that if she violated her engagements they should consider themselves absolved from their oath of allegiance.

The Protestant nobility now resolved to stand by their ministers at the approaching trial, and assembled in large numbers at Perth, thence to proceed in a body to Stirling. But as wise as they were resolute, they first sent a deputation to Stirling, declaring that their aims were peaceful, their only purpose being to attend with their preachers, to join with them in a confession of their faith. Upon this the wily woman succeeded in persuading them to remain at Perth, promising them that the trial should not go on. It seemed hard to distrust a pledge so fairly given, and some, confiding in the word of a woman who never kept it when treachery was more convenient, withdrew to their homes.

Smiling in her sleeve at their credulity, she hastened on the preparations for the trial and further adjusted her schemes of oppression. But, just when all was ready, a huge, terrible shadow fell upon the Stirling conclave. Knox had returned from exile—had landed at Leith—had entered Edinburgh—had hurried to Dundee—had gone to Perth, and was now waiting there with those who had remained to attend the trial at Stirling! Elijah had shown himself to Ahab in the vineyard of Naboth the Jezreelite. And Mary, the Jezebel of the hour, exclaimed, "God do so to me, and more also, if I make him not food for the flames!" She proclaimed him an outlaw and a rebel. The trial went on and the ministers were outlawed for non-appearance. Erskine of Dun stole away from Stirling and hastened to Perth with word of the woman's perfidy. Knox was there preaching with marvellous power.

A riot at Perth furnished what little excuse the regent cared for to advance on Perth with fire and sword. The Reformers, however, sent messengers abroad announcing their peril, and such hosts responded—the Earl of Glencairn alone bringing twenty-five hundred men—that Mary was constrained to ply her valuable promises rather than force. An agreement was concluded by which the town was to be left open to her, the people left unquestioned as to the past, the French army forbidden to enter, and on her withdrawal no garrison to be left behind—nearly every point of which agreement the miserable woman of course violated.

Before withdrawing from Perth, however, THE LORDS OF THE CONGREGATION formed another bond, pledging themselves to mutual support and defence in the cause of religion, or any cause dependent thereupon by whatsoever pretext it might be coloured and concealed. This bond was subscribed, in the name of the whole Church, by the chiefs of the Protestant nobility. This was "THE SECOND COVENANT."

REPUBLICANISM.

Once certify man, from the pages of God's word, that he, together with all his human brethren, is created in the image of his God, and if occasion arise he will shrewdly question the claim of any other man to absolute dominion over him. Show him that king and peasant stand on the same level before God as sinners, but one set of terms of peace with the great King and one heaven open before all; and, especially if he be a Christian, he will rigorously question the fancied birthright prerogatives of a bad monarch to lord it absolutely over him and his. If an Oriental rabble may submissively fill the place of "dumb-driven cattle," a people whose minds have been enlightened and whose intellects have been enlarged and quickened by the mighty truths of revelation will not be long in finding their way to the foundation laws of human freedom, civil and religious. And, especially if driven by tyranny to probe this matter to the bottom, they will ascertain that if legitimate civil government is an ordinance of God the legitimacy of the government in a given case is to be determined by the people. And this is republicanism.

At this time, in Scotland, Mary of Guise occupied the throne, and stood before the people as the embodiment of legitimate governmental prerogative; and had she designed to put the people to school and indoctrinate them in their rights and in the true limits of the royal prerogative, she could have taken no more promising course than that which she actually pursued.

No sooner did she obtain possession of Perth than she considered her engagements with the congregation null and void, and at once proceeded to punish those who favoured the Reformation. Argyle and Lord James Stewart, having remonstrated against her perfidy, and having been rudely repelled with this characteristic reply: "I am not bound to keep promises made to heretics, and I will make little conscience to take from all that sect their lives and inheritances, if I may do it with so honest an excuse," they forsook her and joined the Lords of the Congregation.

These lords now took matters into their own hands and formally invited Knox to come and preach in the Abbey Church of St. Andrew's. Knox, of course, did not hesitate, and the archbishop hurried thither with an armed force and threatened to answer the arguments of Knox with powder and ball, while the queen-regent followed him with her French army. The lords, appreciating the magnitude of the danger and unwilling to lose another Wishart and a much greater than he, put the question to Knox:

"Will you abide with us and take the risk?"

He answered like himself:

"In this town I was first called to preach the gospel; do not hinder me from preaching here again. As for the fear of danger that may come unto me let no man be solicitous, for my life is in the custody of Him whose glory I seek. I desire the hand and weapon of no man to defend me. I only crave audience, which if it be denied here unto me at this time, I must seek further where I may have it."

Heroism like cowardice is contagious, and the lords caught the spirit of the prophet; and the next day, with the armies of the regent thundering on in the distance, Knox preached to a great company of his friends and to "Agrippa, Bernice, chief captains and principal men in the city," to the archbishop himself and many with him, who murdered the preacher in their hearts while they listened with their ears—preached to them of Jesus overturning the tables of the money-changers who had made God's temple a den of thieves. And for three days he thus preached, until the people, being "mightily convinced," tumbled pictures and images out of the church windows and tore down the monasteries. Popery had resorted to violence to crush the reformers, and now popery was forced to taste its own medicine. But the dose was not pleasant to the taste. The archbishop flew to the regent, and she with her troops prepared to fly upon the reformers. But they were soon ready, and this

Jezebel was compelled to make "I dare not" wait upon "I would." Terms were made between the parties, but knowing the perfidy of this woman, the Protestant army took Perth and expelled the regent's garrison, and then Stirling and then Edinburgh. The reforming spirit spread, and in a few days large portions of the realm turned popery out of doors and set up a pure worship.

Matters thus wore on until the perfidies of the regent having exhausted the patience of the Protestant lords, the latter resolved on measures more firmly decisive. On the 21st of October, 1559, they assembled at Edinburgh in such numbers as to constitute a convention of the estates of the realm, and with ungloved hands laid hold of the Gordian knot either to untie or cut it. While matters were under discussion, Knox and Willock were invited to state their views upon the duty of subjects to oppressive rulers. Willock said that the *power of rulers was limited,* both by reason and Scripture, and that *they might be deprived of it upon valid grounds.* Knox assented to these views, and added that the assembly might with safe consciences act upon it if they attended to these three points: first, that they did not suffer the misconduct of the queen-regent to alienate their affections from their due allegiance to their sovereigns, Francis and Mary; second, that they were not actuated in the measure by private hatred or envy of the queen-dowager, but by regard to the safety of the commonwealth; and third, that any sentence they might now pronounce should not preclude her readmission to office if she discovered sorrow for her conduct and a disposition to *submit to the advice of the estates of the realm.*

After this the whole assembly, having severally delivered their opinions, did by a solemn deed *suspend the queen-dowager* from her authority as regent of the kingdom until the meeting of a free parliament, and at the same time elected a council for the management of public affairs during the interval.

Thus Carlyle was not speaking at random when he said that under the influence of Knox and his coadjutors the *people* began to *live.* Already, under the influence of the Reformation, it was rapidly making its way into the consciousness of the world that Christ had been given as "leader and commander to *the people.*" In England the national authorities patched up a sort of Reformation *for* the people—in every other land *the people* took the work legitimately into their own hands. In more ancient times, when the question came up as to a temporary alteration of the law which required the passover to be celebrated on the fourteenth day of the first month, King Hezekiah submitted it to the "princes and all the congregation in Jerusalem," and they decided to hold the feast on the *fourteenth day of the second month* (2 Chron. xxx. 1–3, 22, 23). So in this case the people, by their representatives, took counsel and suspended the reigning monarch from her functions until she should be willing to take counsel with them on matters affecting the weal of the nation.

In these principles and acts of 1559 those of American republicanism were anticipated. Our forefathers, after long and patient endurance and weary and vain petitioning, solemnly suspended King George from his dominion, and themselves constructed a government according to the council of their own will.

These were the principles working like a mighty leaven in the hearts of the people, and, in the words of Hetherington, "let it ever be most gratefully remembered that to the Reformation"—and he might have added to the essential principles of Presbyterianism—"we owe that true civilization which not only strikes off the fetters from the body but cultivates also the mind, which not only liberates men from civil, mental and moral thraldom, but also, elevating them in the scale of existence, renders them worthy to be free. The mind of Knox was too deeply imbued with these great principles and his heart too fearless for him to hesitate in giving a frank avowal of his sentiments, be the danger and the obloquy thereby to be encountered what they might."

THE GENERAL ASSEMBLY.

Organizing forces had long been at work and were now rapidly maturing the fruit. The Church of Christ is one body, a living body, and the indwelling life in that body tends with unbending aim towards visible ecclesiastical union. These forces had already embodied the Church in particular congregations, with their several colleges of ruling elders. The first covenant and the second had rallied these Presbyterian forces, which were now pressing forth toward more complete unification in one *General Assembly.*

The high republican act of suspending the queen-regent had brought the congregation and the government into armed collision, and the latter had appealed to Elizabeth for aid. Well knowing that her own cause was bound up with that of the Scottish reformers, she reluctantly relaxed her parsimonious purse-strings a little, and at first sent money and afterward an army. The French troops retired before the English to Leith; and at length a treaty of peace was made between France and England, in accordance with which the troops of both nations were to be withdrawn from Scotland.

While these events were taking place in the distracted realm other matters were engrossing the thoughts of the queen-regent. The summons had come bidding her to the bar of her God. It is melancholy to see how swiftly the actors in life's drama move across the stage, and how soon they disappear; melancholy to know how many make a record as they pass, the perusal of which torments them on the bed of death. But if the good must die, let us be thankful that the wicked do not live for ever.

On the central hill, in many-hilled Edinburgh, stands the castle, covering some six acres of ground with its spacious esplanade. From its ramparts a magnificent prospect greets the eye. Westward stretches the level country out from the bottom of the crag. Eastward is Salisbury Crag and Arthur's Seat, and on the lower ground, between them, the old quadrangular palace of Holyrood. A splendid place to live in, but the queen-regent was now there to die.

"Shut up in Edinburgh Castle," writes Froude, "cut off from her friends and half a prisoner under the cold neutrality of Erskine, the mother of Mary Queen of Scots had sunk from day to day, her body swollen with dropsy, the visible shadow of death fast closing over her, yet, to the last, going through her daily work with the same cheerful resolution, cool, clear and dauntless, as became a daughter of the house of Guise.

"Her position was forlorn and even tragic—religion had not many attractions for her—her confessor was an abandoned debauchee, whose ministrations must have been a mockery, and it was overlate to learn a new creed."

Finding her end approaching, she "sent for"—Hetherington says, "allowed to be sent to her"—writes Froude, "John Willock, Knox's colleague at Edinburgh, and conversed with him upon the subject of religion. After this, she sent for her priest, confessed, received extreme unction and passed away.

"So ended Mary of Lorraine, once Mary Duchess of Longueville, the wittiest, brightest, fairest ornament of the court of Francis I., now closing the nineteenth year of widowhood and exile in a land of strangers." Her death removed the greatest obstacle to the peace which was now soon concluded.

On the first day of August, Parliament assembled under the anxious eye of gazing Europe. Crowds of people flocked to Edinburgh on the great occasion. The demands of the Protestants were singularly moderate. They asked no sanguinary vengeance upon their adversaries, as Rome would have done in like circumstances, no compulsory laws, enforcing an acceptance of the true religion, no banishments from the kingdom, nor even that the displaced ecclesiastics should be summarily deprived of the means of livelihood, but only that the popish doctrines be discarded, purity of worship and *primitive discipline* be restored, and that the ecclesiastical revenues be applied to the support of a pious, active ministry, the promotion of learning and the relief of the poor. To these demands the Parliament responded by abolishing Romanism, prohibiting the mass under certain penalties, leaving, by their silence, the question of discipline to the clergy, and by adopting, almost without a dissenting voice, the Confession of Faith. But what of the church revenues? For long years they had been employed for the support of graceless ecclesiastics, who not only left, but strenuously kept, the people in ignorance, while by example and precept they corrupted their morality. Why, then, should not these revenues be now put into the hands of pure, godly, patriotic men, to be employed in undoing the deadly work of popery among the people?

These funds would have been amply sufficient for the ends proposed. The papistical system was abolished, and the Protestants, though not unwilling that the Romish ecclesiastics, while they lived, should have adequate support, were quite unwilling that these men, now relieved of all their duties, should still enjoy the whole of their usual income; and, as they passed away by death, the Protestants proposed that the rents of benefices, bishoprics, cathedral and collegiate churches, and those arising from the endowments of monasteries, should be appropriated for the support of ministers, schools and of the poor. But lordly avarice forbade.

Among the so-called Protestant leaders, at this time, was William Maitland, of Lethington—a name that often recurs in this history. Able, ambitious and unscrupulous, he cared little for religion in any form and looked at all questions through purely secular eyes. His own spirit and that of many who acted with him appeared in a sarcasm he uttered on hearing a sermon of Knox: "We may now forget ourselves and bear the barrow to build the house of God." And the readiness of many of the lords to abolish the papacy was due to their desire to appropriate its revenues to their own uses. Accordingly, the revenue question was left at this time untouched, but with too sure a presage that when the hour for action came the interests of education and religion would weigh very lightly in the scales.

The Confession of Faith was prepared by six Johns—Winram, Spotswood, Willock, Douglas, Row and Knox—and, with the Book of Discipline, "took abiding residence in the mind and heart of Scotland, in the deliberate judgment and conviction of its intellect and the fervent regard of its affection."

Already a temporary arrangement had been made for the effective preaching of the gospel among the people. The great chiefs were appointed to preach in the cities, and superintendents appointed to secure as large attention as possible to the wants of the inland and remoter districts.

Thus, at last, after all these years of confusion, woe and blood, Presbyterianism had conquered the obdurate papacy and hung its banners on the topmost towers of the realm.

And now, on the 20th of December, 1560, the leading ministers and laymen, without leave asked of human governments, met together in Edinburgh "To consult upon those things which are to forward God's glory and the weal of his Kirk in this realme." And this was the FIRST GENERAL ASSEMBLY of the Church of Scotland. The truly popular character of this assembly is seen in the fact that while it numbered forty members, thirty-four of the whole were laymen. Parliament had rid the land of Romanism, the Assembly was now to organize, on its sole responsibility to the great Head of the Church, an ecclesiastical system for the nation. To the same men who had drawn up the Confession of Faith was now assigned the task of preparing a system of ecclesiastical government. In this work they betook themselves directly to the Holy Scriptures.

The result of their labours was the FIRST BOOK OF DISCIPLINE. This book recognized four kinds of ordinary and permanent office-bearers in the Church—the pastor, the teacher, the ruling elder and the deacon. The teacher's task was not unlike that of our theological professors. To meet the pressing necessities of the hour, two other officers of a temporary character were added—*superintendents,* who should itinerate and preach, and inspect the conduct of the more uneducated country ministers, and *exhorters* or *Bible-readers*—humble, pious persons, who might instruct their still humbler and less enlightened brethren.

Pastors were to be regularly called by election, examination and admission. To the people belonged the right to elect their own pastor. The minister, elders and deacons constituted the kirk-session. Presbyteries were soon organized, and the General Assembly, composed of ministers and ruling elders, commissioned from different parts of the kingdom, combined in itself the governing powers of the whole Church. Judicious rules for public worship on the Sabbath were embraced in the system—a sermon on Sabbath morning and catechizing in the afternoon, and in the towns a sermon on a week day besides. It was also held imperatively necessary that there be a school in every parish for the instruction of youth in the principles of religion, in grammar and in the Latin language; and it was proposed that a college be established in every notable town.

Such was the Presbyterian protest against the Romish adage, that ignorance is the mother of devotion. Such was the scheme for elevating the degraded Scottish masses into the dignity and character of *a people;* and to carry out this noble plan the revenues of the church were needed; and but for the ignoble covetousness of the nobles these revenues would have been obtained, and an early and glorious salvation wrought out for Scotland. But some of these nobles had already seized upon portions of the Church lands and were filling their pockets with the revenues, and others were casting longing eyes toward a share in the golden spoils. From this fountain flowed many a stream of bitterness in after years.

MARY QUEEN OF SCOTS.

A new chapter now opens before us of this story of conflict. Mary, daughter of James V. and Mary of Guise, was born seven days before her father's death. At the age of eight she was sent to France, educated in a convent, and in 1558 married to the dauphin Francis, who died in 1560, and the following year she returned to Scotland as its queen. Beautiful as ever woman could desire, richly endowed with mental gifts, finely accomplished, her residence of thirteen years abroad, part of the time in a Romish convent, but most of it as a fascinating creature in one of the most flagitiously corrupt and licentious courts in the world, had very poorly fitted her to rule over Presbyterian Scotland. Foreseeing the bearing on the interests of France of her character and course in the turbulent scenes before her, her relations in that country had spared no pains to mould her spirit in accordance with the most rigorous bigotry, and to thorough detestation of the Reformation and its champions. They strove to fill her vision with the glories to be gained in the work of re-shackling the now liberated limbs of Scotland with the fetters of Romanism. Nor did they find their pupil either incompetent or unwilling. Right greedily did she swallow all their teachings. And to all other motives for stifling the Reformation was added the hope of putting the English crown upon her saintly brow and bringing erring England back from her wanderings to the true fold. For this she would need French gold and French armies, all which were promised in lavish abundance.

Scarcely, therefore, had she set foot on Scottish soil when she flung out her colours before the eyes of the nation. On her first Sabbath in Scotland she set her foot upon the act of parliament, and had mass celebrated in Holyrood house. Against this the privy council protested, and Knox, with a voice louder than theirs, in a thundering sermon at St. Giles, declared that "one mass was more fearful to him than ten thousand armed foes." It is not so difficult to conquer men, especially in a good cause—to conquer God in a sinful one, who can hope?

Well for Mary that Romish measure was not dealt out to her. Well has it been said that had Scotland now been in the hands of Rome, and Mary a Huguenot queen, persisting in the exercise of her religion, she would speedily have followed Hamilton, Wishart and Mill to the stake, or have been hurried out of the realm.

The Protestants, however, contented themselves with rigorously protesting, and when Mary heard of Knox's sermon she sent for him that she might set her eyes upon that subject that dared to rebuke his sovereign. She was soon satisfied if not gratified with the sight. Wonderful scene, that interview between the stern prophet and the beautiful

Jezebel! Curious contrast, between the emotions in those two hearts, as they stood gazing into each other's eyes. Two mighty conflicting systems were there face to face—Presbyterian republicanism and despotic Popery.

"Think you," asked the queen, "that subjects having the power may resist their princes?"

"If princes exceed their bounds, madam," he replied, "no doubt they may be resisted, even by power. For no greater honour or greater obedience is to be given to kings or princes than God has ordained to be given to father or mother. But the father may be struck with a frenzy in which he would slay his children. Now, madam, if the children arise, join together, apprehend the father, take the sword from him, bind his hands and keep him in prison till the frenzy be over, think you, madam, that the children do any wrong? Even so, madam, is it with princes that would murder the children of God that are subject unto them. Their blind zeal is nothing but a mad frenzy; therefore, to take the sword from them, to bind their hands and to cast them into prison till they be brought to a more sober mind, is no disobedience against princes, but just obedience, because it agreeth with the will of God."

"Thus spoke Calvinism," writes Froude—"the creed of republics in its first hard form."

And, indeed, this was pretty strong meat for those days and for that queen who had as yet tasted nothing stronger than courtly flatteries and adulations; but strong as it was it is now acknowledged, wherever manly liberty is known, to be as wholesome for the citizen as unpalatable to the despot.

"My subjects, then, are to obey you, not me?"

"Nay," he answered, "let prince and subject both obey God. Kings should be foster-fathers of the Kirk and queens its nursing mothers."

"You are not the Kirk that I will nurse. I will defend the Kirk of Rome, for that, I think, is the Kirk of God."

"Your will, madam," said Knox, "is no reason, neither does your thought make the Roman harlot the spouse of Jesus Christ."

When once the queen contemptuously demanded, "What are you in this commonwealth?" he answered, "A subject, born within the same, madam; and, albeit I be neither god, lord nor baron in it, yet has God made me, how abject that ever I be in your eyes, a profitable member within the same."

"On reading the actual narrative of the business," writes Carlyle—"what Knox said and what Knox meant—I must say one's tragic feeling is a little disappointed. They are not coarse, these speeches; they seem to me about as fine as the circumstances would permit. Knox was not there to do the courtier; he came on another errand. Whoever, reading these colloquies of his with the queen, thinks they are vulgar insolence of a plebeian priest to a delicate, high lady mistakes the purport and essence of them altogether. It was unfortunately not possible to be polite with the Queen of Scotland, unless one proved untrue to the nation and cause of Scotland. A man who did not wish to see the land of his birth made a hunting-field for intriguing, ambitious Guises, and the cause of God trampled under foot of falsehood's formulas and the devil's cause, had no method of making himself agreeable. 'Better that women weep,' said Morton, 'than bearded men be forced to weep.' Knox was the constitutional opposition party of Scotland—the nobles of the country, called by their station to take that post, were not found in it; Knox had to go, or no one. The hapless queen, but the still more hapless country, if she were made happy!

"I am not prepared to say Knox had a soft temper, nor do I know he had what we call an ill temper. An ill nature he decidedly had not—kind, honest affections dwelt in the much-enduring, hard-worn, ever-battling man. That he *could* rebuke queens, and had such weight among those proud, turbulent nobles—proud enough, whatever else they were—and could maintain to the end a kind of virtual presidency and sovereignty in that wild realm—he who was only a subject born within the same—this of itself will prove to us that he was found close at hand to be no mean, acrid man, but at heart a healthful, strong, sagacious man."

After the close of his first interview with the queen, Knox said, "If there be not in her a proud mind and a crafty wit, and an indurate heart against God and his truth, my judgment faileth me."

"He made her weep," said Randolph to Cecil, "as well you know there be of that sex that will do that for anger as well as grief. You exhort us to stoutness. The voice of that one man is able to put more life in us in one hour than five hundred trumpets blustering in our ears."

When advised to more gentleness of manner, Knox answered: "Men deliting to swym betwixt two waters have often compleaned of my severitie. I do fear that that which men term levitie and dulceness do bring upon themselves and others more fearful destruction than yit hath enseued the vehemency of any preacher within this realme."

KNOX ON TRIAL.

In December, 1561, the General Assembly met, at which some of the secular members, who, willing to see popery in its grave could they but be the heirs of its revenues, and not unwilling to be free from its penances could they but enjoy instead the liberty to live in profligacy, and who dreaded the restraints of church discipline, which the assembly was aiming to enforce, questioned the propriety of such meetings without the queen's consent. King Jesus must kneel down and wipe the dust from the sandals of King Cæsar. To this suggestion Knox exclaimed: "Take from us the liberty of assemblies and take from us the gospel! If the liberty of the Church must depend upon her allowance or disallowance, we shall want not only assemblies but the preaching of the gospel." And when the proposition was made to ask the queen to ratify the Book of Discipline, a courtier answered: "Stand content—that book will not be obtained." "Then," said Knox, "let God require the injury which the commonwealth shall sustain at the hands of those who hinder it."

Upon the question of those Church revenues that had so long fattened the Romish beast, the privy council at length came to the sage determination to give two-thirds to the ejected priests during their lives, and to divide the remaining third between the court and the Protestant ministry. "Two parts," exclaimed Knox, "given to the devil, and the third divided between God and the devil. To those dumb dogs, the bishops, ten thousand was not enough, but to the servants of Christ, who principally preach the gospel, an hundred marks must suffice. How can that be sustained?" But the covetous lords cared little for either Popery or Protestantism; but they cared much for gold, and they looked to see their purses replenished with a rich portion of that two-thirds, as one by one the displaced ecclesiastics disappeared beneath the sod. Poor human nature!

The General Assembly met twice in 1562, once in June and again in December. The decrees of the Assembly now went forth as the act of the whole Church. "The haill Kirk appoints and decerns." And they provided by solemn act that

Church discipline should reach to all alike. The "magistrate subject to the rule of Christ" was not to be "exeemed from the same punishment" as the rest, "being found guilty and inobedient."

The work of Church construction went on at a steady pace, and as many priests and persons "*called* bishops" were still acting as ministers, it was determined that they be subject to examination under the eye of the superintendents. Synods were also elected to meet twice a year, with power to appoint and translate ministers, and a committee was nominated to adjust questions of jurisdiction with the privy council.

Encouraged by the papacy on the throne, the papacy in the land, in spite of the act of parliament to the contrary, ventured here and there to celebrate the mass; but such was the storm of public indignation that the cunning queen bent before it and put certain of the offenders in not very uncomfortable ward. She then convoked the parliament, and so effectually did she ply the lords with her wiles that not only was nothing done in favour of, but much to the prejudice of, the Reformation. Knox, of course, thundered out his reprehensions of their conduct, and from his pulpit, in the presence of many of them, he said, "I have been with you in your most desperate temptations, in your most extreme danger. There is not one of you against whom death and destruction was threatened perished, and how many of your enemies has God plagued before your eyes? Shall this be the thankfulness that ye shall render unto your God?" And then he warned them against the proposed marriage of the queen with a papist and the woes that must ensue thereon. For his audacity, the queen summoned him before the council, where she gave him a right queenly scolding, in the midst of which she burst into tears.

The celebration of the mass at Holyrood, while the queen was absent at Stirling, occasioned a slight popular outbreak, for which, wanting revenge, she cited two ministers to trial. Knowing her malignity, Knox, in execution of a commission he held from the Church, sent word to a number of Protestant gentlemen, asking their presence at the trial. For this act the queen sprang upon him like an eagle upon her prey, thinking that the happy hour had arrived to send him after Wishart. A grand assemblage of counselors and lords formed the court that was to try the giant heretic. With intense anxiety the public awaited the result, as a matter involving the life or death of the Reformation, and the palace yard and avenues were thronged with people.

Previous to the trial great efforts had been made to induce Knox to acknowledge that he had committed a fault and to throw himself upon the queen's mercy, but, of course, in vain, as he knew himself innocent of any fault in the matter.

The queen, having been assured by Lethington, her able and astute secretary, that her trouble with the stern Elijah was now virtually at an end, she burst into a fit of laughter as he appeared before the court, exclaiming, with revengeful glee:

"That man made me weep and never shed a tear himself. I will now see if I can make him weep."

Ah! for her soul Knox could weep tears of blood, but for himself he could lose his own blood without weeping.

One of his letters, inviting the attendance of his friends at the trial of the two ministers, was handed him, and the question asked,

"Is this of your writing?"

"Yes, it is."

"You have done more than I would have done," said Maitland.

"Charity is not suspicious," said Knox.

"Well, well," exclaimed the queen, "read your own letter." He did so.

"Heard you ever, my lords, a more despiteful and treasonable letter?" she asked.

"Mr. Knox, are you not sorry, from your heart, and do you not repent that such a letter has passed your pen?" asked Maitland.

"My lord Secretary, before I repent I must be taught my offence."

"Offence! If there be no more but the convocation of the queen's lieges the offence cannot be denied."

"Remember yourself, my lord; there is a difference between a lawful convocation and an unlawful. If I have been guilty in this, I offended oft since I came last into Scotland."

"That was then and now is now."

"The time that hath been is even now before my eyes, though then the devil had a visor on his face and now he comes under the cloak of justice."

At this, her majesty's passions boiled over, and she exclaimed:

"What is this? Methinks you trifle with him. Who gave *him* authority to convoke *my* lieges? Is not that treason?"

O good queen, your appetite for heretical blood cannot be gratified!

"No, madam," said Lord Ruthven, "for he makes convocation to hear prayers and sermon almost daily."

"Hold your peace and let him answer for himself," said the queen.

After further reply by Knox, she answered, "You shall not escape so. Is it not treason, my lords, to accuse a prince of cruelty?" A portion of his letter was then read, in which he had said that the proposed trial of the two Protestants was to open the door to further cruelty.

"So what say you to that?" asked the queen.

All ears were intent to hear his reply.

"I ask your grace, madam, whether obstinate papists are not deadly enemies to the professors of the gospel of Christ?"

Mary was silent but the lords were not. With one voice they exclaimed:

"God forbid that the lives of the faithful stood in the power of the papists! Experience has taught us the cruelty of their hearts!"

Knox went on until interrupted by the chancellor, who said:

"You forget you are not now in the pulpit."

"I am here to speak the truth," said he, "and therefore the truth I speak, impugn it whoso list."

Knox and Mary withdrew and the vote was taken acquitting the defendant. Lethington, enraged, brought back the queen and proceeded to take the vote again in her presence. This was too much for Scotch blood.

"What!" said they, "shall the Laird of Lethington control us, or the presence of a woman cause us to condemn an innocent man?"

A *woman!* This is too republican! But the vote of acquittal was passed again. When the bishop of Ross, who had been the informer in the case, voted with the rest, this "woman" exclaimed:

"Trouble not the child, I pray you trouble him not, for he is newly awakened out of his sleep. Why should not the old fool follow the footsteps of those that have passed before him?"

So it seems that a queen from courtly France could be uncourtly upon occasion as well as stern reformers.

PRESBYTERIANISM NATIONALIZED.

To revolutionize the wrong religious convictions and worship of a nation is a more than herculean task. Often, almost always, this requires not only the highest heroism, great firmness of purpose, vast intellectual power, souls on fire with the truth, but also rivers of blood. The seeds of truth must be moistened with streams from many a martyr's veins, and our present peaceful enjoyment of religious light and liberty was bought for us with blood—the best blood that ever coursed through human veins.

True to the genius of our holy religion, that knows no distinction between sinners of whatever civil rank or social grade, the Scottish Reformers lashed with impartial scourge the sins alike of nobles and peasants. This, of course, was not a little distasteful to the proud and profligate. As the Duchess of Buckingham, in after years, wrote to Lady Huntington: "The doctrines of these preachers are most repulsive and strongly tinctured with impertinence and disrespect toward their superiors, in perpetually endeavouring to level all ranks and do away with all distinctions. It is monstrous to be told that you have a heart as sinful as the common wretches that crawl upon the earth. This is highly offensive and insulting, and I cannot but wonder that your ladyship should relish any sentiments so much at variance with high rank and good-breeding." And the proud sinners of the sixteenth century relished them no better than those of later times.

In 1564 a conference was held between the principal statesmen and the ministers of the Church respecting the freedom of the latter in animadverting in the pulpit upon the morals of the people, small and great—the conference being assented to by the ministers on the express condition that no formal decision was to be made upon the topics discussed. Knox and Lethington were the two champions of the hour—the latter learned, subtle and acute; the former "superior to all fear."

The statesmen urged upon Knox the wishes of the council that he would study greater caution and mildness in his language. To this the prophet replied by drawing a vivid picture of the prevalent vices of the day, and added that none ought to be surprised at the faithful freedom of God's ministers, of sins committed so openly and persisted in so recklessly.

The former disapproved of the manner in which Knox prayed for the queen.

"Ye pray for the queen's majesty with a condition, 'illuminate her heart if thy good pleasure be.' Where have ye an example for such a prayer?"

"Wherever the examples are, I am assured of the rule, 'If ye shall ask anything according to his will, he will hear us.'"

"But in so doing ye put a doubt in the people's heads of her conversion."

"Not I, my lord; but her own obstinate rebellion causes more than me to doubt of her conversion."

"Wherein rebels she against God?"

"In all the actions of her life. She will not hear the preaching of the blessed evangel of Jesus, and she maintains that idol, the mass."

"She thinks not that rebellion, but good religion."

"So thought they who offered their children to Moloch."

"But yet ye can produce the example of none who have prayed so before you."

"Peter said these words to Simon Magus, 'Repent of this thy wickedness.'"

"But where find ye that the Scriptures call any the bond-slaves of Satan, or that the prophets spoke so irreverently of princes?"

"Paul said, 'Behold I send you unto the Gentiles that they may turn them from the power of Satan unto God.'"

No wonder the noble secretary said he was tired, and begged some other one to take his place in the lists. Chancellor Morton cunningly ordered George Hay to answer Knox, but Hay replied that he agreed fully with Knox.

"Marry!" exclaimed the discomfited secretary, "ye are the well worst of the two."

The debate was long protracted, and at last Maitland proposed that a vote should be taken. Against this Knox protested, reminding their lordships that the General Assembly had agreed to this conference on the express condition that nothing should be decided on; and at length the meeting broke up, leaving Knox triumphant and his opponents in deep chagrin at the result.

Toward the end of 1564 Matthew Stewart, earl of Lennox, returned to Scotland after an exile of twenty years. He was of royal blood, and his wife, the Lady Margaret Douglas, was niece of Henry VIII. and uterine sister of James V. of Scotland. Soon after the return of Lennox, he was followed by his son Henry Stewart, Lord Darnley, who was thus the nearest heir to both the English and Scottish crowns, should both Elizabeth and Mary die without issue. As he was a Catholic, the Protestant lords dreaded his union by marriage with Queen Mary. But allowing themselves to be cajoled by her with a promise—the promise of one who made little account of even oaths to heretics—to grant a royal sanction to the legal establishment of the Protestant religion, most of them gave their consent—the earl of Murray, however, half-brother to the queen, resolutely withholding his own. Upon this his good sister the queen resolved upon his ruin.

Early in the morning, "while the drowsy citizens of Edinburgh were in their morning sleep," Mary and Darnley were married in the royal chapel by a Romish priest. To the surprise of those who were permitted to witness the ceremonies, Mary wore a mourning dress of black velvet, "such as she wore the doleful day of the burial of her husband."

"Whether it was an accident," writes Froude, "whether the doom of the house of Stuart haunted her at that hour with its fatal foreshadowings, or whether simply for a great political purpose she was doing an act which in itself she loathed, it is impossible to tell; but that black drapery struck the spectators with a cold, uneasy awe."

Darnley was now proclaimed king without waiting for the consent or dissent of the estates, and naturally favoured his wife in her schemes for the ruin of Murray. The latter had objected to the marriage, and the Scottish Herodias would now have the dissenter's head in a charger. Murray was ordered to court, but not silly enough to enter the lion's den, he was proclaimed an outlaw. He now raised an army of defence, which was attacked and scattered by the forces of the queen, and he, driven from pillar to post, at last took refuge in England. Elizabeth, with accustomed irresolution and meanness, refused aid to those who were fighting her battles in fighting their own.

A month before the queen's marriage the General Assembly had met in Edinburgh. To conciliate the Protestants while her marriage scheme was maturing, she had proposed a conference at Perth. Accepting the proposition, the assembly drew up six articles for ratification by the parliament she promised to call. The marriage having now taken place, she gave her answer to the articles, accompanying it with the declaration that she "neither will nor may leave the religion wherein she has been nourished and brought up." The second of the articles asked for permanent provision for the ministers, that vacant charges be given to qualified persons, and that "no bishopric, abbacy, etc., having many kirks annexed thereto may be disposed to any one man."

To this she answered in effect that she wanted the greater part of the church revenues for her own use.

The assembly met again in December and took the queen's reply into consideration, and transmitted to her their views of the matter, to the effect that they would not that she or any other patron be defrauded of their legal patronages, but that the presentee should always be tried and examined by the learned men of the Kirk; that if the presentation remain in the hands of the patrons, the admission of the presentee should be in the hands of the Kirk; otherwise the patrons could present absolutely whom they pleased, whether the Kirk pleased or not, and "what then would abide in the Kirk of God but ignorance without all order?"

This matter of patronage has ever been, as it must of necessity always be, a thorn in the side of the body of Christ. It was one of the many curses bequeathed by Rome to Protestantism. It was long the policy of the clergy to induce wealthy sinners to ease their consciences by giving or bequeathing at their death large sums of money for the endowment of churches, monasteries and the like. By this act, the donors secured a legal right for themselves and their heirs to nominate, or present, as they called it, the candidate, who was to fill the offices so established and enjoy the revenues accruing from these endowments. When these patronages had largely multiplied, the cunning clergy enabled the holders of this right to buy new spiritual favours by resigning it to them, and thus these patronages became distributed among priests and nobles, courtiers and kings. And often when, say, a bishopric with ample revenues, became vacant, some utterly ungodly man held the legal right to name the new incumbent; and thus the ecclesiastical offices became filled with creatures who were as ignorant of religion as they were destitute of all moral decency. And now the Reformed Church, tied up to the system of patronage, yet strove to secure itself against its obviously corrupting influence by asserting the right to judge of the character of the presentee and exclude the unworthy.

The queen's proposed retention of so large a part of the income of the Church in her own hands they pronounced "both ungodly and also contrary to all public order, bringing no small confusion to the poor souls, the common people, who by these means should be instructed of their salvation." Two-thirds of the patrimony of the Church had already been allowed to the rejected papists during their lives, and now her majesty would retain for her own disposal the fruits of the benefices!

And now, in 1566, thick darkness began to brood over the land. Bloody-minded Romanism, at Trent, had decreed the extirpation of Protestantism, and the League formed for this purpose was sent to Mary, who promptly set her signature to the bond, and measures were taken by her to restore popery in Scotland to all its power and glory. But wickedness is contagious, and in its blindness is very apt to commend its own chalice to its own lips. If Mary longed for blood, she should see it flowing, but from other veins than she desired and designed.

The dark, cunning Italian, Rizzio, this woman's private secretary, had excited the jealousy of Darnley, the queen's weak and despised husband, and he resolved on revenge. He drew certain lords—who hated Rizzio as heartily as he—or they drew him into a conspiracy to rid the world of his rival. The other conspirators required of him, and he gave, a bond declaring that all that was done was "his own device and intention." The deed was to have been done on a certain day, and when it was postponed Darnley declared with an oath that "if the slaughter was not hastened" he would stab Rizzio in the queen's presence with his own hand. At the next appointed time—Saturday night, the 9th of March, 1566—the conspirators surrounded Holyrood Palace, secured the doors, and Darnley entered the queen's boudoir—Rizzio sitting on a chair and the queen opposite him on the sofa. Darnley kissed the queen. She shrank from him, and her eyes fell on the corsletted form of Ruthven entering through the opening in the tapestries. Glaring on Darnley, Mary answered his kiss with the one word, "Judas!" and then demanded of Ruthven the cause of his presence there.

"Let yon man come forth," said he, pointing to Rizzio; "he has been here over long."

"What has he done?"

"He has offended your honour, and your husband's honour, and caused your majesty to banish a great part of the nobility."

Rizzio was dragged out into the darkness to the bottom of the stairs, and stabbed with sixty wounds. From this hour the queen's dislike for her husband deepened into hatred the most intense, and she never rested till she had seen him murdered.

Two or three nights after, at midnight, Mary, accompanied by her husband—whom she tolerated till his time should come—and one servant, left the palace by a subterranean passage, mounted the horses shivering in the cold, and in two hours she was safe at Dunbar, twenty miles away. Thus were her bloody designs against Protestantism frustrated, the blood of her secretary shed, the papal lords scattered, the Protestant lords brought back from England, and the Parliament which was to have done her work prorogued. But as her power of persecuting the Church sank, her fury against the slayers of Rizzio rose, and she now set herself to study revenge. Having gathered an army, she returned to Edinburgh to glut her revenge. While agitated by these fierce passions, she gave birth, on the 19th of June, at Edinburgh Castle, to a son, afterward the noted James VI. of Scotland and I. of England.

During this month the Assembly met, and in view of recent horrors and apparently impending dangers, appointed the first national fast since the beginning of the Reformation. "The haill Assembly, in respect to the perils and dangers wherewith the Kirk of God is assaulted, and that by mighty enemies, considered a general fast to be published throughout this realm in all kirks reformed."

But other horrors were in store for that suffering nation. As soon as the queen recovered her health—in conjunction with the execrable James Hepburn, Earl of Bothwell, wicked as he was weak—she began to mature schemes for the murder of her husband. He lay sick at Glasgow, of a sudden illness, probably the effect of poison, to which the queen seems to allude in a shameless letter to Bothwell from this place, whither she had gone to visit him, in which she asks, "Consider whether you can contrive anything more secret by medicine. He is to take medicine and baths at Craigmiller." In this letter this woman tells Bothwell that her husband's breath "almost killed her," and she "sat as far from him as the bed would allow." She tells Bothwell that she had left her heart with him; calls him her "dear love," and says she can sleep nowhere as she wishes but in his arms. Alluding to Bothwell's young and faithful wife, she says, "we are coupled with two bad companions. The devil sunder us and God knit us together to be the most faithful couple that ever he united." Then she promises to bring "the man" with her, and begs Bothwell to "provide for all things."

And she did bring "the man," her husband, to Edinburgh, and Bothwell met her at the gates, took the man off her hands, and, in spite of his remonstrances, lodged him in "Kirk-a-Field," a roofless, ruined church, with a building adjoining, in which a room had been prepared for the victim. While he lay there Mary frequently visited him. At midnight—Sunday night, February 9—Mary sat with Darnley, while dancing was going on at the palace and while Bothwell, with his servants, was piling up powder-bags in the room below. When all was ready, Bothwell came into the room and gave the signal for Mary to retire. As she rose to go, she said: "It was just this time last year that Rizzio was slain." Wretched Darnley shuddered at her words, and said, "She was very kind, but why did she speak of Davie's slaughter?" Some time after an explosion was heard, and "Edward Seymour was blown to pieces, and the bodies of Darnley and his page were found forty yards beyond the town wall, under a tree."

Not long after Bothwell was divorced from his

wife, and Mary, the murderess of her former husband, was married to Bothwell the murderer.

The nobles flew to arms to protect the infant king, whom Bothwell would soon have hurried out of the world to make way for his own heirs, and whom the mother loved too little to care to protect. To meet these the queen gathered a small army, and the parties met near Preston. But finding her troops little disposed to shed blood in such a cause, she sent to the confederates to treat with them, while Bothwell fled with all precipitation toward Dunbar, and at length to the Shetland Islands, where he turned pirate. From thence he went to the Continent, where he was cast into a prison, and at length died, detested by all who had not forgotten him.

The queen gave herself up to the confederates, and as she entered their ranks, dressed, as Buchanan says, "in a short shabby robe that scarcely reached below the knee," the cry arose, "Burn the harlot! burn the murderer!"

The soldiers also held up to her view a standard on which Darnley's dead body was painted, and near the body the infant king praying to God to avenge the death of his father. She was conducted to Edinburgh, and thence, after two days, by a decree of the nobles, she was sent prisoner to Lochlevin castle. From Lochlevin she escaped to England, where she fell into the hands of the merciless Elizabeth.

The bitterest and most powerful foe of the Church being now disabled and banished by her own crimes, the lords, at the meeting of the assembly in July, specified certain articles in favour of the Reformation, the adoption of which they promised to secure at the next lawful parliament. The earl of Murray, who had now returned from exile, was appointed to the regency. In December, Parliament met; at the opening of which Knox preached, urging the legislators to begin their labours with the affairs of religion, that God might prosper them the more in the arduous work of restoring order in the confused and shattered realm. Heeding the admonition, the Parliament solemnly re-ratified the acts of 1560, abolishing the papacy and establishing true religion in the land. It was further provided that no prince should ever be admitted to the exercise of authority in the realm without first taking an oath to support the Protestant religion, and that none but Protestants should be admitted to any office excepting such as were hereditary or held for life.

To the Church alone was assigned the duty to examine and admit candidates to the ministry, though the ancient lay patrons might yet *present* their favourites. Parliament also ratified the ecclesiastical jurisdiction claimed and exercised by the Assemblies of the Church. The thirds of incomes from the benefices were appointed to be paid into the hands of collectors nominated by the Church, who, after paying the salaries of the ministers, were to account for any surplus to the exchequer.

A few days after this meeting of Parliament the Assembly met and appointed commissioners to co-operate with the six members of Parliament, or secret council nominated by the regent, for such affairs as concerned the Kirk and its jurisdiction. It also degraded from the ministry "Adam, *called* bishop of Orkney," for marrying the queen to Bothwell, and called John Craig to account for publishing the banns of marriage between them, and in view of all the circumstances of the case approved his course; and it subjected the countess of Argyle to censure for having given assistance and countenance to the baptizing of the infant king after the popish fashion.

Thus man proposeth and God disposeth. Mary had laid her cunning schemes to sweep Protestantism with a bloody besom from the land, and the breath of God had swept popery away instead. Mary slew her husband to marry Bothwell, and Bothwell, her instrument in the bloody deed, had also divorced his lawful, faithful wife to marry Mary, and the two thus united were soon to lord it over Scotland, Church and State, from Holyrood Palace; and now Protestantism held all the reins of power, and Bothwell was gone in one direction, an execrated fugitive, to a foreign prison and a dishonoured grave, and Mary was gone, an execrated fugitive, in another direction, to England—to execution!

Presbyterianism was now become the acknowledged religion of the realm—sanctioned, not created by the authorities of the kingdom. Man proposeth—God disposeth! And let all the people say, Amen!

THE TULCHANS.

If the darkest hour is just before the day, the brightest dawn is often darkened by quick-gathering clouds, to be followed by a day of wrathful, desolating storm.

For the hour, in Scotland, the skies were very bright, and spring promised abundant bloom and bountiful harvest. The Church, victor over all her foes, was mistress of the field. Neither papal monarch, state council nor Parliament under the manipulation of ungodly Lethingtons, threatened invasion of her rights. Her assemblies possessed unchallenged spiritual jurisdiction, and her untrammelled ministers were free to proclaim, where they would and as often as they pleased, the "holy evangel" of Christ.

Even during the troublous times now passed the Church had enjoyed a not discouraging growth. In the first General Assembly, in 1560, there were but six ministers, and this was one-half of the whole number of Protestant ministers then in Scotland; while now, seven years after, the Church could number two hundred and fifty-two ministers, four hundred and sixty-seven readers and an hundred and fifty-four exhorters.

In the mean time, improvement in doctrine and discipline, as Hetherington writes, "was not less rapid, steady and decided. Offenders of every kind and degree were compelled to yield obedience to sacred authority; noblemen and ladies of highest rank submitted to disciplinary censures; lordly prelates were constrained to bow their unmitred heads before the Church's rebuke; over the refractory members of its own body—over one even of its early champions, Paul Methven—its power was extended in the impartial administration of even-handed spiritual justice. That there must have been a marvellous amount of the divine influence accompanying all the exertions of the Church, when the walls of her temples were thus built in troublous times, we cannot doubt."

But the seeds of evil were rapidly germinating under the calm sky—bloody civil wars impending between the queen's party and that of the king—the friends of the Church to fall, the good regent to be assassinated, and Knox to die—and maladministration under other regents, strong or weak, and wicked whether weak or strong.

But, worst of all, foes to the Church were to spring up within her own household. As there was one traitor among the twelve apostles, so in all ages there are tares among the wheat, in pulpit and in pews. The ancient, and in many countries still prevalent, system of admitting to the communion on external rather than internal grounds, upon a recital of the catechism and the creed, rather than upon probable evidence of heartfelt piety, has always resulted in disaster—disaster to the persons thus admitted, and, through such of them as passed into the offices of the Church, sad disaster to the whole Church.

In the exciting times of the early Reformation little inquiry was made of applicants for church-membership and office, beyond merely external qualifications; and many of the so-called Protestant lords—even those who legislated as ruling elders in church courts—were the merest ecclesiastical politicians, willing enough to be rid of the papacy, but more willing still to serve themselves, even at the expense of sound Protestantism. The divisions and commotions and corruptions embosomed in such seed were not long in making themselves manifest.

In the mean time, while the partisans of Mary on the one hand, and those of the regent on the other, were engaged in keeping the realm in ebullition, the General Assembly were active and vigilant.

In July, 1568, they passed an ordinance prescribing the qualifications of membership in their body and the methods of election; and another suppressing a book entitled the "Fall of the Roman Kirk," in which the king was named as the "Supreme Head of the Primitive Kirk;" for from first to last Christ's sole headship in his

Church has been the favourite watchword with Scotch Presbyterians. They also demanded more ample provisions for the support of the ministry—a demand to which "THE GOOD REGENT" would have listened if he could.

But this magnanimous man, beset with snares and schemes for his assassination, had more than enough to do to maintain a position becoming more and more precarious, and to discharge the secular duties of an office becoming more and more arduous. Lethington, the faithless, joined the queen's party and became a chief schemer in all her unscrupulous intrigues. But the regent held on his way, reforming abuses, maintaining public order, administering justice and defending everybody but himself. The queen's agents, however, were as remorseless as he was kind and conscientious; and, finding it impossible to compass his death by open assault, they at length took a lesson from the conduct of the queen and resolved upon assassination. Hamilton of Bothwellhough, a nephew of the archbishop of St. Andrews, whose life Murray had once spared, undertook the task of murdering his benefactor. Like a bloodhound he followed his victim from place to place. He hunted him from Dumbarton to Glasgow, and from

Glasgow to Stirling, and from Stirling to Linlithgow, where the archbishop had a house not far from the house in which Murray was accustomed to lodge. In this house the assassin concealed himself to watch his opportunity. The regent was warned of this on the very day of the murder, but he despised danger and trusted his life with his God. As he rode along on his horse, the murderer, from behind a curtain on the balcony, took aim and shot him, and then, escaping by a back door through the garden, fled to his accomplices and was received with warm congratulations.

Thus died James Stuart, earl of Murray, son of James V. and half-brother of Mary Queen of Scots —a high-minded, enlightened Christian statesman, who well earned the title affectionately bestowed upon him, "The Good Regent"—and with him fell a bright star from the banner of Presbyterianism in Scotland. He was succeeded in the regency by Matthew Stuart, the earl of Lennox and grandfather of the young king. The realm, now divided under two factions—the one supporting the claims of the exiled queen, and the other those of the king and the regent—was devastated by civil wars; the two parties being so equally matched that neither could gain decided advantage over the other. Of course the Church lent all her influence to the king's party, but could do little more than preach and pray amidst the ceaseless din of clashing arms. Knox was a special object of hatred to the murderers of Murray. When news of the regent's death reached Edinburgh, Knox was overwhelmed with distress, for it had been through his intercession that the life of the murderer had been spared by the earl, and in a sermon on the day following he thus poured out his heart:

"Thy image, O Lord, did so clearly shine in that personage that the devil and the people to whom he is prince could not abide it, and so to punish our sins and our ingratitude thou hast permitted him to fall, to our great grief, in the hand of cruel and traitorous murderers. He is at rest, O Lord—we are left in extreme misery."

As Knox was preaching at the weekly conference, he found in the pulpit a paper containing these words: "Take up now the man whom you accounted another God, and consider the end to which his ambition hath brought him." During the sermon, Knox said:

"There is one present who has thrown into the pulpit a paper exulting over the regent's death. That wicked man, whosoever he be, shall not go unpunished, and shall die where there shall be none to lament him."

Maitland of Lethington, on his return from church, said to his sister,

"That man is raving, to speak thus of one he knows not."

She, suspecting her brother, replied with tears: "None of that man's denunciations are wont to prove idle."

Maitland died in Italy, having "no known person to attend him."

At the funeral of the regent, Knox preached to a weeping audience of three thousand persons, on the text, "Blessed are the dead which die in the Lord." And the General Assembly, at its meeting, the month following, ordered that the assassin be publicly excommunicated in all the chief towns in the kingdom.

Such were now the number, power and malice of the enemies of Knox in Edinburgh that he was persuaded to retire for a while to St. Andrew's; and on his disappearance they circulated reports, some that he would never preach again, some that "his face was turned into his neck," and some that he was dead.

But the fall of the Good Regent was neither the

only nor the worst calamity that befel the Church. Foes without can be met and vanquished, but what shall be done with covert foes within the citadel? Greedy nobles were hungering for the income of the Church. Several of the popish incumbents had died, and the question now arose as to the disposal of the funds thus freed from papal grasp. The Church claimed that, as they had been consecrated to religion, they should now be employed in supporting pastors and teachers. To this the ignoble nobility would not listen, though as yet they dared not openly attempt their secularization.

But where there is a will there is a way. Whenever did avarice fail of cunning to help itself to forbidden gold? The credit of solving the arduous problem belongs to James Douglas, earl of Morton, and afterward regent. Able, ambitious, avaricious and rapacious, he was well capable of conceiving and executing any scheme that promised either power or profit. Accordingly, on the death of the popish archbishop of St. Andrew's, Morton obtained a grant empowering him to dispose of the archbishopric and its revenues. Not daring to formally hold the benefice himself and feed his purse with the income, he induced John Douglas, rector of the University of St. Andrew's, to take the office of archbishop, with the understanding that he, Morton, should have the lion's share of the revenues.

Thus the way was open for the infliction upon the Church of a set of ungodly officers, whose titles and duties were alike disallowed by Presbyterianism, and for the diversion of the ecclesiastical revenues into secular and avaricious hands.

Through this transparent scheme Knox saw at a single glance, and, being unable to attend the meeting of the Assembly at Stirling, in August, 1571, he wrote to them:

"And now, brethren, because the daily decay of natural strength threateneth my certain and sudden departing from the misery of this life, of love and conscience I exhort you; in the fear of God I charge and command you that ye take heed unto yourselves and to the flock over which God hath placed you overseers. Unfaithful and traitorous to the flock shall ye be before the Lord Jesus Christ if, with your consent directly, ye suffer unworthy men to be thrust into the ministry. This battle will be hard, but in the second point it will be harder; that is, that, with the like uprightness and strength in God, ye gainstand the merciless devourers of the patrimony of the Church. If men will spoil, let them do it to their own peril and condemnation, but communicate ye not with their sins by consent nor by silence; but with public proclamation make this known to the world, that ye are innocent of the robbery whereof ye will seek redress of God and man. God give you wisdom and stout courage in so just a cause!"

The Assembly sent a remonstrance to Parliament against this scheme of Morton, and loudly protested against Douglas taking a seat in that body as lord-bishop, on pain of excommunication. Morton, however, whose will was not easily resisted, secured his admission and commanded him to vote as archbishop on pain of treason. Thus Parliament took the first step toward the displacement of Presbyterianism, which had been, under God, the regenerator of Scotland, and the substitution of Episcopacy, which never entered the realm but as a curse.

While thus spiritual war raged within the Church, civil war was making havoc in the realm without. While Parliament sat at Stirling, the queen's party, in a body about five hundred strong, entered the town without resistance, attacked the house where Morton was lodging, and, setting it on fire, killed several of his servants, and at length took him prisoner, together with the regent, whom they slew. But the governor of the castle, rallying a few men, drove them out of the town; and the nobles elected John Erskine, earl of Mar, as regent. Mar was little disposed to hostility to the Church, but, as he had himself seized a portion of her patrimony, and as he was also greatly under the influence of Morton, little aid could be looked for from him in the great struggle in which she was now engaged.

Powerful, however, as Morton was, he sometimes found himself something else than victor in his conflicts with the Church. The tithe-collectors of St. Andrew's having refused to pay them into the hand of his creature Douglas, Morton secured from the regent an injunction forbidding their collecting them. But Erskine of Dun procured the annulment of this prohibition by an earnest remonstrance to the regent, in which he says:

"There is a spiritual jurisdiction and power which God has given to his Kirk and to them that bear office therein; and there is a temporal jurisdiction and power given of God to kings and civil magistrates. Both the powers are of God, and most agreeing to the fortifying one of the other if they be right used. But when the corruption of man enters in, confounding the offices, usurping to himself what he pleases, nothing regarding the good order appointed of God, then confusion follows in all estates. The Kirk of God should fortify all power and authority that pertains to the civil magistrate, because it is the ordinance of God. But if he pass the bounds of his office and enter within the sanctuary of the Lord, meddling with such things as appertain to the ministers of God's Kirk, then the servants of God should withstand his unjust enterprise, for so they are commanded of God."

The distinction here drawn between State and Church is clear and fundamental, but it was a long day before the precise boundaries of and relations between these two jurisdictions was well understood; and wherever Church and State are in any way formally united, they are of necessity, to a most harmful degree, confounded.

Erskine, in the same letter, deplores "the great disorder used in Stirling, in the last Parliament, in creating bishops, placing them and giving them a vote in Parliament, in despite of the Kirk and high contempt of God, the Kirk opposing herself to that disorder."

On the 12th of January, 1572, a convention of

the superintendents and certain ministers was convoked by the regent at Leith to consult together about the affairs of the Church. This convention, mistaking its own powers, appointed a committee to confer with the privy council, and agreed to ratify the conclusions they might come to in accordance with their instructions. So difficult is it to be always wise—so hard to see a clear way through cloudy complications—so rarely are the children of the kingdom true children of Issachar that have understanding of the times, to know what Israel ought to do! A joint committee of six ministers and six of the council—a self-constituted body without all authority from the Church—undertook to settle matters of national importance between Church and State. And they agreed upon a subtle scheme for setting up Mortonism in the Church, by which, under unlawful ecclesiastical forms, the patrimony of the Church might gratify the greed of avaricious lords. The titles of archbishop and bishop were to be retained, and the bounds of dioceses to remain as in old popish times, until the king's majority or until Parliament should determine upon the matter; the archbishops and bishops, to be chosen by an assembly of learned ministers, to have like jurisdiction with the superintendents, and be subject to the General Assembly in spiritual and to the king in secular matters. Like arrangements were made respecting abbacies, priories and the rest, and the holders of the larger benefices to have place in Parliament. This arrangement was at once confirmed by the regent, and the Church turned into a conglomerate of Presbytery, Prelacy and Popery.

Now the scheme of Morton was realized. Ambitious ecclesiastics would fill the offices, draw the revenues and pay over the chief share to the patrons through whose influence they came into place.

This scheme soon received from the wits of the day a designation which covered it with merited ridicule, and showed how well its ends and aims were comprehended by the popular mind. In the Highlands it was then not uncommon to deceive refractory cows into yielding their milk, by stuffing the skin of a departed calf with straw and placing it beside the cow as her own offspring; and now Janet had little difficulty in safely filling her pail. The name given to this surreptitious calf was Tulchan. And no sooner did the popular mind comprehend this new procedure than it saw that the diocese was the cow, and the bishop the stuffed calf, that meekly stood by while the patron filled his pail with the revenues. Hence these ecclesiastical tools came to be called *Tulchans.*

Morton's Tulchan, Douglas, was first ordained and installed in the archbishopric of St. Andrew's. Knox was invited by Morton to inaugurate Douglas, and he replied to the invitation by anathematizing both Douglas and Morton; and in the Assembly which met at St. Andrew's the following month he entered his protest against the election of Douglas, and "opposed himself directly to the making of bishops."

Patrick Adamson said that there were three sorts of bishops—"my lord bishop, my lord's bishop and the Lord's bishop. My lord bishop was in the papistrie, my lord's bishop is now when my lord gets the benefice, and the bishop serves for nothing but to make his title sure, and the Lord's bishop is the true minister of the gospel."

In August, the Assembly met at Perth and passed the Leith arrangement under consideration, and protested that the heads of articles therein should be received only as an interim, till farther order be obtained from the king, regent and nobility, for which they would press as occasion served. This, however, was rather a bowing before the storm than a manly, indignant opposition, and the poor Church reaped the harvest of their cowardice.

To this Assembly, Knox—now near the end of his career—addressed a farewell letter, replete with solemn counsel and wholesome advice, though he abstained from advising them to a course of opposition to the articles of Leith, for which he knew their courage and ability inadequate.

And now another calamity befel the Church, in the elevation of Morton, the originator of Tulchanism, to the regency on the death of Mar, who was worn out with the anxieties and toils of guiding the ship of state during the dark, stormy period of disorder and civil war.

But the greatest sorrow of all—as it at the same time deprived the Church of her Elijah and left a timid, time-serving ministry in the hands of Ahab, in the person of the regent—was the death of Knox. Morton was scarcely seated in the regency when Knox was laid in his grave. For long he had been sighing, "Call for me, dear brethren, that God in his mercy will please to put an end to my long and painful battle. For now, being unable to fight, I thirst an end before I be more troublesome to the faithful; and yet, Lord, let my desire be moderated by thy Holy Spirit. The day approaches, and is now before the door, for which I have frequently and vehemently thirsted, when I shall be released from my great labours and innumerable sorrows, and shall be with Christ. And now, God is my witness, whom I have served in the spirit in the gospel of his Son, that I have taught nothing but the true and solid doctrine of the gospel of the Son of God, and have had it for my only object to instruct the ignorant, to confirm the faithful, to comfort the weak, the fearful and the distressed by the promises of his grace, and to fight against the proud and rebellious by the divine threatenings." Go tell Grange, once courageous and constant, that "John Knox remains the same man now that he is about to die that ever he knew him when able in body, and wills him to consider what he was and the estate in which he now stands, which is a great part of his trouble."

To Morton, he said:

"Well, God has beautified you with many benefits which he has not given to every man. And therefore, in the name of God, I charge you to use all these benefits aright, and better in time to come than ye have done in times bypast. If ye shall do so, God shall bless you and honour you; but if ye do it not, God shall spoil you of these benefits, and your end shall be ignominy and shame."

On the 21st of November, three days before his death, he spoke at intervals such words as these:

"Come, Lord Jesus. Sweet Jesus, into thy hands I commend my spirit. Be merciful, Lord, to thy Church which thou hast redeemed. Give peace to this afflicted commonwealth. Raise up faithful pastors. Grant us, Lord, the perfect hatred of sin. Oh serve the Lord in fear, and death shall not be terrible to you. Nay, blessed shall death be to those who have felt the power of the death of the only begotten Son of God."

On Sabbath, the 23d, he said:

"If any be present, let them come and see the work of God. I have fought against spiritual wickedness in heavenly things and have prevailed. I have been in heaven and have possession. I have tasted the heavenly joys where presently I am."

Monday, November 24, 1572, was his last day on earth. When asked if he felt pain, he replied:

"It is no painful pain, but such a pain as shall soon, I trust, put end to the battle." He asked his wife to read the fifteenth chapter of first Corinthians; on hearing which, he said:

"Is not that a comfortable chapter? Oh what sweet and salutary consolation the Lord hath afforded me from that chapter!" About five o'clock he said to his wife:

"Go, read where I cast my first anchor;" when she read the seventeenth chapter of John's gospel. At ten o'clock prayer was offered, and he was asked if he heard it. He answered:

"Would to God that you and all men heard as I heard. I praise God for the heavenly sound." About eleven he gave a deep sigh, and said, "Now it is come." Being now speechless, he was requested to give a sign that he was supported by the promises, and he lifted one of his hands and died without a struggle.

A vast concourse of the people and all the nobility in the city attended his funeral; and, at the grave, the regent Morton said, "There lies he who never feared the face of man."

The departure of Knox was a blow to the Church, under which "it reeled and staggered like a storm-tossed vessel when the pilot's hand has ceased to guide the rudder," while the same event gave new life to Morton, who fancied that there was no one left for him to fear. Taking the imperious, selfish Elizabeth of England for his example, he proceeded to deal with the Scotch ecclesiastics as she dealt with her bishops. Finding that Presbyterian elders are much less easily manageable than prelatic bishops, he set himself to change the whole ecclesiastical system into a pliant, serviceable prelacy. The road to this lay through the multiplication of tulchan bishops, and filling church offices with unprincipled sycophants; and along this road he steadily walked. And at the same time, to reduce the power of the Church and increase his own, and also—a matter of chief aim with him—to enrich himself, he drew into his own hands the thirds of the benefices, promising to pay the pastors himself. And then he joined two, sometimes three, and sometimes four parishes together, and through his pliant tools, the tulchans, he appointed one minister to preach in each by turns, paying *one* salary and pocketing the rest.

Against this wickedness the Assembly remonstrated more or less energetically, and did what it could to exercise control over the tulchaus. In this struggle the Scotch spirit rose somewhat, and the Assembly remonstrated earnestly with the regent, and placed the tulchan bishop of Dunkeld under censure for improper conduct. The rigour of these measures was largely due to one on whom the mantle of the departing Knox had fallen—Andrew Melville.

THE MELVILLES.

The truest test of doctrines and principles is their influence on men, their character, and thence on their conduct. By their fruits shall ye know them. For man is very largely what the contents of his mind make him. Physically, he is somewhat the creature of climate; mentally, he is somewhat as his physical nature provides for and allows. But this is true only as to the intrinsic character of his powers. And whatever these be, they are at first mere capabilities, without either skill to act or tools to work with. Tools and skill must come by exercise upon things without. The caterpillar will weave of itself and out of itself a marvellous cocoon, but not until it has fed liberally upon the leaves that form its appropriate food. And the human mind, however naturally endowed, can put forth nothing worthy either of itself or its Creator until it has gone forth in the exercise of its powers and fed upon the truths that offer themselves for its action. These truths, gathered up and stored away in the mind and there digested by meditation, develop the powers and put into their hands the materials with which it may erect its structures, and form the enginery with which to subdue other minds to its own way of thinking, and thus mould and shape the actings of society. The larger this store of truths acquired and mastered, and the greater their intrinsic magnitude, the more truly is the possessor a man.

Nature is a vast volume of truths, well worthy our study, for they all come from God. But if light from created objects is bright and life-giving, how much more that which rays into the mind from God, the luminous centre of all! If it enlarges and elevates the mind to study the creature, how much more to study God! Thus religion is one of the most efficient of educators. "But if the light that is in thee be darkness, how great is that darkness!" To substitute for God something that is not God, whether a creature of God or of the perverted imagination—a dream, a nonentity—and with it engross the highest faculties of the soul, is at once to cheat the spirit with delusions and to dwarf instead of develop and enlarge its powers.

One of the many charges that reason and religion lay at the door of Romanism is, that it keeps the people out of the fruitful fields of truth, and sends them forth to starve in the dry, herbless deserts of error and human dreams. Visit any province where it works its unhindered will, and what grovelling worms they become! But Protestantism withdrew Luthers, Zwinglis and Calvins from mumbling masses, counting beads and kneeling before pictures and images, and confronting their minds with the grand verities of revelation, converted them into kings unto God.

And for the people of no country did the Reformation a greater work than for those of Scotland. From the beginning there was not wanting in that land of cloud and storm, wild glen, rock and mountain, a natural intellectual energy second to that of no other country; but not only had Romanism taken no step for its development—not only had it suffered the masses to lie enveloped in ignorance—but in its grovelling mummeries had enfeebled, degraded and dwarfed their powers. But the era of the Reformation there was the era of *men.* The play of its vast and mighty truths upon the mind of her commons advanced them into the condition of *a people,* endowing them with intelligence, developing their acuteness and harnessing their energies to the car of truth. And the hitherto despotic nobles soon learned that a power was growing into existence which must in future be consulted in matters in which it was expected to bear a part, and which not unfrequently laid a resistless prohibition upon aristocratic turbulence and crime. And not unfrequently, when the sagacity of king and nobles, and even of some of the time-serving ministers, was at fault, that of the new Protestant people discerned a plain path of progress. And here and there noble forms arose above the common mass, and became the Elijahs and Elishas of their day; and among many other such were the Melvilles, Andrew and James, uncle and nephew.

Andrew was born in 1545, the youngest of nine sons. When only two years of age his father fell in battle, and his mother dying soon after, he was left to the care of his oldest brother, Richard, who, with his wife, acted the parent to the parentless child. Of weakly habit of body, he displayed uncommon energy of mind, and was enabled through his brother's aid to pursue a course of liberal education. At the age of fourteen he entered St. Mary's College of the University of St. Andrew's, and, at the close of his course there was pronounced the "best philosopher, poet and Grecian of any young master in the land." Having acquired what learning he could at home, at the age of nineteen he went to France, and spent two years at the University of Paris, when that institution was at the height of its prosperity. Thence he went to Poictiers, where he was at once made regent of the College of St. Marceon. Three years after we find him at Geneva, in the chair of Humanity at the Academy. Here he rose to distinction as an Oriental scholar; studied law under some of the most famous teachers of the time; thoroughly discussed the great questions of civil government, and there drank in those doctrines of republicanism, civil and religious, which in after years in Scotland he so ably and faithfully illustrated. Here, also, he formed the acquaintance of many of the master spirits of the day, and a life-long attachment to his noble friend, Theodore Beza. In 1574, at the urgent request of his friends, he returned to Scotland—when King James was eight years old and Morton was regent—bearing a letter from Beza to the General Assembly, in which his friend wrote that Melville was equally distinguished for piety and erudition, and that the Church of Geneva could give no stronger proof of its affection for her sister Church in Scotland than by suffering herself to be bereaved of him, that his native country might be enriched with his gifts. Here he was soon appointed by the General Assembly principal of Glasgow College, where, by his talents, energy and success, he made himself felt and admired throughout the kingdom. Distinguished as he was for scholarship, he became even more distinguished for his knowledge of theological and ecclesiastical principles, as taught in the Word of God and illustrated in the Genevan Church. Master also of a strong voice, a fluent elocution, a cogent, incisive diction, and great dialectic skill, and of great ardour of mind, what he knew he could so utter as not only to leave his hearers in no doubt as to his meaning, but also to work conviction in even unwilling and prejudiced minds. Though low of stature and slender in person, he possessed great physical energy, and, as will be seen, was able, when aroused, by his amazing intrepidity, to overawe even the bad, imperious Morton, the inflated king and any number of noble sycophants who clung about the court. And withal he was, next to Knox, the great champion of Presbyterianism, and of such zeal and ability in this cause that he was wont to be called the *episcopomastix*—the bishop-scourger.

James Melville was about ten years the junior

of his uncle; the son of Richard, that brother of Andrew to whom the latter was indebted for a home and an education. Living in the same house, uncle and nephew came to love each other with a true fraternal affection, and James clung to his uncle Andrew with unswerving fidelity through all the hardships of a most eventful career, and left on record many of the facts we know respecting him. Entering college, the youth was so overcome to find that he could not understand the lectures delivered in Latin that he burst into tears, seeing which the regent took him in charge and put him in the way of soon mastering the difficulty. Hearing Knox preach at Aberdeen, he resolved to enter the pulpit. This being contrary to the wishes of his father, he wrote a sermon and placed it where he knew his father would find it, and by this stratagem succeeded in his desires. In physical stature and cast of countenance he strikingly resembled his uncle, though in talents and learning he was inferior, and in temper of spirit the two differed as Luther and Melancthon. James was mild in disposition and courtly in demeanour. Guilelessly upright and conscientious, he was true as steel in his fidelity to his friends and to the cause of his Master. These two men we shall often encounter in the stirring scenes of subsequent history.

The Assembly which met in March, 1575, found again its courage, and with its courage its strength reviving; it passed an act requiring the knowledge of Latin in every person appointed to a benefice, for the tulchan bishops had already sanctioned the introduction of even servants and children as holders of benefices. The convention of estates, tired of the unsettled condition of ecclesiastical affairs, urged that some definite scheme be fixed upon to remove the perplexing uncertainties constantly resulting in controversy and collision; and the regent sent to the Assembly a demand that they ratify the Leith system or draw up a plan upon which they would unite and by which they were willing to abide. They accordingly appointed a committee to frame an outline of policy and discipline, and report the result to them, for even the bold Morton did not venture to impose a system upon the Church.

In the Assembly in August the question as to bishops was taken up and discussed; and Melville asked:

"Have bishops, as they are now in Scotland, their functions from the Word of God or not?

and ought the chapters appointed for electing them to be tolerated in a Reformed Church?

"He was satisfied," he said, "that prelacy had no foundation in Scripture, and that its tendency was extremely doubtful, if not necessarily hurtful. The words *bishop* and *presbyter* are interchangeably used in the New Testament, and the popular arguments for episcopacy are founded on ignorance of the original language of Scripture. It was the opinion of Jerome and other Fathers that all ministers of the gospel were at first equal, and that the superiority of bishops originated in custom and not in divine appointment.

"The same principles which justify, and the same measures which led to the extension of the bishop's power over all the pastors of a diocese, will justify and lead to the establishment of an archbishop, metropolitan or patriarch over a province or kingdom, and of a universal bishop or pope over the whole Christian world.

"The maintenance of the hierarchy in England he could not but consider as one cause of the rarity of preaching, the poverty of the lower orders of the clergy, pluralities, want of discipline and other abuses, which had produced dissensions and heart-burnings in that flourishing kingdom. And he was convinced that the best and only way of redressing grievances in Scotland was to strike at the root of the evil by abolishing prelacy and restoring that parity of work and authority which existed at the beginning among all the pastors of the Church."

Thus spoke the episcopomastix, and his words went deep into many minds. Knox was still alive! But on this subject the yet too timid Assembly dared no very decided reply. Morton now used his utmost endeavours to shut the mouth of Melville. It was little to be rid of Knox if his successor was to stand in his place. Accordingly, he plied Melville with courtesies and bribes. He offered him the living of Govan, and then, on the death of Douglas, Archbishop of St. Andrew's, he offered him that tulchanship. He would have given him anything but the regency and the Church revenues, both of which he wanted for himself. But he found that he could no more easily cajole than he could daunt the honest, intrepid Melville.

In the next Assembly the question of Melville respecting the title of bishop was partially answered as follows: "The name of bishop is common to all who are appointed to take charge of a particular flock in preaching the Word, administering sacraments and exercising discipline with the consent of their elders, and this is their chief function according to the Word of God." To the discussions on this subject six tulchan bishops listened, and had no word to say in defence of the titles they bore, themselves well knowing, and knowing that all others knew, that the prelatic feathers they wore were the gaudy decorations of sycophants, who, while disloyal to their Church, fawned on wicked worldly lords, and were the mere channels through which the money of the Church flowed into the coffers of their masters.

The Church and the regent soon came again into collision. Adamson, who had spoken so sarcastically about "my lord's bishop," when the opportunity presented itself to him of becoming a lord's bishop, could not resist the temptation, and, on Morton's presentation, accepted the archbishopric of St. Andrew's. The Assembly required him to submit to their examination. He refused because his master forbade. The Assembly then forbade the chapter to proceed in the matter, and the chapter proceeded in spite of the Assembly's prohibition. Then, at the meeting in April, 1577, it interdicted his lordship from the exercise of his tulchanship until regularly admitted by the Church, and a commission was appointed to summon him before it and adjudicate upon his case.

The regent, having failed to bribe, now attempted to intimidate Melville. The former complained that the Church was kept in confusion by certain persons bent on introducing their own fancies and foreign laws. The latter replied that he and his brethren took Scripture, and not fancy, for their guide. Morton said that the Assembly was a body of the king's subjects, and that it was treasonable for them to meet without his permission. Melville replied that if this were so, then Christ and his apostles were guilty of treason, for they called together great crowds and taught them without permission of the magistrates. Morton, biting the head of his staff, growled, in that deep undertone which marked his occasional fits of cold, black, ruthless anger, "There will never be quietness in this country till half a dozen of you be hanged or banished."

"Tush, sir!" answered Melville; "threaten your courtiers after that manner! It is the same to me whether I rot in the air or in the ground. The earth is the Lord's. My country is wherever goodness is. I have been ready to give my life where it would not be half so well expended. Let God be glorified; it will not be in your power to hang or exile his truth." Knox was dead, but Morton might say again, "Here is one that does not fear the face of man!"

Knowing that others would catch this spirit, the regent dissembled with the Assembly in regard to their new book of policy, but he got his tulchan Adamson to frame a series of captious questions, to which he demanded their reply. But by this time he had made himself so odious by his avarice and tyranny to the mass of the people and of the nobility that the earls of Argyle and Athol induced the young king to call a council of the nobility at Stirling to consider the condition of affairs, to which council only the enemies of Morton were invited. Paralyzed by the knowledge of his crimes and the consequent strength of his foes, he wrote to the king, begging to be allowed to resign the regency. Delighted at this turn of affairs, the council determined that his resignation should be accepted, and that the king, now twelve years old, should assume the reins of government. Hardly, however, had Morton sent his resignation than he regretted it; but it was now too late to mend the matter, for the young king, flattered with the suggestion of the council, accepted it, because he said he saw no other way through the complicated disorders of the realm. The king, however, gave him a full pardon, and declared him incapable of being accused and brought to trial for anything he had done, the nobility pledging themselves, under a bond of five hundred thousand pounds, to procure a ratification of this pardon and assurance at the first meeting of Parliament. Thus fell this bold, unscrupulous, tyrannical regent, and the State and the Church passed, on the sixth of March, 1578, under the sway of King James VI.

JAMES VI.

King James was a man whom Presbyterianism can never forget, and never remember but with mingled contempt and indignation. His father was the wicked, silly, wretched Darnley. His mother was the beautiful, accomplished, licentious Mary Queen of Scots. He was born during that fearful period of her life between the murder of Rizzio and the murder by her and Bothwell of her husband. He was baptized according to Romish forms. He was reared amidst the smoke and battle of ever-blazing civil war. That he should become something very good, very bad or very great, there was no little reason to expect. And during his early years there were some signs of promise and hope. Before his mother's marriage with Bothwell, he was committed to the custody of the earl of Mar in Stirling castle, where he was kept during successive regencies to the time of his succession to the throne at the age of twelve; his education conducted, under the direction of Alexander Erskine, by George Buchanan, a man of wonderful versatility of talent, of varied and profound learning, aided by three others of the most distinguished scholars in Scotland. Such advantages probably made of the royal youth all that the material was capable of. "He discovered an aptitude for the languages," and outstripped most youths of his age in general knowledge. But his manhood soon dissipated all hope of good. Excessively vain, he was always boasting of his kingcraft. He was ungainly in person and a boor in manners, and deficient in personal courage, "stammering, slabbering, shedding unmanly tears, trembling at a drawn sword, and talking in the style alternately of a buffoon and a pedagogue. Of dignity and elevation of mind he had no conception. His tastes, opinions and habits were alike low and vulgar." Without vigour of mind or any attribute of statesmanship, he had not sense enough to refrain from pretentious claims to authority which he had no power to enforce. Utterly perfidious, he was a low despot. In his books, "The Free Law of Free Monarchies" and "Basilicon Doron," he claimed that a free monarchy is the government of a free and absolute monarch, in which the will of the sovereign is above all law, and that a principal part of his function consisted in ruling the Church.

Such was the character now under course of development with which the Church was destined to deal.

The commission appointed to prepare a complete system of discipline reported to the Assembly, in April, 1578, and the report having been carefully considered and discussed was adopted by the Assembly, and became the well-known "SECOND BOOK OF DISCIPLINE," and from that time it has been the authorized standard of the Church of Scotland. The Assembly also ordered that "the bishops" be henceforth addressed in the same style as other ministers, and that, in case of vacancy, the chapters should elect no other till their next meeting. It was also ordered that the book be laid before the king and council; and commissioners were appointed to conduct any conference that might be desired. Perhaps, in their circumstances, it was necessary to seek the royal signature to their book as a defence against worldly, wicked nobles. But in our day we cannot help feeling that a more bold and decided course, asserting what they would adhere to without reference to the secular power, would have been wiser and safer.

In the following June the Assembly did what they should, as we think, have done long before—in forbidding from thenceforth all election of men to the unscriptural, and in Scotland illegal, office of bishop. It further ordained that those in office should submit to the Assembly in matters relating to "the corruption of that estate of bishops in their own persons under pain of being excommunicated." To this the so-called bishop of Dunblane at once submitted.

The result of the conference between the Church commissioners and those of the Parliament respecting the Book of Discipline was, on the whole, satisfactory, and the Parliament then sitting at Stirling ratified and approved all the acts and statutes previously made, agreeably to God's Word, for the maintenance of the "true Kirk of God."

But now a dark shadow fell upon the Church. Morton reappeared upon the scene and was taken into favour by the king, who was always a mere chameleon, taking on the hues of the persons and circumstances immediately around him. Through his influence, the changeful monarch arrested the Assembly in its exercise of discipline upon the tulchan bishops, and forbade them to proceed to excommunication for disorder and disobedience. But the next Assembly took its rightful stand, and, while remonstrating with his majesty against his interference with their inherent rights, proceeded with its work. Thus Presbyterian republicanism stood face to face with wilful monarchy. The next Parliament sustained the Assembly.

But the veteran sinner, Morton, acquired a disastrous influence over the weak and fickle king, and by flattery made himself potent among the intriguing, wire-pulling courtiers. With Morton, Esme Stewart, duke of Lennox—brought up in France a Romanist, but now a nominal Protestant—and Captain James Stewart, afterward earl of Arran, a bold, licentious, crafty, criminal, ambitious politician, shared in the control of the royal puppet.

Seeing how things stood, the Assembly passed an act declaring the pseudo-prelacy illegal and destitute of all warrant in the Word of God, a mere human invention, introduced by folly and corruption, and tending to injury; and ordered all holders of such pretended office to resign their positions, and appointed the places and times at which they should appear before the provincial synods and signify their submission to this act. This act was passed, after full discussion, without one dissenting voice. The mantle of Knox had now fallen on the Assembly. And such is the majesty and might of courage, when on the side of right, before the year closed the whole tribe of tulchans, with the exception of five, had submitted.

In 1581, the Assembly, without waiting longer on king, council and Parliament, ordained that the SECOND BOOK OF DISCIPLINE be formally registered among the permanent laws of the Church, and copies thereof to be taken by each of the presbyteries. Feeling the influence of the Assembly, as James always felt every wind that blew, he requested it, through his commissioner, to bring the ecclesiastical discipline into more effective exercise over the realm, and the Assembly at once erected thirteen presbyteries, and recommended the early extension of the system over the kingdom. Thus unwittingly did James help to build the walls he afterward sought in vain to overthrow.

The Assembly also ratified "*Craig's Confession of Faith*"—known also as "*The First National Covenant of Scotland*"—as an open protest against the more or less open hostility of the duke of Lennox and other nobles to Presbyterianism. This covenant was signed by the king, his household, and by the greater part of the nobility and gentry of the realm.

In that great standard, the SECOND BOOK OF DISCIPLINE, it is asserted that Christ has appointed a government in his Church distinct from that of the State—to be exercised not by civil, but by ecclesiastical officers; that civil government exists for the promotion of external peace, ecclesiastical for the direction of men in matters of religion; that both should co-operate with and fortify each other; that in external matters, ministers are subject to the State, in religious matters magistrates are subject, like other men, to the Church. It divides the management of church affairs into three branches—doctrine, discipline and distribution: for the first, preachers are ordained; for the second, ruling elders with the preachers; and, for the third, deacons to manage the benevolent and other funds of the Church. The name bishop is equally applicable to all pastors. These office-bearers are to be admitted by election and ordination, and none to be obtruded upon the people contrary to their will. The ruling officers are to be grouped first into presbyteries, for inspection and discipline of the churches within their bounds; second, into synods, which include more or fewer presbyteries, and are larger presbyteries; and, over all, the General Assembly, composed of commissioners, ministers and elders, to represent and act for the Church as a whole. Appeals may lie from the lowest through all above to the highest court, the General Assembly, from which there is no appeal. The Assembly may meet at its own option as to time and place. The patrimony of the Church includes what has been appropriated to her use, to divert which to secular purposes is a crime. Besides these matters various abuses are specified as needing removal.

Such is the thoroughly scriptural and presbyterial form of government and discipline adopted by the mind and into the heart of Scotland, and which, when wrested from the people by violence, has always been regrasped when better days came and circumstances allowed. It has been hated by men in proportion to the worldliness and wickedness of their heart and character, and loved in proportion as they have loved Christ and his cause.

It was therefore, of course, hated and dreaded by King James and his unscrupulous courtiers, and by those "cringing sycophants, the tulchan bishops." For under it the bishops lost their lordly titles, the avaricious nobles the rich gains of tulchanism, and the king his despotic mastery over the Church. Hence they resolved to measure strength with the Assembly when opportunity should offer, and it soon offered; for, in June, of this very year, Boyd, archbishop (so called) of Glasgow, died, and the duke of Lennox secured from the council a grant of the revenues. But for this he must have a tulchan; and after some searching Lenox found a creature "reckless and knavish" enough to serve the turn, in the person of one Robert Montgomery, minister of Stirling—a "vain, feeble, presumptuous" man—who stooped to become the "base instrument of a licentious courtier's sacrilegious avarice."

The Assembly interposed, called Montgomery to its bar, forbade him to accept the office and ordered him not to leave his charge at Stirling, and remitted the case to the Presbytery of Stirling to be dealt with according to its merits.

But the lords were not to be so easily beaten at their game, and the Synod of Lothian was cited before the privy council for interfering with Montgomery in obedience to the Assembly. They appeared and protested their readiness to yield all lawful obedience to the government, but declined the judgment of the council as incompetent to act in a case purely ecclesiastical.

In April, 1582, the Assembly met and were encountered by a mandate from his majesty forbidding them to proceed against Montgomery. They answered, like men, that they must do their duty. Then came the king's messenger-at-arms, commanding them to desist on pain of rebellion. They responded to the despotic mandate by ratifying the sentence of the presbytery suspending Montgomery from the ministry, and by finding eight charges against him proved, and declaring him liable to deposition and excommunication. Upon this the wretched culprit hastened to the Assembly, and, acknowledging that he had offended against God and the Church, begged that the sentence might not be pronounced, and promised to play the tulchan no more. The sentence was accordingly suspended, and the Presbytery of Glasgow was charged to watch the conduct of Montgomery, and, if he violated his promise, to appoint one of their number to proceed with the excommunication. How refreshing to see Presbyterianism truly itself in the presence of civil despotism!

But the contest was not yet over; for on the adjournment of the Assembly, Montgomery, not able to withstand the temptation to the dignity within his reach, broke his promise; and when the Presbytery of Glasgow met to pronounce the penalty, he, with an order from the king to stay their proceedings, entered the house at the head of an armed force, and, when the presbytery refused to obey the order, dragged the moderator from his seat, beat him and cast him into prison. But the presbytery went on notwithstanding, found him guilty and transmitted the result to the Presbytery of Edinburgh, which pronounced the sentence and published it in all surrounding churches.

A proclamation from the council pronounced the excommunication null and void. The ministers of Edinburgh were insulted, and John Dury banished from the capital and forbidden to preach.

But these tyrannical measures, instead of breaking the spirit of the Church, only increased their courage and resolution. An extraordinary meeting of the Assembly convened and transmitted to the youthful tyrant on the throne a manly remonstrance, in which they said:

"Your majesty, by device of some councillors, is caused to take upon you a spiritual power and authority which properly belongeth unto Christ, as only King and Head of the Church, the ministry and execution whereof is only given unto such as bear office in the ecclesiastical government in the same. So that in your highness' person some men press to erect a new popedom, as though your highness could not be full king and head of this commonwealth unless as well the spiritual as temporal sword be put into your highness' hands—unless Christ be bereft of his authority, and the two jurisdictions confounded which God hath divided, which directly tendeth to the wreck of all true religion."

With such bold and honest plainness could Presbyterianism speak to the king upon his throne! This remonstrance was put into the hands of Melville and others to present to the king. Such was the indignation of the courtiers when informed of these proceedings that many people feared for the lives of the deputation, and some begged them not to venture into the lion's den. But Melville answered:

"I am not afraid, thank God, nor feeble-spirited

in the cause and message of Christ; come what God pleases to send, our commission shall be executed."

When they had read their remonstrance to the king in council, Arran, with a fierce frown upon his wicked brow, looked over the assembly and exclaimed:

"Who dares subscribe these treasonable articles?"

"We dare!" said Melville, and walking up to the table, put down his name, and in this was at once followed by the other commissioners.

The scowl on Arran's face sunk at once from that of "domineering sternness" to that of awed and "baffled malice." The commission was dismissed, and certain Englishmen present were amazed at the bold front of the men of God, and could hardly believe that armed men were not at hand to defend them.

When they were gone, a warrant was given to Lennox to hold a chamberlain's court at Edinburgh, to "inquire into the late sedition and have its authors duly punished."

Darkness seemed now gathering over the Church. The king, in the hands of the ungodly Arran and Lennox, seemed ready to follow their counsels even to blood.

But while man proposeth, God disposeth. Again, as so often in the history of the Church of Scotland, the wickedness of its foes spent itself upon themselves. While Presbyterianism was battling it for God and his cause, the nobles were maliciously intriguing against one another. The wicked Morton, after regaining his power, at last fell into the hands of the merciless Arran and was brought to execution, saying, in almost the very words of Wolsey, "Had I been as careful to serve my God as I was to serve the king's weal, I had not been brought to the point I am to-day." But Arran and Lennox had made themselves as odious to the great body of the nobles as Morton was to them; and their turn was now to come. Stimulated by the heroic boldness of the ministers, the Protestant nobles shook off their cowardly supineness, and resolved to rescue the king from the grasp of these two corrupt favourites. Accordingly, they came upon his majesty as he was engaged in hunting, and invited him to Ruthven Castle. The king unsuspectingly complied. But when, the next morning, he prepared to betake himself again to the field, the nobles met him and presented a memorial against the tyrannical conduct of the favourites. The king answered graciously, and was about still to go forth to his sport when he was informed that he must remain where he was. Upon this he threatened, expostulated and burst into tears. To his tears the Master of Glammis answered:

"It is no matter of your tears; better bairns weep than bearded men."

Hearing of the "Raid of Ruthven," Lennox set out full of arrogance, and, narrowly escaping an ambush on the way, reached Ruthven Castle, attended by a single servant. Here he would have been slain upon the spot but for the intercession of the earl of Gowrie, and he was permitted to retire, and soon went to France and died of fatigue or chagrin, or both together. Arran was sent to confinement in Stirling Castle. The king, as usual, submitted to circumstances, and issued a declaration that he was under no restrictions—that the lords had done good service to himself and the commonwealth. A proclamation was also issued annulling all the late despotic measures and staying all hostile proceedings against the Church. Thus the chamberlain's court was not held, and the heroism of Melville and his compeers was abundantly rewarded.

When the Assembly next met, the lords connected with the Raid of Ruthven sent to them a deputation to explain the grounds of their conduct, asserting, one and all, that they were moved thereto by the evident dangers gathering around both Church and State, and asked their approval. Before replying, the Assembly sent to the king to know his judgment in the matter. The king having answered that in his opinion religion and his own person had been in peril, and that it was the duty of all to unite in their rescue and in reforming the commonwealth, they passed an act declaring their approbation of the enterprise.

The Assembly then entered upon the trial and deposition of the corrupt prelates, and the wretched Montgomery again submitted, begging pardon and reinstalment in the Church and ministry. The convention of the estates soon met, and in the fullest manner sanctioned the Raid of Ruthven and relieved its participants from all actions, civil or criminal, against them in the matter.

For the present all was quiet, and the Church was encouraged by the king to go forward in the work of reformation. It seemed as if the Court and the Church were henceforth to be as one, and the morning star of hope shone brightly out upon the sky.

CLOUDS—STORM—SUNSHINE.

True to his constitutional fickleness and hypocrisy, James continued for a while to smile on the Church, while at the same time he chafed under the restraints of her pure doctrine and scriptural discipline, and longed for the companionship of those who, while they corrupted his morals, fed his vain soul with honeyed flatteries. In our day a royal smile goes for what it is worth, but then even Scotchmen had not yet shaken off the traditional semi-superstitious regards for the purple. Hence the Protestants allowed themselves to be so beguiled by the king's apparent friendliness as to relax their vigilance and leave an open door for the execution of his subtle designs.

Having secretly invited such lords as he thought he could trust to meet him at St. Andrew's, he slipped quietly away thither, took possession of the castle, and then, contrary to the advice of his best friends, he invited the return of the infamous Arran and threw himself into his arms. The worst enemy of both Church and nation was now once more in power. So suddenly did the bright skies gather blackness! An insidious pardon was offered to the actors in the "Raid of Ruthven," whose conduct had been formally approved by the king, nobles and the General Assembly, on condition that they submit with repentance and confession! Then they were required, by a new proclamation, to surrender themselves prisoners, and all who refused were denounced as rebels. Arran soon got himself appointed governor of Stirling Castle, and induced the poor silly king to take up his residence there, and thus put himself under the full personal control of this wicked earl. Hostilities were commenced also against the Church. Andrew Melville was cited before the privy council for certain alleged treasonable expressions. He appeared and proved his innocence. But they, proceeding to a formal trial, Melville protested that, as a minister, he should be first tried by his brethren. This reply angered the king and made Arran furious. But Melville was not a man to quail in the presence of despots. Unclasping his Hebrew Bible from his girdle, he threw it upon the table, saying:

"These are my instructions; see if any of you can judge of them or show that I have passed my injunctions."

Seeing that he could not be frightened into the withdrawal of his protest, they found him guilty of declining the judgment of the council and of behaving irreverently before them, and condemned him to imprisonment in Edinburgh Castle, and to be punished in person and goods at his majesty's pleasure. Learning that Arran was preparing to send him to Blackness Castle, kept by one of his creatures, where Melville easily divined what fate would await him, he fled to Berwick.

The kingdom was startled by these measures as by a thunderpeal! The ministers prayed in the pulpits for Melville, and the lament was loud and universal among the godly that the misled king had driven from the realm its most learned man and the ablest defender of its religion. The Assembly, which met in April, was imperiously commanded to rescind its act approving of the Raid of Ruthven, and to pass another condemning it as treasonable. They had barely courage enough to decline obedience to these mandates, and broke up and withdrew cast down and dispirited. Knox was in his grave, Melville in exile, and heroism had departed with them.

The council raged with fury. They ordained that the accused preachers should be arrested without legal formalities, and it was declared treasonable to hold correspondence with those who had fled. The earl of Gowrie, for his part in the Raid of Ruthven—though he had been expressly pardoned by the king—was seized and executed, and his estates divided among the friends of Arran. A parliament was called at Edinburgh to sit with closed doors, and the Lords of the Articles sworn to secresy. Knowing the malignity of James and Arran, the ministers awaited with dread the doings of this body. To mitigate the wrath of their persecutors, they sent the temperate David Lindsay to entreat the king that no law affecting the Church should be passed without consultation with the Assembly, and Arran arrested him in the palace courtyard and sent him prisoner to Blackness Castle. Others sent to Parliament were denied admission. The dark council, including Adamson and Montgomery as bishops, went on in their works of darkness, and enacted the "Black Acts of 1584," which asserted that to decline the judgment of king or council in any matter was treason —that to impugn or seek diminution of the power and authority of the three estates was treason—prohibiting any assembly, except the ordinary courts, to consult or determine any matter, civil or ecclesiastical, without special commandment and license from the king—declaring that bishops, and others whom the king might appoint, should have control in ecclesiastical matters—that to censure the conduct of the king or council was gross treason.

When these acts were proclaimed, Pont and Balcanquhall entered a public protest at the market-cross, Edinburgh, and fled the kingdom, while Arran raged and issued orders for their arrest. Nicol Dagleish, a distinguished scholar, was arrested and tried, as for a capital offence, for praying for his persecuted brethren. This charge failing, he was arrested on another, tried and condemned to death, and, though not executed, was shut up in a cell, from whose window he could see the scaffold on which he was sentenced to die. Professors in the colleges were banished or thrown into jail.

The exiled pastors wrote to their congregations. The cowardly magistrates of Edinburgh sent the letter to the king, and his majesty had a letter drawn up casting reproach and contempt upon the ministers, and thanking God that the people were now relieved from wolves, and begging the king to give them good pastors in their stead, and then endeavoured to get the chief inhabitants in Edinburgh to sign it! Sixteen craven-spirited persons put their names to this letter.

The reign of terror wrought a double work—driving the best men out of the kingdom, and stirring up a spirit within the realm of mighty, though for a while smothered, indignation. The recreant Adamson drew up a bond binding all ministers who subscribed it to submit to the king's power over all estates, spiritual and temporal, and ordering all to sign it within forty days. Even this bond a few subscribed. But the vengeance of James was not yet sated, and he begged of Elizabeth to drive the poor refugees out of her kingdom, which he well knew she was wicked enough to do if a sufficient reason offered. Civil war now broke out between Arran and the oppressed nobles, and the plague added its horrors to the darkness of the times.

At length the exiled lords returned, joining with the insurgents in Scotland, and, advancing upon Stirling, published a proclamation enumerating the crimes of Arran, and declaring that they had taken up arms to deliver Church and State from their oppressors. They took the town by surprise, and came to terms with the king in the castle. Arran fled, and was deprived of his title and estates, and the fickle king took his *deliverers* to his bosom!

This revolution delivered the Church from persecution, but the lords, having attained all they cared for, did little to free her from the yoke of the black acts of Arran's infamous Parliament. During these hours of gloom some of the ministers displayed even a rashness of courage, which damaged rather than helped the good cause. James Gibson, minister of Pencaitland, in a sermon at Edinburgh, declared:

"I thought that Arran and Lady Jezebel, his wife, were the persecutors of the Church, but now I find that it was King James himself. As Jeroboam and his posterity were rooted out for staying the worship of the true God, so I fear that if our king continue in his present course, he shall die childless and be the last of his race." For this he was sent to prison. During a sermon against bishops, in the High Church, Edinburgh, the king rose and offered to bet his kingdom that he could disprove what the preacher had said!

In April, 1586, the Synod of Fife excommunicated Adamson, tulchan archbishop of St. Andrew's. Adamson was a man of parts and culture, but of doubtful private character and immoderately ambitious, and, from being an orthodox Presbyterian, for the sake of a bishopric had become a zealous prelatist. This tulchan, finding himself excommunicated by the ever-faithful Synod of Fife, proceeded to excommunicate Melville and several others. The matter came before the Assembly in May, and, after a long struggle with the kingcraft of James, it reversed the sentence of the synod; and while denying all scriptural ground for Prelacy, declared that it must be tolerated if forced upon them by civil authority. They, however, persisted in compelling Adamson to beg pardon for his imperious conduct, to promise submission to the Assembly, and to conduct himself as a pastor ought, suitably to the character of a bishop *as described by Paul*—that is to say, as a Presbyterian preaching elder.

As Queen Mary was now in the cruel grasp of Elizabeth, James insisted that the ministers should pray for her. A solemn fast was proclaimed for her, and the so-called bishop of St. Andrew's was directed to officiate at St. Giles' on the occasion. But the ministers prevailed upon John Cowper to take possession of the pulpit and forestall the bishop. The king, coming in in the middle of the prayer, stopped Cowper and told him to withdraw or else pray for the queen. He replied that he would do as the Spirit of God directed. The captain of the guard then put him out, and, as he withdrew, he exclaimed:

"This day shall be a witness against the king in the great day of the Lord."

In July, 1587, Parliament met, on which the venerable Erskine of Dun, the last of the original Reformers of the Church, attended as commissioner to favour the interests of religion. This Parliament ratified all the laws passed in favour of the Reformation during the minority of the king, and annexed all the unappropriated lands of the Church to the Crown. This act was a sword with two edges, one of which James did not see. It at once—and this he saw with delight—robbed the Church of her rightful revenues, but at the same time—which he did not see—gave a fatal blow to bishoprics, as it took away their support, and rendered vain all his subsequent efforts to restore the work of Prelacy, to which James was becoming more and more inclined. For already he saw that Presbyterianism and royalty could hardly be harnessed to the same chariot; and, furthermore, he now scented the rich game across the borders in the crown of England, to which he was heir, and which the declining years of Elizabeth was bringing hourly toward his hand. But the same Parliament also transferred, with these Church lands, the patronage attached to them, thus giving into godless hands the power to present candidates for great numbers of pulpits, and opening the way for corruption in the ministry, and for many a hard struggle between the patrons and the State behind them and the vigilant and resolute Church authorities.

Stirring times in the whole civil and religious world were now drawing on. The persistent though semi-popish Protestantism of England, and especially the judicial murder of Mary Queen of Scots, had at length concentrated the bigoted energies of popery into ripe conspiracy, and the Great Armada was getting ready to sail for the overthrow of Protestant power. James, though tampered with by Philip of Spain, had sense enough to see that his own interests were bound up with those of England.

But while King James, with characteristic indolence and love of ease, was trifling away his time, the Assembly held an extraordinary meeting, and sent a deputation to him to offer their services and to rouse him to action. The childish monarch, offended at this seeming reproach, refused to receive the deputation, and petulantly asked if they meant to dictate to him and threaten him with their power? But, listening to wiser councils, he named a committee of the privy council to co-operate with the Church commissioners in making provision for the public safety. Thus Presbyterianism as such, identified as it was with the people's liberties, and finding its own interests deeply involved with the general good in this hour of great national peril, did not wait to respond to the call of the government for aid, but took the initiative, and, pledging all its powers to the work, called with a trumpet voice upon the government and nation to bestir itself for the national salvation.

A bond was drawn up and signed by the ministers, and by all ranks of nobles and subjects for co-operation, recognizing religion and the State as involved in the same peril, and pledging themselves to maintain both against all foes at home and abroad. A popish insurrection in Scotland was promptly suppressed. And now news came that the Armada had sailed! A meeting of the estates was immediately summoned; a general enrolment of the whole population fit for arms was ordered; officers appointed and watchers for the seaports, and a system of beacons and signals adjusted to give timely notice of the appearance of any hostile ships—the whole Protestant population warmly seconding every measure of the government. This activity, however, was due much more to Maitland, the chancellor, than to the fickle, half-imbecile monarch.

At length the Armada arrived in the Channel. Sir Francis Drake, with his lighter vessels, hung on their flanks and cut off several vessels. While anchored before Calais, fireships were sent in among them, which threw them into confusion, during which the English attacked them, and, aided by a storm, sent devastation through the whole fleet. In their consternation the Spaniards swept northward, where a violent tempest scattered and wrecked them among the Hebrides and on the coasts of Scotland and Ireland. A very few of the relics of this proud Armada found their way back to Spain, leaving behind in the ocean's angry bosom some representative of almost every considerable family in the kingdom, and thus it was that popery swept Protestantism from Britain! Great were the rejoicings both in England and Scotland, and in the fervour of their gratitude the people of Scotland treated the wretches who were wrecked on their coasts with great humanity, and sent them home to their friends.

The zeal of the Church in this great crisis produced a transitory effect on the impressible James.

An insurrection of papists, with the design of seizing the king and gaining control of his person, was put down. The Assembly excommunicated Adamson for solemnizing marriage between the popish earl of Huntly and a lady of the Lennox family.

The danger of invasion past, the king bent his thoughts on marriage with the Princess Anne, second daughter of Frederick II. of Denmark. Married by proxy, the princess set sail for Scotland, but a violent storm, attributed by James to the witches of Norway and Scotland, drove the fleet into a part of Norway, near Upsal, where it was determined that the bride should spend the winter. But the king, though in great dread of the witches, resolved to venture his sacred person within their power, and, setting forth with a fine retinue, reached the princess after a stormy voyage of five days. On Sunday, the 24th of November, he was married, and early in May following he arrived at Leith with his bride.

Before leaving Scotland, the king appointed a provisional government to act during his absence, at the head of which he placed the duke of Lennox, and, as an extraordinary member of the council, he named Robert Bruce, one of the ministers of Edinburgh, declaring that he reposed greater confidence in him and his brethren than in all the other members of the council. During the six months of his absence the country was more tranquil than it had been for many years, much of which James himself attributed to the influence of the clergy, and in his letters to Bruce he told him that he considered him worth a quarter of his kingdom, and that he should reckon himself beholden to him while he lived for his services, and would never forget the same. Subsequent events showed how much the words of a king are sometimes worth.

The return of the king was celebrated with all manner of festive rejoicings. At the coronation of the queen three sermons were preached—one in Latin, one in French, one in English. The Tuesday following the queen made a public entry into Edinburgh amid the enthusiasm of a rejoicing people. The following Sunday, after sermon in the High Church, the king rose and thanked the ministers for their fidelity, confessed the indiscretion of his youth, and promised truer fidelity to Kirk and State as a married man.

In the Assembly, which met in August, he pronounced his famous eulogium upon the Church of Scotland. With hands uplifted and in a temporary rapture, he said:

"I praise God that I was born in such a time as in the light of the gospel, and in such a place as to be king in such a Kirk, the sincerest Kirk in all the world. The Kirk of Geneva keepeth Pasch and Yule, and what have they for them?—they have no institutions. As for our neighbour Kirk in England, their service is an ill-said mass in English. They want nothing of the mass but the liftings. I charge you, my good people—ministers, doctors, elders, nobles, gentlemen and barons—to stand to your purity; and I, forsooth, so long as I brook my life and crown, shall maintain the same against all deadly."

The Assembly were in transports, and for a quarter of an hour nothing was heard but praising God and praying for the king. It was honeymoon with the king and honeymoon with the Kirk; but, alas! the poor Kirk afterward found occasion to sigh with the afflicted husband: "For six months after my marriage I thought I should have devoured my darling wife, and ever since I have been very sorry that I did not."

For the present, however, all was bright. Zion had shaken herself from the clutches of her foes, and her face was radiant with peace and hope. And now old "Bishop" Adamson, the able and virulent enemy of his Church, deprived of support by the transfer of the revenues of his bishopric to the Crown, reduced to poverty and neglected by the king, of whose worst measures he had always been a warm advocate, tortured by remorse and wasted by immoralities, recanted his episcopal sentiments, confessed sorrow for his sins, and drew out the rest of his miserable life in dependence upon the charities of Andrew Melville, whom he had often and bitterly persecuted.

"GOD'S SILLY VASSAL."

When the Church becomes entangled in unholy alliance with the State—unless, as in England, it sinks to passive vassalage—its history is sure to be chequered by harrassing conflicts of jurisdiction which mislead her judgment, embitter her temper, waste her time and impair her energies.

Graham, of Hallyards, was accused of certain fraudulent transactions which exposed him to censure as a minister of the gospel and to trial and punishment as a citizen. Under the former phase of the case, the Assembly arraigned him, as it was their right and duty to do. Under the latter, the State arraigned him, as was its right and duty. It would seem as if there were here no room for collision; but each asserted priority of jurisdiction in the case—the Church, that as a minister Graham must first come before them; and the Court that, as a subject he must first appear at their tribunal. In this, undoubtedly, both were in the wrong. Both Church and State had the right to act at their own convenience; nor need the judgment of the one, whatever it might be or whenever given, prevent the other from either passing the accused through an impartial trial or from inflicting a penalty according to the verdict. The Assembly, however, maintained its own claims and passed upon the matter, and then the Court of Sessions tried the cause in their own way.

During the absence of the king the Church and nation had peace; on his return the latter was rent with civil broils, giving reason for a wish that James might have frequent occasion to go abroad, and that his return might not be hastened. A fierce quarrel arose between the wicked Huntly and "the bonnie earl of Murray," the handsomest man of his age and son of the "Good Regent." Blood flowed freely, and the silly king, instead of quelling the disorder, spent his time in the discovery, arrest and examination of witches, and burning them. One of the witches accused Bothwell, and the king had him arrested. Bothwell escaped, and, raising a party, attacked the palace, but was driven off. Huntly told James that Murray was among the assailants, and, setting off with a troop to arrest Murray, killed him. The next morning James set out a-hunting as if nothing had happened, but such was the general indignation that he sent for some of the ministers and protested to them his innocence in the matter. They replied that he might clear himself by promptly punishing the real offenders. But his indolence in the matter only increased the general indignation. And now in his perils the cowardly king threw himself into the arms of the Church, which saw that the time had come to insist on reformation and formal release from some of their burdens. The Assembly accordingly drew up articles embodying their requests, and presented them to the king, at the same time begging him to enter upon a path of righteous dealing, that thus he might avert the wrath of God.

When the Parliament met it ratified the General Assemblies, synods, presbyteries and sessions of the Church, declaring them, with the jurisdiction and discipline belonging to them, to be thenceforth just, good and godly—all statutes, acts and laws, canon, civil or municipal, to the contrary notwithstanding. It ratified and embodied also some of the leading propositions of the Second Book of Discipline. It ordained that General Assemblies be held once a year, or oftener as occasion might call; the time and place of meeting to be named by the king or his commissioner, or, in case of their absence, by the Assembly itself. It gave into the hands of the Church all matters of doctrine and discipline according to the Word of God. It declared the act of Parliament, granting commissions to men as bishops, and other judges in ecclesiastical causes, appointed by the king, to be null and void; and ordained that patrons should present their candidates to presbyteries, who were not to reject those they deemed fitted for the office; and should the presbytery refuse to induct a qualified minister the presentee, might retain the income of the benefice in his own hands. And this act Hetherington pronounces the *great charter of the Church of Scotland.*

We, in our land and day, while taking into account the peculiarly difficult position of our venerable fathers of the Scottish Church, yet cannot look without impatience and vexation on the scene where the Church accepts with thankfulness, at the hands of a Parliament the rights which God had given before Parliaments came into existence.

This act of Parliament was, no doubt, a great blessing to the Church, but the power that gives may recall, and in accepting the boon at such hands the Church virtually acknowledged the right of Parliament in the case, and put itself largely at its mercy. And in the clause allowing the patron to retain the income of a benefice when a qualified minister was rejected by the presbytery, who was to be the judge as to the rejected man's fitness? The patron, or some secular court, or the king, or, at all events, some other power than the presbytery, and thus in any case, the liberty of the Church was gone and her purity put in jeopardy. May the great Head of the Church hasten the hour when the Church everywhere shall free herself from all formal alliance with the State, and act freely in all matters in the independence that belongs to her!

But vexatious and disastrous complications multiplied. The king's word was a breath from a vain and treacherous heart, and of no more binding force with him than his dreams; and, knowing this, the Church took little comfort from the existence of the "Great Charter" on the records of the realm.

In 1592 a general alarm spread through the kingdom from the known presence of plotting priests and Jesuits. An extraordinary meeting of ministers was convened at Edinburgh to take measures for defence. Andrew Knox, minister of Paisley, having secret intelligence of a conspiracy, hastened to the island of Cumray and seized George Kerr, as he was just embarking for Spain. Letters from priests in Scotland were found upon him revealing an extended conspirary of the most perilous character. Spain was to land thirty thousand men on the western coast of the kingdom—part to invade England and part to act with Huntly, Errol and Angus for the suppression of Protestantism and the establishment of popery in Scotland.

With this information, the privy council united with the ministers in issuing letters calling upon all patriots to hasten to Edinburgh. The king also was earnestly besought to hasten thither. Angus was arrested. Upon the king's arrival he fretted like a spoiled child at the zeal of his subjects, and resented their conduct as an invasion of his prerogative. They replied like men; and when the king saw the extent of the danger his vexation turned against the conspirators, and he called Angus a "traitor of traitors." A proclamation was issued specifying the general nature of the conspiracy, and commanding all to abstain from intercourse with popish priests on pain of treason, and the array of the country was ordered to meet the king by the 20th of February at Aberdeen. And as the king lay under suspicion of lack of zeal—and there can be no doubt that the wretched man would have been easily content to have popery restored, or anything else that would at once make him a thorough despot in fact as he was in spirit, and leave him to enjoy his childish pleasures—he thought it necessary to purge himself, as far as words would do it, by a formal prohibition of any attempt to procure pardon for the conspirators. Graham of Fintry was brought to trial and executed, but Angus escaped and joined the conspirators in arms. The king now marched northward, and on his arrival at Aberdeen the conspirators retired to the mountains and sent their ladies to intercede for them; and, notwithstanding his solemn bond to the contrary, James received them with kindly courtesy, telling them that if their husbands would submit to trial they should suffer no wrong. In favour of the enemies of his country, and its religion, James generally made an exception to his general rule, and kept his word.

In April the Assembly met at Dundee, without the king's order. The king, by his commissioner, complained of this as an infringement of the act of 1592, requiring its meetings to be held only by his majesty's appointment. The Assembly assented, but stirred up his royal mind by way of remembrance with the hint that by the act in question they were at liberty to meet on their own motion if he were not present in person or by his commissioner. Other points of disagreement between them demonstrated an utter lack of harmony, and made it evident that open rupture could not be very long delayed.

In July, Parliament met for the trial of the popish lords, but Angus and Kerr had been allowed to escape; and after playing with the subject for a while, the king allowed the traitors to return to their castles in the full enjoyment of their liberty, excepting a prohibition to appear in certain towns in the realm; and the whole proceeding deepened the conviction in the public mind—the king was much more popish than Protestant in his principles and sympathies.

The Synod of Fife, at its meeting in September,

with true Presbyterian independence and fidelity, resolved that if the king sheltered the traitors from civil censure, they would visit them with that of the Church. And as Angus and Errol had subscribed the Confession of Faith within its bounds, and were thus within its jurisdiction, and within its bounds Huntly had murdered Murray, the synod excommunicated them, and sent notice of what they had done throughout the country; they further made arrangements to hold a general meeting of commissioners from the different counties—of noblemen, gentlemen, burgesses and ministers—at Edinburgh, in October. Poor James was sorely tried by the resolute fidelity of these Fife presbyters, and, on a visit to Lord Hamilton, poured out his piteous complaints: "You see, my lord, how I am used. I have no man in whom I can trust more than in Huntly. If I receive him, the ministers will cry out that I am an apostate; if not, I am desolate."

"If he and his associates are not enemies to the religion, ye may receive them," said Hamilton.

"I cannot tell what to make of that, but the ministers hold them for enemies. Always I would think it good that they enjoyed liberty of conscience."

Aroused at hearing the royal hypocrite thus prate of liberty of conscience, Hamilton exclaimed:

"Sir, then we are all gone! then we are all gone! If there is not another to withstand them, I will!"

Alarmed at his earnestness, the king forced a ghastly smile and meekly replied:

"My lord, I did this to try your mind."

After such dissimulation the most credulous could put no trust in the king. However, on his setting out to quell some disturbances on the borders, he lavished upon the faithful those treasures which with him were exhaustless—fair and false promises, assuring them that he would show no favour to the conspirators.

On the very day when this promise was given the king admitted the conspirators to his presence at Jala, and made arrangements with them for their trial. The convention, now in session at Edinburgh, sent commissioners after the king to Jedburgh to tell him manfully of their displeasure at his conference with the traitors; to demand that his pledges to them, in so far as they were calculated to defeat the ends of justice, be annulled; and to say that his faithful subjects would sooner lay down their lives than allow the land to be overrun with popish conspirators.

At this the king turned like a wolf at bay and denounced the convention as an unlawful assembly, inveighed against the Synod of Fife for their decrees of excommunication, and threatened to call a Parliament and overthrow Presbytery and establish Prelacy. James well knew that while elders ruled in the Church his despotic instincts could never be gratified.

To this furious philippic, James Melville replied in manly spirit, and the heat passing off, the king dismissed the commissioners with another batch of royal promises.

The convention of estates, meeting at Linlithgow in October, appointed commissioners to try the conspirators at Holyrood, where these traitors were ordered to give satisfaction to the Church, and to embrace Protestantism within a certain time or leave the realm, and all further process in the case was dropped. Six commissioners from the Church were present at this mock trial, and among them Melville, who took advantage of the occasion to read the king one of his sharp, incisive lectures, reproving him for his harsh words respecting the chief actors in the Reformation and his own best friends, and for his partiality to the enemies of both; and pledging himself to prove that the king's advisers in these matters were traitors to the Crown and realm, and engaging, if he failed, to go himself to the gibbet.

As usual, in the issue of this trial the king displeased all but the foes of the nation and its religion. All knew that the criminals could easily enough comply with the terms of their release, and the next day obtain absolution from the papal authorities both for their seeming offence and from all obligation to submission after it became convenient to throw off the mask. The motives of James for this course were many. In the first place, courage was not one of the few virtues of the king, and he feared to deal out justice to the conspirators. Then Huntly, as the head of the popish party in Scotland, wielded considerable influence, and as James was looking to the crown of England, where the popish party was strong, he was anxious not to offend either. Besides, the despotic principles of the Romanists were much more in harmony with his own than the free, indomitable spirit of Presbyterian Protestantism, and with all he was inflated with a childish pride in craft and cunning, and was thoughtful for any opportunity for its display. All these reasons combined to induce that "line of policy which he pursued all his life, and left as a dire heritage to his successors, which they followed till the ill-omened race reaped the baneful fruits of generations of falsehood and oppression, and became extinct after years of exiled, discrowned, unhonoured, unpitied wretchedness."

In the Assembly that met in May, 1594, on the question of appointing commissioners to the king, the nomination of James Melville as one of them was objected to on the ground that the king suspected him of giving money to the infamous earl of Bothwell, an illegitimate scion of the royal race, the successor in title and character to the murderer of Darnley, to enable him to raise troops against the king. Melville told the Assembly that in the general he sought no such appointments, but now he insisted on being appointed that he might clear himself of the slander. He was appointed, and when the commissioners were about to retire from the presence of the king, Melville rose and asked his majesty if he had anything to lay to his charge. The king said he had not. Melville expressed his gratification, and added that if there were any present that traduced him to his majesty, he desired they would now speak their minds while he was present to defend himself. No one made reply, and then the king took him into his cabinet, conversed with him with great familiarity, and then, dismissing him with warm commendations, doubtless sat down to chuckle over this additional demonstration that he was indeed the very emperor of kingcraft.

As the twofold effect of James' weakness and tergiversation, the popish rebels were soon again in arms, and found abettors in Parliament, and even in the council-chamber of the king. Appearing for the Church before the Lords of Articles, Melville urged to manly and decisive measures. Addressing the king, he said:

"Sir, many think it a great matter to overthrow the estate of three so great men, but it is a weightier matter to expel out of the country three far greater—to wit, true religion, the quietness of the commonwealth and the prosperous estate of the king. If ye lords can get us a better commonwealth and a better king, we are content that the traitorous lords be spared; otherwise we desire ye to do your duty."

Thus spoke the Church in the hour of national peril, as a Church worthy of the name will always speak when the immeasurable interests of society and religion are at once threatened by the incursion of foreign or the uprising of domestic foes.

Melville then objected to the presence among those counsellors of some who lay under suspicion of sympathy with the rebels.

"Whom do you mean?" asked the king.

"One who laughs across the table."

"Do you mean me?" asked Kinloss.

"If you confess yourself guilty, I will not clear you; but I meant Inchaffray."

"Now, Edward," said James to Kinloss, "that is Judas' question—*Is it I, master?*"

Argyle, having been sent against the rebels, was defeated, and James, with a great show of zeal, set out toward Aberdeen, taking with him both Andrew and James Melville to see his zeal for the Lord. But his money soon gave out, and none had confidence enough in his sincerity to entrust him with either men or money, and now, as so often, the Church sprang into the breach. James Melville hastened southward to raise contributions, and with such speed and success that the king was enabled to keep the field. But scarcely had Melville gone on this errand when his privy counsellors almost persuaded the royal weathercock to change his purpose and spare his enemies. But Andrew Melville, by his cogent reasonings and earnest remonstrances, made such an impression upon the army officers present that the king gave orders for the dismantling of Huntly's castle of Strathbogie, and the rebels soon after quitted the kingdom. Thus, as usual, any little manliness shown by this king can be traced directly to the counsels and energy of the Kirk he so disliked; and had his majesty been blessed with but a reasonable share of common sense, he would have seen that her principles were those of honour, energy and prosperity. But so little harmony existed, or could exist, between such a man as James and a true Presbyterian eldership, that the latter was always compelled to stand at the sentinel's post to watch against royal encroachments, and the former was always as keenly on the watch for opportunities to chain the Church to the steps of his throne.

From the time of the regent Morton it had been the constant aim of men in power to unite several parishes under one incumbent, and then appropriate the extra salaries to their own use; and, not satisfied with this, they would even so reduce the income of the one pastor as almost to starve him, while they consumed the spoil thus wrested from him.

To remedy these ills, the Assembly of 1595 appointed certain ministers to inspect the condition of things in the parishes, and report, at a convention to be held at Edinburgh, some plan by which the iniquity might be prevented. The result was a scheme called the "constant plat," which, had the king been faithful to his oaths, might have saved both him and the Church no little evil. The king, indeed, promised to ratify the scheme, but made his promise the occasion of a further display of his boasted kingcraft.

In March of the following year a scene was enjoyed in the Assembly of touching and memorable interest. John Davidson, a devoted minister of Prestonpans, whose mind had been deeply affected by the prevalent disorder and corruption in the Church, induced the Presbytery of Haddington to overture the Assembly upon the matter. The overture touched the heart of every member of the Assembly, and a paper was drawn enumerating the evils to be reformed in the persons and lives of the ministers, the offences in the court of the realm, the corruptions in the estates and in courts of justice. On motion of Melville, the means of reaching the desired reformation were agreed upon. As all true reformation should begin at home, the Assembly agreed to hold a meeting by themselves in the Little Church at Edinburgh on Tuesday, the 30th of March, John Davidson to preside, for the purpose of personal confession and humiliation. And so searching were the words of Davidson in his opening discourse that tears were wrung from every eye. At length he called upon them all in their seats to bow the head and each make secret confession before God. For a quarter of an hour a profound and solemn stillness pervaded the Assembly, broken only by sighs and sobs. The service lasted for three hours, when, at the call of Davidson, the whole Assembly arose to their feet, and, lifting up the right hand to God, pledged themselves to walk more warily and be more diligent in their several charges. "There have been many days of humiliation for present judgments or imminent dangers, but the like for sin and defection was never seen since the Reformation."

At the order of the Assembly the service was repeated throughout the Church—in synods, presbyteries and congregations—"until all Scotland, like Judah, of old, rejoiced at the oath."

At the meeting of the Synod of Fife, David Ferguson addressed the meeting. He was one of the first six ministers engaged in the Reformation, and now the sole survivor. He told them that he had engaged in the work when the name of stipend was unknown, and when they had to encounter the united opposition of the civil and ecclesiastical authorities, without all support from rank and power, yet they persevered, and God had crowned their efforts with success. Davidson and Melville also addressed the synod, and all felt that God was with them of a truth.

Thus does God newly anoint his chosen with grace preparatory to trial. This outburst of sunshine was the prelude of storm and disaster, and was granted that his saints might remember when the dark days were upon them that the sun unextinguished still sat enthroned in glory behind the clouds, and that, in God's own time, the storm would pass and the rainbow of peace once more span the skies.

After this scene of devout humiliation, the Assembly adopted the "constant-plat" scheme, which provided that the whole of the tithes should be regarded as the patrimony of the Church, to be expended in the support of the ministry, of the poor and of a national system of education. But King James cared more for pleasures unresisted by church censures, and power unlimited by church liberty, and his wicked ministers more for the gratification of their avarice than for education, the poor or Christ's ministry, and hence, as usual, they took one side of this question and the Church the other. And now rumours of another Spanish invasion filled the air, and the king ordered military musters; and the preachers, as usual in the front rank of patriotism, exhorted the people to arms. In the midst of these commotions news came that the popish lords had re-entered the kingdom, and the people's hearts sank within them as the conviction forced itself upon the mind that the false-hearted king was privy to their return. Most of the king's counsellors were known papists. The king, as was easy with him, protested his innocence. If any believed him, they soon saw their folly, for at an early day a meeting of the privy council was called at Falkland, to consider terms for the submission of the traitors. Certain ministers, whom the court thought it could trust, were invited to the meeting; but among them, of his own accord, came Andrew Melville! When the king saw him, he felt as Ahab did when he saw Elijah: "Hast thou found me, O mine enemy?"

"Sir," said Melville, "I have a call from Christ and his Church, who have special interest in this convention, and I charge you and your estates, in their name, that you favour not their enemies, nor make citizens of those traitors who have sought to betray their country!"

But the council agreed that the traitors might be restored on certain conditions. But afterward, finding how unpopular this advice of the council was, the king declared he did not mean to act upon it. And yet, shortly after, he did act upon it, and the terms of restoration were solemnly ratified. Such was the creature with which godly men had to deal!

The Church was not irresolute, and commissioners of the Assembly and certain gentlemen met at Cupar in Fife, and sent a deputation to remonstrate with the king. James Melville, on account of the courteousness of his manners and the respect the king had shown him, was appointed their spokesman. But scarcely had he begun to speak when the king broke out in denunciation of the Cupar meeting as seditious, and of the commissioners as agitators. James Melville was about to reply, when his uncle, Andrew Melville, seeing that the crisis demanded not a Melancthon but a Luther, stepped forward and addressed the king. The latter bade him be silent. But the lion was aroused. Catching the king by his robes, he said:

"Thou God's silly vassal! we always humbly

reverence your majesty in public, but now in private, seeing you in danger of your life and crown, and the country and the Church going to wreck, we must discharge our duty or be traitors to Christ and you. There are two kings and two kingdoms in Scotland—King James, the head of the Commonwealth, and Christ Jesus, King of the Church, whose subject James VI. is, and of whose kingdom he is not king, lord nor head, but a member. Sir, those whom Christ has commanded to watch over his Church have power and authority to govern his spiritual kingdom. We will yield to you your place and give you all due obedience, but you are not the head of the Church; you cannot give us that eternal life which we seek for even in this world, and you cannot deprive us of it. Sir, when you were in your swaddling-clothes, Christ Jesus reigned freely in this land in spite of all his enemies. His officers and ministers convened for the ruling and welfare of his Church, which was ever for your welfare, defence and preservation, when these same enemies were resolving your destruction. And now, when there is more than extreme necessity for the discharge of that duty, will you hinder and dishearten Christ's servants and your most faithful subjects? The wisdom of your council, which I call devilish, is this: that you must be served by all sorts of men—Jew, Gentile, Papist and Protestant; and because the Protestants and ministers of Scotland are over-strong and control the king, they must be weakened and brought low by stirring up a party against them. But, sir, if God's wisdom be the only true wisdom, this will prove mere mad folly. His curse cannot but light on it; in seeking both you shall lose both; whereas, in cleaving uprightly to God, his true servants would be your sure friends, and he would compel the rest counterfeitingly and lyingly to give over themselves and serve you."

THE KIRK UNDER THE HEEL OF THE KING.

James was now thirty years old. A despot by constitution, he could not brook the bold, manly freedom of Presbyterianism. Licentious and frivolous, he could not endure a Church that in her censures spared not even the vices of a king. The facile dispensations of Rome were much more to his taste. But, by nature a coward, he was often compelled to make "*I dare not* wait upon *I would.*" But now strengthening passions and larger experience made him more bold, and he set his heart upon humbling the Church at his feet.

However, awed by the manly address of Melville, the king lapsed again into a more favourable mood, and gave his royal word that he had no previous knowledge of the return of the popish conspirators; that he would hear no proposals from them till they had left the kingdom, and that even then he would show them no favours till they had satisfied the Church. "But the Church got only words and promises—her enemies got the deeds and effect."

Seeing measures taken to restore the popish lords, the commissioners of the Assembly met in Edinburgh, warned the presbyteries of the impending perils, specified the means of arresting them, and summoned an extraordinary council to sit in Edinburgh during the crisis, and, if need arose, to convoke the Assembly. On the ninth of November the commissioners had an interview with his majesty, at which he plainly told them that there could be no agreement between them and him until "the marches of their jurisdiction were rid," and they concede to him that the preachers should not introduce matters of State into their sermons—that the Assembly should not convene without his command—that no act of it should be valid till ratified by him, and that no Church court should take cognizance of any act punishable by the criminal law of the land. His first step toward his proposed dominion in the Kirk was upon the neck of

David Black.

This faithful minister of St. Andrew's had said something in a sermon disparaging to the religious character of Queen Elizabeth, and the English ambassador was induced to lay in a complaint against him. Accordingly, he was summoned before the privy council upon a vague charge of "uncomely speeches in divers sermons." To this he objected, as illegal and inquisitorial. He was then told that the charge related only to what he had said about the English queen. The English ambassador expressed himself satisfied with Black's explanation, and withdrew from the matter; but the court, determined on its plans, laid in new charges against him, covering a space of two or three preceding years. Discerning well the whole scheme, the commissioners resolved on resistance to measures evidently aimed at the enslavement of the whole Church, and drew up a declinature of the council's original jurisdiction in the case, which declinature, accepted by Black, was also signed by above three hundred ministers. The court, of course, refused to recognize the declinature, and, having found Black guilty, banished him beyond the Tay until his majesty should decide upon further punishment.

On the morning of the trial the commissioners presented a solemn address to the king and council, calling on God to witness between them and their malicious opposers, protesting their loyalty and their purpose to serve him as faithful subjects, appealing to the king's own knowledge of their conduct in other trying times, accusing the king's enemies of urging on this matter far beyond his original intent, beseeching him to remit the case to the decision of the Assembly, and warning him that if he proceeded to abridge the liberty of the Church, the wrath of God would be kindled against him.

As the trial proceeded, interview followed interview between the king and the commissioners, but James would accept of nothing but complete submission on the part of Black and his friends. The ministers replied that if the matter "concerned only the life of Black, or of a dozen others, they would consider it of comparatively trifling importance; but, as it was the liberty of Christ's gospel that was concerned, they could not submit, but must oppose even to the hazard of their lives." As

Bruce thus spoke the wretched king was moved to tears, but his remorse soon passed away under the goadings of his courtiers, who assured him that he had gone too far to retrace his steps.

The king ordered the commissioners to leave Edinburgh, and an act of council ordained that ministers before receiving their stipend should subscribe a bond to submit to the king and council as often as they were accused of seditious or treasonable doctrine, and commanding all magistrates to imprison any ministers whom they should hear uttering such language from the pulpit. A convention of the estates and a General Assembly was ordered to meet in Edinburgh on the 15th of February following, to take into consideration the "whole order and policy of the Kirk."

In December the alarming rumour was spread that Huntly had arrived and had been admitted to the royal presence. The alarm was increased by the fact that twenty-four of the most zealous citizens had just been ordered to leave Edinburgh. A meeting of barons, burgesses and ministers sent a deputation to the king, then in the Tolbooth, with the lords of session. Bruce, their spokesman, said:

"We are sent to lay before you the dangers that threaten religion."

"What dangers see you?"

"That Huntly has been admitted to your majesty."

"What have you to do with that? and how durst you convene against my proclamation?"

"We dare do more than that," said Lord Lindsay, "and will not suffer religion to be overthrown."

Upon this the king withdrew, and the deputation returned to the meeting to make their report. While considering what should be done some one entered the church and exclaimed:

"Fly, fly, save yourselves! the papists are coming to massacre you!"

Just then the cry was heard in the streets, "To arms! to arms!" and some one in the Assembly called out, "The sword of the Lord and of Gideon!" The Assembly rushed in a panic into the streets, and for a time all was wild confusion; but by aid of the ministers and magistrates the disturbance was soon quelled without injury to any one.

The incensed king posted the next morning to Linlithgow, discharging first a Parthian quiver-full of proclamations, ordering all in public office to repair to him, strangers to leave the city, the ministers of Edinburgh to enter into confinement in the castle, the magistrates to apprehend them, and declaring the tumult to be a cruel and barbarous attempt against king, nobility and council at the instigation of certain seditious ministers and barons.

To carry out this stroke of kingcraft his majesty came back in January to Edinburgh at the head of an army breathing out threatenings and slaughter: he would raze their city to the ground and sow it with salt, and erect a monument there to perpetuate the memory of such treason. The terrified citizens trembled before the king in his well-feigned wrath, and surrendered all their liberties into his hands, and were then graciously forgiven. The ministers also bowed before the storm and withdrew from the capital.

From the neck of David Black the king now stepped upon the neck of the Assembly, and inaugurated a system of Church corruption in the

Perth Assembly.

To open the way Secretary Lindsay published in the king's name fifty-five captious questions for discussion, and a convention of the estates and a meeting of the Assembly was summoned to meet at Perth in the following February.

In the mean time the Church displayed her old heroic spirit. The Presbytery of Haddington suspended a minister for agreeing without their consent to an arrangement with the privy council for supplying the pulpits of Edinburgh. The Synod of Lothian testified their dissatisfaction with the king. Though denied their stipends till they had subscribed the king's bond, scarce one could be induced to subscribe. The Synod of Fife answered his majesty's propositions, remonstrated with the king against holding the extraordinary meeting of the Assembly, but, if the meeting should be held, instructing the presbyteries under their charge to send commissioners, but forbidding them to acknowledge the lawfulness of the Assembly, or to consent to its handling the matter of Church polity.

His majesty, running his eye along this bold front of Scotch Presbyterianism, and conscious of his lack of boldness to confront it with force, easily fell back upon his constitutional cunning and favourite kingcraft. Sir Patrick Murray was sent out among the distant presbyteries, whose members, remote from the great centres, and poor withal, had rarely attended the Assembly, and by playing upon their ignorance and little jealousies, and by promises and flatteries, succeeded in gaining for his master an Assembly the majority of which could be easily manipulated by the king into his measures.

Andrew Melville could not be present, but James was there and ready to do his duty. After three days' debate, the court intriguers succeeding in carrying an affirmation that the Assembly was a lawful one. James Melville, disgusted with the weakness of some of his brethren and with the corrupting arts with which the Assembly was controlled, withdrew from the body. The Fife commissioners remained, but under protest against the lawfulness of the meeting. Answers were now obtained to the king's questions, such as satisfied his majesty for the present, and paved the way for such other and more decided innovations as the king had in view.

This Perth Assembly was remarkable as the first in which kingcraft wrought its will by corrupting the membership. "Coming to Perth," writes James Melville, "we found the ministers of the north in such numbers as was not common in Assemblies, and each one a greater courtier than another; so that my ears heard new notes and my eyes saw a new sight, to wit: flocks of ministers going in and out at the king's palace late at night and betimes in the morning. Sir Patrick Murray, the diligent

Apostle of the North, made all the northland ministers acquainted with the king. They began to look big in the matter, and find fault with the ministers of the south and the popes of Edinburgh, who had not handled matters well, and had almost lost the king." Thus the silly flies were entangled, leg and wing, in the royal spider's web.

Grieved, but not surprised, Andrew Melville, with certain of his brethren, held a meeting at the time and place for the regular meeting of the General Assembly, and then adjourned.

The Dundee Assemblies.

James called the General Assembly together at Dundee in May, and, though with the utmost difficulty he succeeded in carrying through his measures, the Assembly was induced to declare the Perth Assembly lawful and regular, and, with certain explanations, to approve of its acts and to give guarded replies to some of the king's questions. They even consented to receive back again the popish lords on certain conditions, and appointed a committee of fourteen ministers, any seven of whom might convene with his majesty to make arrangements respecting the ministers of St. Andrew's and Edinburgh, the providing of stipends for the ministers throughout the kingdom, and to give the king advice concerning the weal of the Church throughout the realm. Thus a feather was plucked from the eagle's breast wherewith to wing an arrow to its heart, and this was "a needle formed to draw in the episcopal thread." Nearly all the commission were the devoted tools of the king. Through them his majesty called presbyteries before him, reversed their decisions and restored a suspended minister to office. And now the king expressed the desire that the Kirk should have a share in the government of the nation—that is, that by its commissioners in Parliament it should assent to his measures of absolutism. To this end he induced the commissioners to request, and the Parliament to grant, that the Church might have a voice in the supreme council of the nation, and Prelacy was declared to be the third estate in the kingdom—that such ministers as his majesty should raise to the Prelacy might sit and vote in Parliament—and that bishoprics, as they became vacant, might be given to those who would act as preachers and ministers, the spiritual powers of the bishops to be adjusted by his majesty and his majesty's General Assembly. Thus the royal rogue succeeded in handing Presbytery over, bound hand and foot, to

Prelacy, and the whole scheme was a deadly blow to liberty, civil and religious.

Over these proceedings the Synod of Fife held long and earnest conference, disapproving of the whole matter—the Melvilles, the patriarchs Ferguson and Davidson denouncing it, and the latter exclaiming:

"Busk, busk him as bonnilie as ye can, and fetch him in as fairlie as ye will, we see him well enough; we see the horns of the mitre."

At another meeting of the Assembly, at Dundee, in May, 1598, well packed by the king with his northern legion, this act of Parliament came under consideration. Before the Assembly proceeded to business every practicable member was personally manipulated by the king. But armed as the king was by an act of Parliament and the assent of his commissioners, and the subserviency of the members of the Assembly, there was one man whose presence and influence he sorely dreaded, and that man was Andrew Melville. When his name was called on the roll of the Assembly, his majesty denied his right to sit. Melville made his defence. He had a commission from his presbytery, and would not betray his right. Davidson reminded the king that he was not president of that body.

But with James might was instead of right, and he ordered Melville to his lodgings and then from the city. Knox, of Melrose, boldly said that this interdiction proceeded from fear of Melville's learning.

"I will not hear one word on that head," said the king.

"Then," said Davidson, "we must crave help of Him that will hear us."

A week having been spent in efforts to mould the Assembly to the king's wishes, his majesty introduced the business of the hour in a speech, in which he applauded his own services to the Church, protested his anxiety for her welfare, and disclaimed all intention of intruding popish or Anglican bishops into the Church. He only desired that certain of the best and wisest ministers, appointed by the Assembly, should have an honourable and influential place in the council and Parliament of the realm.

The question was, "Is it necessary and expedient, for the welfare of the Church, that the ministry as the third estate should, in the name of the Church, have a vote in Parliament?" A warm and protracted debate ensued, in which all the best and ablest ministers united in rejecting the wealth, rank and power thus offered them. Gladstanes pleaded the power of heathen priests in ancient Rome. Davidson answered:

"The priests were consulted, but they were allowed no vote."

"Where have you that?" asked the king.

"In *Titus Livius*."

"Oh! You are going from the Scriptures to Titus Livius!" sneered the king, as if the Scriptures detailed the duties of Roman priests.

The question, being put to vote, was carried by a majority of ten; many of the elders in the majority, as was asserted, being without any commission. Davidson, who had refused to vote, laid in a protest against the proceedings of this and the two preceding Assemblies, on the ground that they were not free, but overawed by the king, and restricted in their privileges. This protest was signed by forty and more ministers.

The Assembly then chose fifty-one ministers—according to the number of the ancient bishops, abbots and priors—to represent the Church, to be elected partly by the king and partly by the Church. But, before they had gone far in adjusting the matter of the elections, the ministers began to see whither things were tending and drew back a little, and the king, fearing to press them too hard, referred the subject to the next Assembly.

In the numerous meetings for conference among the ministers that ensued, such opposition to the scheme was developed that the king postponed the proposed meeting of the Assembly to give further time for kingcraft.

In November, 1599, he called a conference of ministers at Holyrood, that he might learn in advance what arguments were likely to be urged against his plan when the Assembly should meet. At the opening of the conference the king signified that the largest liberty of discussion would be allowed. A chief question discussed was, "Is it consistent with the nature of their office, and the provisions of Scripture that gospel ministers undertake a civil function?"

On this question Melville deduced the history of the blending of civil and ecclesiastical functions under the Papacy, and warned the king to take heed lest he set up a power that would yet cast him and his successors down.

Then came the question as to the duration of this office; one party pleading for annual elections, the other for official position during good behaviour.

The orthodox party held that permanent civil office and emolument would corrupt the incumbent—make him the tool of the king and the enemy of the Church.

"There is no fear but you will all prove true enough to your craft," said the king.

"God make us all true enough to Christ," answered Melville.

"There is nothing so good but it may be suspected of evil."

"We doubt the goodness of the thing, and have but too much reason to suspect its evil."

"We will not admit ministers but for life. If you refuse this you lose the benefit."

"The loss will be small."

"Ministers will then be in poverty and contempt."

"It was their Master's case before them. Better poverty with sincerity than promotion with corruption."

"Then others will be promoted to their place who will ruin the Church."

"Then let Christ, the King of the Church, avenge her wrongs."

At the next morning the moderator summed up the points in the debate, and intimated that the mind of the conference was in harmony with the wishes of the court. A murmur of dissent ran around the hall, and Melville asked if any one could imagine that a matter of such weight could be settled in such a conference, where the Scriptures had been rather profaned than solemnly handled? At this the king politely told Melville that he lied, and adjourned the conference with the threat that he would leave the refractory ministers to poverty, and of his own act fill the vacant bishoprics with men who would serve him and the realm.

The Melrose Assembly.

At Melrose the Assembly met, in March, 1600. It was very full, and all felt that king or Kirk was now to win a victory of decided results. Andrew Melville was on the spot. The king sent for him and reproached him as a troubler of the Church. Melville pleaded his commission. The king threatened. Melville withdrew, putting his hand to his neck and saying:

"Sir, it is this you would have, and you shall have it before I betray the cause of Christ."

Forbidden to sit in the Assembly, he remained near by to assist by his counsels. The great question was, "Shall ministers sit in Parliament?"

Seeing that the vote would go against him, James interfered and said that the question had been already settled, and withdrew it from farther consideration.

The vote on the duration of the office went for annual elections, yet kingcraft secured a modification of the minute that gave James all he wanted, and at the close of the Assembly he got the minute approved by the house. The voters, however, were to have the name simply of commissioners. The Church was to nominate six in each province, of whom the king was to choose one, and the commissioner was to propose nothing in Parliament, convention or council without the express sanction of the Church, nor vote for any measure prejudicial to her interests. He must report his action to the Assembly, and submit to its censure without appeal. He should have no power in presbytery but what belonged to other ministers; with various other restricting provisions, calculated, if faithfully observed, to make the measure as harmless as possible.

But, as one of the king's sycophants wrote, "It was neither the king's intention nor that of *the wiser sort* to observe these cautions." To demonstrate this, the king called a meeting of the commissioners of the Assembly, in October, to advise with him about filling the Edinburgh pulpits, and "such other things as he thought to be for the weal of Church and king, at the next Parliament." To open the way for the outcarrying of his plans, the royal trickster rid himself of the presence of James Melville by securing his appointment on a committee to transact some business without the body, and during their absence he obtained the nomination of David Lindsay, Peter Blackburn and George Gladstanes to the bishoprics severally of Ross, Aberdeen and Caithness; and this proceeding was carefully concealed from those absent members until the meeting was dissolved, and these bishops, so appointed, sat and voted in the next Parliament! James dreamed that night that he was crowned the Solomon of kingcraft.

Thus, whatever else the king neglected, he was shrewd enough to watch the Church, being always present at the sittings of both commission and Assembly, and ever ready to "regale his friends" with delicate specimens of royal wit—calling one member a "seditious Knox," another "a liar"—saying to one, "that's witchlike," and to another "that's anabaptistical."

All this while James was looking wistfully toward the English throne, and was striving in every way to conciliate the powerful Romish party in both kingdoms. He even sent a secret embassy to the pope; and, restoring to Archbishop Beaton the temporalities of the see of St. Andrew's, sent him ambassador to the court of France.

It was at this time that he issued his masterpieces, "The Free Law of Free Monarchies" and "Basilicon Doron," in which he affirmed that a chief duty of the monarch consists in ruling the Church—to judge when a preacher wanders from his text—to forbid ecclesiastical councils except by his consent—that no man is to be more hated by a king than a proud Puritan—that parity in the ministry is irreconcilable with monarchy, and the mother of confusion—that Puritans were democratic in their principles—that Parity should be banished and Episcopacy set up, and that all who preached against bishops should be punished. How could Romanists and Prelatists longer doubt that the author of such doctrines was just the man to be king of England?

The "Gowrie conspiracy" put a new scourge into the hand of the royal persecutor. Alexander Ruthven and John, earl of Gowrie, men of great popularity and acknowledged piety, seem to have formed some sort of a conspiracy with reference to the king. Its aim is yet a mystery, though papers subsequently discovered prove that it was no part of that aim to shed the king's blood.

The king's story was this: "On his way a-hunting, Alexander met and induced him to accompany him to his house, where his majesty was set upon by the brothers, both of whom were slain in the struggle. The earl was run through the body, but no blood was seen, because, said the king, the victim had in his pocket a bundle of magical parchments; when these were removed, the blood gushed out!" As the absence of these popular men was very convenient to the king, and as no imaginable motive could be suggested for any attempt on their part at his life, many believed that the king himself was the only guilty one. And the known want of veracity of the monarch, and his furious resolve that all should believe his story, increased the suspicion against him. At Edinburgh he vowed vengeance on all who would not express belief in his tale. A form of public thanksgiving for his marvellous deliverance was dictated by the king and enjoined upon all ministers. The ministers of Edinburgh were not unwilling to give thanks that the king's life was preserved, but, as they did not fully believe what he wished them to express, they modified his form of thanksgiving. Five of them were promptly banished and forbidden to preach in Scotland. Four soon submitted, but Bruce would not submit, and was banished the kingdom, and though allowed afterward to return, he was never forgiven.

In 1601, two months before the appointed time, James, having failed in his embassy to the Pope, and feeling the odium increased by the slaughter of the earl of Gowrie, called a meeting of the General Assembly at Burntisland. At this Assembly a faithful, forcible letter was read from John Davidson. The spiritual confusions and disorders of the land came under consideration, during which James was attacked with one of his temporary paroxysms of piety. He rose in the Assembly, and, with tears in his eyes, confessed his offences, and lifting his hand, vowed that he would live and die in the religion of his country and defend it against all adversaries. At his request, the Assembly followed his royal example, and this vow was ordered to be mentioned from the pulpits on the following Sabbath for the edification of the realm. But sore experience kept the Assembly this time from going into any ecstasies over the matter. It soon adjourned, and James laid off his piety and took up the sword of persecution.

In 1602, the king, on his own authority changing the time and place of meeting, summoned the Assembly at Holyrood House in November. James Melville gave in a protest against this arbitrary procedure. The Assembly, however, by its acts showed that the spirit of true Presbyterianism yet survived. With this year ended James' residence in Scotland, and this Assembly was the last Assembly recognized by the Church of Scotland as free and lawful for a dismal period of thirty-six years. The Church now lay prostrate under the heel of the king.

"THE BLACK SATURDAY."

Toward the close of April, 1603, Queen Elizabeth closed her eventful life and reign together, and James VI. of Scotland became James I. of England, and was proclaimed "king of Scotland, England, France and Ireland." The ministers waited on him with their congratulations, though too well assured that in the hands of the English Prelacy his disposition toward the Church of his country could be no way improved. They listened, however, to his farewell speech, in which he assured them of his approbation of the Church of

Scotland, and his purpose to maintain it in its present form.

The honesty and sincerity of James, and the contrast between Presbyterianism and Prelacy, received a noted illustration at the Hampton Court Conference, held soon after the king reached London. It lasted three days. On the first day bishops and deans only were admitted, and the king felicitated himself before them that he was now come into the promised land, that he sat among grave and reverend men, and was a king, not as formerly without state, nor in a place where beardless boys could brave him to his face; and said that he had called this conference not with any thought of innovation, but to take some trifling notice of alleged irregularities. On the second day five ministers were admitted and two bishops and six or eight deans. While Dr. Raynolds was speaking like a man, Bancroft, bishop of London, fell on his knees, begging the king to stop the schismatic's mouth. As Raynolds proceeded the king interrupted him, saying that he found them "aiming at a Scots' Presbytery, which agrees as well with monarchy as God and the devil. Then Jack and Tom and Will and Dick shall meet, and at their pleasure censure both me and my council. Therefore pray stay one seven years, and if then you find me pursy and fat and my windpipe stuffed, I will perhaps hearken to you."

Then turning to the bishops, he said: "My lords, I may thank you that these Puritans plead for my supremacy, for if you were out and they in place, I know what would become of my supremacy, for—No bishop, no king." Then rising from his seat, he added to Dr. Raynolds: "If this be all your party have to say, I will make them conform or I will harry them out of this land, or else worse."

The Prelatists were in ecstasies. Bancroft fell on his knees and protested that "his heart melted for joy that Almighty God, of his singular mercy, had given them such a king as since Christ's time had not been."

Tidings of these events, and of the king's declaration in Parliament that he detested the Puritans, that their "confused form of policy and parity made them a sect insufferable in any well-governed commonwealth," did not serve to reassure the Scottish mind and heart.

Ere long the Scottish Parliament met to consider the basis of union between the two kingdoms.

The Synod of Fife asked liberty to hold a General Assembly, and when this was refused they addressed the Church commissioners in Parliament, and adjured them to defend the government of the Church, and vowed "before God and the elect angels" that they would rather die than allow Presbytery to be overthrown. Nor was their appeal in vain. Parliament passed an act prohibiting the commissioners for union from treating of anything that concerned the religion of the realm.

Resolved on keeping the Kirk under his royal heel, James forbade the Assembly to meet according to appointment at Aberdeen in July, but the Presbytery of St. Andrew's sent their commissioners, who met and protested that they had done their duty, and that any dangers arising from the cowardly neglect of others should not be imputed to them. When the Synod of Fife met, so many commissioners were present from all parts of the kingdom that it was almost a General Assembly. At this meeting and at the one held afterward at Perth, the parliamentary bishops were charged with hindering the meeting of the Assembly, to prolong their own powers and avoid its censures for their misconduct. The sycophant Gladstanes hastened to convey information of these matters to the king, and secured from him an order for the imprisonment of the Melvilles for their fidelity in the matter—an order, however, which the privy council dared not execute.

All haters of liberty detest popular assemblies, and to the Stuarts nothing was more odious than parliaments and presbyterial courts. Accordingly, when the time drew near for the meeting of the General Assembly in 1605, James prorogued it without naming any day for its gathering. This violation of repeated parliamentary enactment in the case, looking evidently to the abolition of the Assembly, the overthrow of Presbytery and the perpetuation of the bishops' term of office, pricked the matter to the core, and challenged the Kirk to action or death. They preferred the former; and when the day arrived for the meeting of the Assembly nine presbyteries were present by their commissioners at Aberdeen. To this meeting the king's commissioner presented a letter from the privy council, addressed to "the brethren of the ministry convened at their Assembly in Aberdeen." Before hearing the letter read they constituted the Assembly, and during the reading of the letter a messenger-at-arms entered and bade them dismiss on pain of rebellion. The Assembly declared their readiness to obey if the commissioner would name the time and place for a future meeting. He refusing, the moderator named Aberdeen as the place, and the last Tuesday of September as the time, for the next meeting, and the Assembly adjourned. Thus nobly did the Assembly war against principalities and powers and spirits of wickedness in high places.

Of course James was not overpleased. Indeed, his wrath knew no bounds. By this time he was warm in his English nest, made soft by prelatic feathers. At first he had seemed to waver a little. Even James did not like to change his coat in an hour. And during the very brief period of his seeming vacillation it is said that a stern old Puritan chaplain treated his majesty to a sermon on the text, James i. 6: "He that wavereth is like a wave of the sea, driven with the wind and tossed." But he was now happily beyond the reach of tormenting Puritan sermons, and when he heard of the bravery of the ministers and ruling elders at Aberdeen, he ordered the arrest and imprisonment of fourteen of the most loyal ministers, and John Forbes, the moderator, and John Welsh, the son-in-law of Knox, were confined in separate cells in the Castle of Blackness. Declining the jurisdiction of the privy council, they were indicted for high treason. Six were found guilty and thrown into prison to await his majesty's will, and orders soon came from the despot to proceed with the remaining eight.

The heroic conduct of the ministers sent a thrill through the heroic heart of Scotland, and the despotic conduct of the king filled that heart with indignation. Proclamations forbade the people, on pain of death, either to pray for the imprisoned ministers or to call in question the justice of their sentence, but the people only prayed the more and the more loudly denounced the sentence. The clouds were gathering, and James, hearing the distant thunders, gave orders for the release of the eight, and sent the six, after fourteen months' imprisonment, into exile.

Such a taste of Episcopacy did not intoxicate the people with its sweets. If such were its beginnings, what would be its ending? While thus John Welsh, through whose zealous preaching of the gospel hundreds had been converted, was incarcerated in a prison cell, a wretched Romish abbot was set free. "Not this man, but Barabbas!" Strangely supposing that the Kirk was now humbled, James, urged on by his bishops, convoked the synods on the same day in different parts of the kingdom, and tried to seduce them into the adoption of five articles whose object was to shield the bishops from Church censures for their illegal conduct. But, the Synod of Angus excepted, they all referred the matter to the General Assembly.

The Parliament held in August, 1606, took another step up the prelatic ladder, and an act was passed opening with a preamble declaring the king to be "absolute prince, judge and governor of all estates, persons and causes, spiritual and temporal;" declaring that the wealth and lands formerly possessed by abbots, priors, etc., in virtue of which those persons had acted as members of Parliament, should be alienated from the Church and erected into temporal lordships; erecting seventeen prelacies and restoring the bishops to their ancient honours. This act pleased all but the Church and its friends. It pleased the king, for it acknowledged him as despot. It pleased the mercenary lords, as it enriched them; and the bishops, as it clothed them with the glories of lords over God's heritage. Against these proceedings Melville and forty-one other ministers laid in a solemn, earnest protest, in which they reminded the Parliament that they were not lords over the Church, and conjured them not to overthrow the religion of the land by erecting a hierarchy which "had uniformly proved the source of idlenesss, ignorance, insufferable pride, pitiless tyranny and shameless ambition."

The Melvilles also drew up a paper containing the reasons for the protest, in which they say: "Set up these bishops once (called long since the Prince's led horse), things however unlawful and pernicious, if favoured by the king, shall be carried through by his bishops without regard to the other estates. And the reason is, that the bishops have their lordship and living from the king. Deprave me once the ecclesiastical estate, which has the gift of knowledge and learning beyond others, and the rest will be easily miscarried. If any succeeding prince please to play the tyrant, these bishops shall never admonish him as faithful pastors, but, as they are made by man, they must and will flatter and please man. The pitiful experience of this in times past makes us bold to give warning for the time to come."

How well grounded these anticipations were is seen in, among other things, a letter of Gladstanes', one of the king's archbishops, in which he writes: "I find myself so overwhelmed with your majesty's princely benignity that I could not but repair to your majesty's most gracious face, that so unworthy a *creature* might both see, bless and thank *my earthly creator!*"

Though James had accomplished much, much yet remained to be done in the work of transmuting Presbytery into Prelacy. The Parliament had wrought well to his will, but as yet Episcopacy stood condemned by the Church, and the king's bishops enjoyed legally little more than the name. Their rank was, as in the Scripture, simply that of pastors, and no superior spiritual power was lodged in their hands; and the desired revolution on this point could be wrought only by the General Assembly. But of this there could be no sure prospect while the veteran leaders of the Kirk were within speaking distance of their brethren. Hence two problems invited solution at the hands of kingcraft: first, the removal of these leaders from the realm, and, second, the corruption or intimidation of the Assembly. Neither of these problems was arduous to the royal manipulator. Accordingly, a peremptory and insidious mandate from the king ordered the Melvilles, and others who had been already imprisoned or banished, to repair to him at London to consult with him upon ecclesiastical affairs. The king's two archbishops, Gladstanes and Spotswood, followed them. On the 20th of September they were allowed to kiss the monarch's hand, and the king rallied Balfour on the length of his beard, which, he said, had grown prodigiously since he had had the pleasure of seeing it in Scotland.

"The cat doth play and after slay."

Two days after, they met his majesty again, when they were asked for an account of the "pretended Assembly at Aberdeen," and of the means of obtaining a peaceable meeting of the General Assembly." On these points they were to give answer the next day. The next day they met in the presence of earls and nobles, with English prelates behind the tapestry. First, James bade his creatures Gladstanes and Spotswood give their views, which, of course, were all his majesty desired. Andrew Melville was then called upon to speak, which he did for one hour, and, as he spoke the honest truth, of course he disagreed with the king. The others followed in the same strain. The lord advocate then spoke of the trial of the ministers for treason in such terms that Andrew Melville took fire and on his knees begged to speak again. This being granted, he poured his spirit forth in one of those bursts of honest, eloquent indignation and power for which he was so famous. Of the lord advocate he said that the arch-enemy himself could not have done more against the saints of God than he had done; and now, said he,

"You must needs show yourself, *Ο Κατηγορος των Αδελφων*."

"What's that he said?" asked the king. "I think he calls him anti-Christ. Nay, by God, it is the devil's name in the Revelation of the well-beloved John."

Then rising hastily, he said, "God be with you, sirs."

Recollecting himself, he turned and asked the ministers what was needed to pacify the dissensions of the Church. With one voice they answered:

"A FREE GENERAL ASSEMBLY."

The predetermined result was that Andrew Melville was shut up for four years in the Tower, James was forbidden to return to Scotland and the others to return to their parishes, and thus the "crafty tyrant cut down the tallest."

Surely now the road was clear for the panting steed of the king to the crowning heights of complete despotism. But even yet much remained to be done. Nothing must be left to Scotch piety and pertinacity. The king's bishops were sent post-haste to gather an Assembly at Linlithgow, but carrying a mandate with them naming those who should be commissioners. The ministers in London asked a *free Assembly*, and as a free monarchy was one in which the king was free to do as he pleased, so a free Assembly was one in which the king's will should have free play. Some of the presbyteries refused to grant commissions to the king's nominees; others elected them, but charged them to take no part in the decision of any ecclesiastical question. The king ordered, and against much opposition the Assembly ordained, the appointment of *constant moderators* in presbyteries, and that his bishops should be moderators of the presbyteries within whose bounds they resided—these "constant moderators being the little thieves within to open the doors to the great thieves without." The poor Synod of Angus was the only synod that obeyed. The king raged and stormed, and his bishops did all the king bade; ministers were thrown into prison, but the presbyteries would not appoint the constant moderators.

In 1609 a Parliament at Edinburgh empowered the bishops to fix the salaries of ministers, and made Spotswood a lord of session, and thus the prelates climbed the throne, being now holders of the ministers' purses, constant moderators in spite of the Kirk, visitors of presbyteries, and soon royal high commissioners; for in 1610 a commission was issued to the king's two archbishops to hold two courts of high commission, the instrument and embodiment of sheer tyranny. No fixed forms of law or justice guided their proceedings. They had the power of receiving appeals from all ecclesiastical courts, of citing before them any accused of immorality, heresy, sedition or any other offence, and of inflicting any punishment, civil or ecclesiastical; and thus did the king put himself in possession of the liberties, goods and persons of his subjects. The "free monarchy" was realized.

One of the king's packed Assemblies was held in June at Glasgow. In obedience to the dictation of James, the Aberdeen Assembly of 1605 was condemned, the right of calling and dismissing Assemblies given to his majesty, the bishops were declared moderators of diocesan synods, and other acts were passed completing the overthrow of the Kirk. These acts, though kept secret till the time came to enforce them, stirred up no little ferment in the realm, and this gave pretext for further persecution.

Thus, after ten years, by the exercise of arbitrary power, by bribery, by dissimulation, treachery and persecution, was Episcopacy established in Scotland.

In 1617, after an absence of fourteen years, the king favoured his native country with a visit, and with instinctive Stuart fatuity gave a preliminary thrust at the prejudices of those who were expected to welcome him, by sending on in advance some cartloads of wooden statues of the apostles, to be set up in Holyrood. On his arrival he found that all his kingcraft had not fully replaced the Presbyterian thistle of Scotland with the lawn of Prelacy. True, the deputy town-clerk of Edinburgh greeted him at the West Port with salutations, as the "bright star of our northern firmament, the ornament of our age;" but the ministers met him with a protest, adopted at a meeting held for the purpose, against a proposal to the effect that the king, aided by the prelates and ministers, should have power to enact ecclesiastical laws and thus abolish the General Assembly. For this, David Calderwood was cited before the High Commission. But he declined its jurisdiction.

The king demanded:

"How dared you to take part in that mutinous meeting?"

"When that meeting is pronounced mutinous, it will be time enough to answer that question."

"What moved you to protest?"

"A proposition of the Lords of Articles to destroy our General Assembly."

"But this is disobedience!

"We will yield passive obedience to your majesty, but not active obedience to unlawful regulations."

"Active and passive disobedience—what is that?"

"That is, we will rather suffer than act."

"I'll tell thee, man, what is obedience. When the centurion said to one, Go and come, and he obeyed. That is obedience. I am informed you are refractory, and attend neither synod nor presbytery, nor in any way conform."

"I have been in confinement these nine years; so my conformity or non-conformity in that point could not very well be known."

"Good faith! Thou art a very knave! See these false Puritans—they are ever playing with equivocations!"

The result was, that Calderwood was banished, and that in the winter, the king gently remarking that "should he be drowned on the voyage, it might save him from a worse end."

During his stay in Scotland the king showed the effect of his residence among English prelates in a proclamation commanding that his subjects should not be prevented from "dancing, leaping, vaulting, exercising archery, having May games, Whitson ales or morris dances after divine service on Sundays." And now followed

The Five Articles of Perth:

Namely, *kneeling at the communion, the observance of holidays, episcopal confirmation, private baptism, and the private dispensation of the Lord's Supper.*

To prepare the way for the adoption of these, the whole force of kingcraft and bishopcraft, of despotism spiritual and temporal, was brought to bear upon the prospective membership of the General Assembly, a meeting of which was ordered at Perth on the 25th of August, 1618. They met in the Little Kirk, in which a long table was placed in the centre, on each side of which benches were placed, with another for the moderator and the king's commissioner at the head. The seats were filled with the nobility and prelates, and the poor ministers stood up behind them! Spotswood took the moderator's seat without election. The commissions of the ministers were handed in, but not examined in public—a prudent procedure, for many of them were illegal. The moderator ordered that the nobles, and others who were present without other commissions than the mandate of the king, should be considered as members of the body. The dean of Winchester read a letter from the king, in which his majesty assured them that he would be satisfied with no "mitigations, delays or shifts, nor indeed with anything short of a direct acceptation of the articles in the form he had sent."

When these articles were laid before the body, there were not wanting, even there, some who faithfully stood up for the right. At this the moderator poured forth a furious tirade, sneering at the suggestion that any of the ministers would submit to expulsion from their charges rather than submit to the will of the king in this matter; "and if any do," he said, "I wish the king would make him a captain, and never one of these braggers would come to the field." So apt scholars were the king's prelates in the school of coarse abuse and overbearing tyranny.

When the faithful ministers attempted to speak, their voices were drowned by the clamors and jeers of courtly barons and gentry. The question was at length put in this form:

"Will you consent to these articles, or will you disobey the king?" and the moderator added that the name of every man who voted against them should be sent to the king! The articles were passed—forty-five ministers, one doctor and one nobleman voting in the negative. These articles, thus forced upon the Church, the Court of High Commission at once began to enforce at the point of the bayonet.

The Black Saturday.

August 4th, 1621, saw these articles ratified by Parliament. For three years now had the Church been "harried" by the High Commission, and plied with every instrumentality cunning could devise and cruelty wield, and now Parliament met at Edinburgh to do the bidding of its imperious master in riveting the chains upon its limbs. The faithful ministers assembled at Edinburgh and petitioned against the act. The petition was cast into the fire and the petitioners into prison. Others met in private and expressed their views, and they were ordered instantly to leave the city. At length the day arrived when the deed was to be consummated. As the parliamentary procession moved from the palace to the Tolbooth a few spectators in the streets looked on in silence, while the inhabitants generally remained at home shut up in their houses. At last the vote was taken and the infamous measure passed—fifteen lords, fifty-four commissioners of shires and burghs voting in the negative. The morning had been cloudy, and as the day advanced the gloom deepened and clouds gathered in dense masses over the city. The king's commissioner rose from his throne, and, in the usual method, stretched out the sceptre to touch the acts and thus seal their ratification. Just then a keen flash of forked lightning darted through the gloom, followed by a second and a third, and three terrific peals of thunder made the old building shake and the guilty legislators tremble! Rain followed in deluging sheets, and hailstones of enormous size rattled upon the roof and against the walls, imprisoning for an hour and a half the wretched conclave in its hall of sin. The prelates likened it to the thundering of Sinai at the giving of the law, but the people remembered the day for a long time as THE BLACK SATURDAY.

Had James been there, he would have ordered a series of counter-incantations to exorcise the city of Presbyterian witches, but his majesty's head that day was pillowed on the soft bosom of English Prelacy.

THE DEATH OF JAMES.

The king survived this consummation of his crime against the Kirk—which he had eulogized as the sincerest Kirk of all the world, and over and over again pledged his word to God and man to defend—a little less than four years, a period of unrelenting tyranny. The people had long been growing restive under the despotism of the High Commission, as depending solely upon the will of the king, but now James elegantly wrote to Spotswood:

"The greatest matter the Puritans had to object against the Church government was that your proceedings were warranted by no law, which now by this last Parliament is cutted short, so that hereafter that rebellious, disobedient and seditious crew must either obey or resist God, their natural king and the law of the country. Lose no time to procure a settled obedience to GOD and to US. The sword is put into your hands; use it, and let it rust no longer." But Spotswood needed no such injunction to keep the sword from rusting. He loved to make and see it bright.

A similar epistle was sent to the privy council,

enjoining all officers of the state, on pain of dismission, to aid in turning the grindstone while the archbishop sharpened and furbished his sword. Very many of the burgesses, however, refused to act, and their places were filled with those who were more pliant.

While this storm of persecution was beating down upon the Church, incessant rains kept the grain from growing, and succeeding winter floods swept away farm-houses, bridges, cattle and men. Perth was surrounded with water. Famine followed and reduced many of the opulent to beggary. John Welsh, now fourteen years in exile, his health fast failing, his wife begged of James permission to breathe once more his native air. James asked:

"Whose daughter are you?"

"The daughter of John Knox!"

"Knox and Welsh! The devil never made a match like that!"

"It's right like, sir; we never asked his advice."

"What children did your father leave?"

"Three, and they were all lasses."

"God be thanked! Had they been lads, I had never possessed my kingdom in peace."

"But give him, sir, his native air!"

"Give him the devil!"

"Give that, sir, to your hungry courtiers!"

"Well, he may return if he will submit to the bishops."

Lifting up her apron, she said, "I would rather keep his head here!"

So poor Welsh died in exile.

In the mean time the bishops hunted up every minister their keen scent could discover, and sought to constrain his subscription to the Perth articles, aiming thus to bend the adverse will of the people by the example of the venerated pastors; and, judging others by themselves, they doubted not that their opponents would quail before the newly-furbished sword. Met in High Commission, they summoned five godly notables before their bar. To the summons George Johnson, of Ancrum, sent this reply:

"If my age of seventy-three years, and my infirmities, a swelling in both my legs, a constant fever after travelling in the open air, with other miseries attendant on old age, may not hold me excused from coming to Edinburgh, I take me to God's mercy." This old man the kind bishops deprived and banished to Annandale. David Dickson, of Irvine, eminent for parts and piety, protected by an earl and pleaded for by his people, was banished to Turriff, and all the rest were made to feel the keen edge of the prelatic sword. Finding the pastors too bold and true to bow, they tried their power upon the people, insisting especially on the kneeling at the communion, as the most visible acknowledgment of the authority of royal and prelatic tyranny; and many a scene of confusion and disgrace occurred in the house of God, and in the presence of the bread and wine, as the persecutors enforced and the people resisted what they regarded as a popish ceremony. A few yielded to gratify the dignitaries, but the greater part either abstained from the communion-table, or resorted to altars where they could participate with New Testament simplicity.

But true Presbyterianism is not wont either to submit to ecclesiastical or secular tyranny, or long to smother its indignant protests. The dullest apprehensions could not choose but see that the assumed power of the prelates meant the death of all freedom. The nobility found that their constitutional rights were dreams in the eyes of those who now lorded it over God's heritage, and the muttering of coming thunder was heard among the cloudy masses of the people, and the sea began to swell under the force of a gathering storm. Nor was any oil poured on the troubled waters by the king's proposal to marry the prince to a Spanish Romanist, nor by the royal favour to Papists to smooth the way for this abominable alliance.

Further force was added to the national discontent by the conduct of the king and his prelatic minions in the case of William Forbes, who, having been recently placed over one of the churches of Edinburgh on account of his anti-Presbyterian principles, was accused of uttering sentiments in favour of the papacy. The bishops, of course, sided with Forbes, who was proudly indignant that the people should venture to question his official acts or utterances. At the solicitation of the bishops a thundering mandate from the king bade a select number of the privy council to put the murmuring citizens on trial for their audacity, and one magistrate was imprisoned in the Castle of Blackness till he could pay a ruinous fine; and five other eminent citizens were imprisoned or banished to remote parts of the country.

The prelates, finding that they were only sowing dragons' teeth, begged now of the king relief from the "conventicles" to which the faithful ministers of the surrounding country resorted for purposes of prayer and consultation; and in answer to their petitions there came a royal proclamation reprehending in severe terms those citizens who listened to the "turbulent persuasions of restless ministers," and strictly prohibiting all private conventicles. Soon after, a letter of censure came from the royal hand, threatening the town of Edinburgh with the removal of the courts of session and justiciary, if the magistrates did not give better obedience to the articles of Perth themselves and better enforce their observance upon others.

But the cup of James was now full. If the saints die, the grave will not yield its claim on sinners;

"Death lays his icy hand on kings;
Sceptre and crown must tumble down,
And, in the dust, be equal made
With the poor crooked scythe and spade."

The 27th day of March, 1625, found King Death darkening with his huge shadow the palace-door of King James, nearly fifty-nine years after his birth in Edinburgh Castle, while his mother was meditating the murder of his father in love for her seducer and in revenge for the death of Rizzio. His reign, in a political point of view, had been one succession of humiliations to his people. In Scotland all was turbulence and strife, and "on the day of his accession to the English throne," writes Macaulay, "our country descended from the rank she had hitherto held, and began to be regarded as a power hardly of the second order. From the time of his accession he shunned hostilities with a caution that was proof against the insults of his neighbours and the clamours of his subjects. Not till the last year of his reign could the influence of his son, his favourite, his Parliament and his people combined induce him to strike one feeble blow in defence of his family and religion."

The portraits left of his person are not flattering. "He was of middling stature, more corpulent through his clothes than in his body, though fat enough; his clothes ever being made too large, and his doublets quilted for stiletto-proof; his breeches in great plaits and full stuffed. His eyes were large, ever rolling after any stranger who came into his presence"—fearing he might prove a king-killer—"insomuch as many for shame have left the room. His tongue was too large for his mouth, which ever made him speak full in the mouth and made him drink very uncomely. He never washed his hands—only rubbed his finger ends with the wet end of a napkin slightly. His legs were very weak, making him ever lean on other men's shoulders. His walk was ever circular."

But physical defects are soon forgotten if mind and character challenge admiration. Unhappily, James' body was the best part of him. His disregard for truth was unblushing. He was ostentatious in his profanity and lascivious conversation and conduct, driving, by his own example, all decency from his court. In spirit he was crafty, mean, selfish and vindictive. Indeed, few kings have lived whose characters would not gain by comparison with his. Such was the idol of English Prelacy—the one whom the fawning Gladstanes called his *earthly creator*—to whom Bancroft, bishop of London, said "that he was such a king as since Christ's time hath not been." At last, however, the time came for his removal. An intermittent fever seized him, and as he sank the wretches who had flattered him so profusely while fawning sycophancy was sure of its reward, miserably deserted him; and it is said that even medical attention was lacking, and that some "empirical prescriptions, which in his impatience he caused to be administered," hastened the end he was so anxious to defer. "Thus," in the language of Hetherington, "he departed, leaving a kingdom sunk from glory to disgrace; filled with the elements of private strife and social discord; a son the heritor of his despotic principles and of all the evils they had engendered, and a name lauded by a few prelatic flatterers who could term him their 'earthly creator,' the 'Solomon of the age,' but scorned by the haughty, mocked by the witty, despised by men of learning and genius, and not hated only because pitied and deplored by the persecuted yet loyal Church of Scotland." Nor can charity concede to his memory even the poor privilege of oblivion.

CHARLES I.

"The king is dead—long live the king!" On the arrival in Scotland of the news of the death of James a general mourning was ordered, the chapel and palace of Holyrood were hung with black, the new king proclaimed with the usual ceremonies, and the chief ministers of state set off for London, less to assist in burying the old monarch than in crowning and soliciting favours from the new one.

Charles I. was a man of medium size, his aspect grave and pale, with a painful weakness of eyes. In intellect he was far superior to his father, and he displayed considerable taste for literature and the arts; and his domestic life was without a stain.

But, affecting the gravity of the court of Spain in his behaviour, he not only despised the civilities and affabilities which endear a prince to his people, but sullen, if not morose, in his temper, his manner in bestowing a favour was so ungracious that "it was almost as mortifying as the favour was obliging." Inheriting his father's despotic temper, he was fond of high, rough measures, though lacking "the skill to conduct them and the genius to manage them." He hated all that offered counsels of prudence and moderation, even when necessity compelled him to listen to such counsels. Thus he was extremely wilful and looked upon all contradiction as rebellion. "Faithlessness was the chief cause of his disasters and is the chief stain on his memory. He was in truth impelled by an incurable propensity to dark and crooked ways. It may seem strange that his conscience, which, on occasions of little moment, was sufficiently sensitive, should never have reproached him with this great vice. But there is reason to believe that he was perfidious not only from constitution and habit, but also on principle. He seems to have learned from the theologians," his prelatic counsellors, "whom he most esteemed, that between him and his subjects there could be nothing of the nature of a mutual contract; that he could not, even if he would, divest himself of his despotic authority, and that in every promise he made there was an implied reservation that such promise might be broken in case of necessity, and that of the necessity he was the sole judge."

Such was the character of the monarch with whom high-spirited Presbyterianism was now to deal, and who had inherited from his father a realm that now rested on a volcano.

For a time, the death of their beloved master, in whose favour they found their life, paralyzed the energies of the prelates and afforded a brief breathing-time to the persecuted Church. The banished ministers came back to their homes, full of zeal and love and cordially welcomed by the people. When James breathed his last, the Court of High Commission, which his will had created, also died, and the relief the godly thus experienced only increased their detestation of despotism and its ministers.

But relief soon returned to the bishops and apprehension to the Church. Charles had sought a wife in Romish Spain, and had found one—lovely, accomplished and strong-willed—in papal France. Nor was it long before a breathless courier rushed in at the gates of Edinburgh, bringing mandates from Charles that made the heart of Archbishop Spotswood leap for joy: "Go right on in the old path, and carry into execution all the ecclesiastical laws of the old reign!" At this the prelatic bells pealed out their exulting clang, and those of right and religion tolled an appalling knell. Then came a royal proclamation commanding conformity to the Articles of Perth and menacing the disobedient with rigorous penalties; and then a royal mandate to the town council of Edinburgh, commanding them to allow as magistrates none but the subservient.

During the preceding reign, liberty, civil and ecclesiastical, found some small security in the mental weakness and cowardly timidity of the king. He was a great blusterer, but his spirit not unfrequently evaporated in the blustering. But Charles, stronger of mind and the incarnation of obstinacy, acted instead of blustering, and that with a quiet tenacity of purpose that only yielded to the axe that took off his head. He early resolved that the sham Prelacy of Scotland should emerge into the solid and real Prelacy of England, and to do this he saw that the bishops, with their titles, must have the handling of the tithes. The apostles were not overburdened with incomes, but their successors in a prelatical establishment had almost as well be without mitres as without money. In the first year of his reign, therefore, he startled both the Church and the nobility by a proclamation revoking "all the acts of his father in prejudice of the crown;" the nobles, as they read therein a significant hint that many lands in their possession were likely to slide from under their grasp, and the Church as seeing the hammer lifted that was to rivet the fetters of Prelacy upon the free limbs of the nation.

After this startling intimation had had time to work, he proceeded to measures calculated, in his view, to curb the intractable, turbulent temper of the Scotch nobility. He remodelled the courts, the privy council and the constitution of the exchequer, introducing certain of his pliant prelates into the two latter; created a commission of grievances or Scottish Star-Chamber, and raised from the dead the Court of High Commission. Thus the machinery was erected, put in order and committed to willing, relentless hands, which was to torture Scotland, Church and State, into conformity with the ideal in the royal mind. A gleam also of the old kingcraft appeared in the order, allowing all the ministers admitted before the Assembly of 1618 to withhold consent to the Perth Articles, on condition that they would refrain from publicly assailing the king's authority and his form of church government. What might have been the effect of this bribe in undermining opposition, the zeal of the younger prelates, whose palates were whetted for the spoils, prevents us from knowing. It was found impossible to restrain hounds keen of scent and game in view.

These younger prelates, seeing that advancement quickly followed the display of zeal, caught the ritualistic fever, and soon nothing was heard among them but plans for the introduction of prelatic novelties. Success turned their heads and filled their hearts with pride. Many of them, destitute alike of piety and learning, put on offensive airs, disdaining association with their flocks, and aping the manners of, and courting association with, the court class, and thus deepening the general disgust.

In 1628 a deputation was sent to the king by the Synod of Edinburgh, begging relief from compulsory submission to the Articles of Perth, and especially from the necessity of kneeling at the sacrament, to which the mass of Presbyterian knees would not bend. As might have been expected, however, his majesty regarded the petition as little short of downright rebellion, and ordered condign punishment upon the petitioners. The result was that the sacrament of the Lord's Supper was not administered in Edinburgh that year.

Things being now ripe, in the judgment of Charles, to set his machine in action, he sent the earl of Nithesdale to hold a convention of the estates and gain their consent to the resumption by the Crown of all the tithes and Church property which came to it at the Reformation, or which had been shared among the leading nobles during the last two reigns. Thus the king would acquire the metal needed to gild his bishops up to the point of orthodox, prelatic splendour, and root the order in the constitution of the government. But this was a tender point. Many of those nobles could say in all sincerity, "He who takes my religion takes trash, but he who takes my purse had as well also take my life." With some of them, however, higher motives prevailed. Presbyterianism had taught them freedom, and this measure was another step toward absolutism; and they resolved to resist even unto death. The convention met, filled with scowling lords. Nithesdale proposed his measure, pledging all who would consent with the special favour of his majesty, and threatening the refractory with the most vigorous measures. But at a private meeting of the enraged nobles it had been agreed that should the earl press this measure, he and his adherents should be slain on the spot. Lord Belhaven, blind by age, asked to be placed by the side of one of Nithesdale's men, and, being set beside the earl of Dumfries, he held him fast by one hand as if needing support in his weakness, while with the other he clutched a dagger concealed in his bosom, resolved, when the signal should be given, to bury the dagger in the heart of his victim. Nithesdale, however, quailed under the frowns of the barons, and gave up the attempt. But with a wisdom peculiar to the Stuart race, the act, upon consent to which the king's agent dared not insist, was published in spite of their dissent, and thus became an additional wedge between the crown and the realm, and an additional bond among the people.

The experience of Spotswood compelled him to see what the king was too wilful and haughty to acknowledge—that the Scottish spirit might be goaded farther than would be safe for him who used the goad, and the visible scowls and audible murmurs of discontent constrained him within certain bounds of moderation. But the more sanguine prelates, blinded by covetousness and zeal, whispered—through Laud, who was now the king's conscience ecclesiastical—into the monarch's ear counsels that better suited his imperious temper, and thus Spotswood began to feel the shadows of a royal cloud. John Maxwell, minister in Edinburgh, able and unscrupulous, led the advanced wing and secured the confidence of Laud, and the violent measures of this party greatly deepened the growing discontent. In 1636, this Maxwell, after consultation with Laud and Charles, brought with him to Edinburgh a royal letter to Spotswood, directing him to convene the prelates and those ministers most under their power, and inform them that the time was drawing near when Scotland must put on the prelatic yoke of England and remodel the whole Church order after the English pattern. This bearding the lion in his den, however, was a task the prelates dare not yet undertake, and the matter was postponed. In July of this year, at a convention of the estates, the faithful ministers presented a paper of grievances of which they asked redress, which, although supported by several of the nobility, was contemptuously left unread. In the mean time, efforts sufficiently futile were made to introduce organs, choristers, surplices and other such novelties. And as death vacated one and another of the ecclesiastical offices, new and more zealous incumbents took the places of the departed. Law was transferred from the see of Ross to the archbishopric of Glasgow, and Maxwell made bishop of Ross, and then a lord of session, and then a lord of exchequer, and then a member of privy council; and who could now doubt that he was a true successor of the apostles?

While the king and his prelates were thus getting their machine in working order preparatory to the final act of exterminating Presbyterianism and saddling the nation with English Prelacy, God, by his providence and Spirit, was rooting the former more and more deeply in the minds and affections of the people, and making the latter more and more odious. Under persecution true piety has ever shown a tendency to deepen and brighten, and rarely have God's ministers shown a zeal so unquenchable and a fervour more seraphic than when hunted like the partridge upon the mountains. Among the noblest of Christian spirits of those days was Robert Bruce. Driven from point to point by Royalty and Prelacy, he had kindled new fires of devotion among the people, and many a young preacher had been imbued with a heavenly heroism by the fervent breathings of his soul. Another, of kindred spirit, was David Dickson, pastor in the town of Irvine, who, allowed to return from exile to the bosom of his half-idolizing flock, proclaimed with such unction and power the unsearchable riches of Christ that a mighty revival sealed and crowned his labours. "Persons under deep exercise and soul-concern came from all the parishes round about Irvine to enjoy the benefit of his ministry." He began a series of services on Mondays, market-days in Irvine, so timing them that the crowds who came to town on that day could attend upon them before market-hour. To these services others also came from distant parts of the country, and not a few removed their families to Irvine and settled there to enjoy the ministrations of this able and favoured pastor. This looked little like an acceptance of Prelacy. After his sermon on Sabbath evenings crowds waited to converse with him about their souls. The work of grace spread into the adjoining parish of Stewarton, and thence from spot to spot along the valley through which the Stewarton water runs; and under its power "many most abandoned characters, mockers of everything bearing the semblance of religion, were completely changed." This remarkable work of grace began the very year Charles put on his crown, and lasted for about five years. Profane ribaldry called it "the *Stewarton sickness.*" Scarce a Sabbath passed without evident conversions or some convincing proof of the mighty power of the Word. "And truly this great spring-tide, as I may call it, of the gospel, was not of a short time, but of some years' continuance; yea, thus like a spreading moonbeam, the power of godliness did advance from one place to another, which put a marvellous lustre on those parts of the country, the savour whereof brought many from other parts of the land to see the truth."

"In the upper ward of Lanarkshire," in the parish of Schotts, two hundred and thirty years ago, there stood a Presbyterian manse, occupied by Mr. Hance, the pastor. One day, about the year 1630, the year in which King Charles made his first motion toward the actual imposition of the English liturgy upon Scotland, a carriage, containing certain ladies of rank, driving past this manse, broke down, and the pastor, coming to the aid of the disabled travellers, took them into his house and attended to the repairing of their carriage. While there the ladies remarked the comfortless condition of the manse, and soon after had a new manse built for the minister on a more eligible site. The grateful pastor then waited on the ladies, expressed his grateful sense of their kindness, and asked,

"Is there any way in my power by which I can do you service?"

"Yes," was the reply; "send out invitations to an administration of the Lord's Supper at your church, and request such and such ministers to assist on the occasion, and we shall be amply repaid."

He gladly consented, and the ministers came, the venerable and persecuted Robert Bruce among them; and the people came from far and near, an immense number of the choicest Christians in the land, with crowds of curious spectators. Richly-blessed preparatory services were followed on the Sabbath, June 20, 1630, by a precious communion season—so precious that at its close the people could not separate and resolved upon services the following day. But who should preach? Why not Bruce? Why not some other notably scarred veteran confessor? In the vast assembly was a young minister not yet ordained, only licensed by the Presbytery, and on him, in the providence of God, the lot fell. He received the intimation with consternation. How could he preach to all that mass of piety, ability and learning. He thought over it during the night, and in the morning resolved on flight. He stole away into the woods, and was now where, on turning his head, he could just see the church in whose yard the crowds were assembling to hear him. Just then a voice darted into the ears of his soul: "Was I ever a barren wilderness or a land of darkness?" It was the voice of God. Cost what it might, to that voice he must give heed. Taking his stand before the crowd, he preached one hour and a half upon the text in Ezek. xxxvi. 25, 26, "Then will I sprinkle clear water upon you," etc. As he was about to close, God from the clouds sprinkled the congregation with a dash of rain, and the people began to flutter. Glancing at the agitated crowd, he exclaimed:

"What! a few drops of rain discompose you! What if they were, as we all deserve, drops of fire and brimstone?" and for another hour he poured forth his soul in fervid torrents of exhortation and warning, and the result was the conversion of about five hundred souls. Sunday night had been spent in prayer, and here was the answer; and this work of grace overflowed through all the surrounding country. One said, "Was it not a great sermon we heard?" another said, "I never heard the like of it!" This was not the way to prepare the people for Prelacy.

Livingston, whose services were so blessed upon this occasion, was, of course, an especial mark for the shafts of prelatic enmity. Called by the people of Torpichen to be their pastor, he was hunted thence by Spotswood, because he would not subscribe the Articles of Perth. But, as in earlier days, when these holy men were scattered abroad by persecution, they went everywhere preaching the Word, and so the holy fire was spread by the very efforts made to extinguish it. Livingston and Blair, and Rutherford and Douglass, and Gillespie and Dunbar, and Hogg and Dickson, and many other like holy clouds, driven to and fro by the winds of persecution, dropped gracious showers on many a thirsty field, and the wilderness was made glad for them and the desert blossomed as the rose.

Thus it is that when the enemy comes in like a flood the Lord lifts up *his* standard against them. Charles and his minions were adjusting the laws, creating and filling offices and girding their loins for victory, but God, through his ministers, was at the same time deepening the faith of the people, feeding their hunger for the bread of life, and, by this very feeding, increasing that hunger and deepening their resolves to turn the anticipated victory of their foes into overwhelming discomfiture!

THE MINE PREPARING.

Before the keystone of the prelatic arch was laid, Charles determined to pay a visit to the scene of his future triumph. And taking with him his evil genius, Laud, on the 17th of May, 1633, he set out from London, his train consisting of "thirteen noblemen—the vice chamberlain, secretary of state, master of the prince's purse, two bishops, a clerk of the closet, two gentlemen ushers of the prince's chamber, six chaplains, two physicians, two surgeons, one apothecary, sixty-one yeomen of the guard, eight cooks, seventeen musicians," and others, in all about five hundred—and swept northward through England with the state of an emperor. At length, on Saturday, the 15th of June, he entered Edinburgh by the West Port, and was welcomed with that enthusiasm so easy to worshippers of royalty and so hard for simple republicanism to understand. On Tuesday he was inaugurated in the midst of ceremonies that too ominously reminded the Scottish masses of the meretricious gewgawry of Rome—bishops arrayed in long, silken, embroidered robes, with white rochets, lawn sleeves and loops of gold—an altar on which were placed two chandeliers and two unlighted wax tapers and an empty silver basin, and behind it a rich tapestry on which a crucifix was embroidered, the bishops as they passed bowing the knee. Spotswood set the crown on the king's head, while the poor archbishop of Glasgow, who had not decked himself with becoming tinsel, was violently pulled from his seat by order of the lamb-like Laud.

Charles had no reason to be dissatisfied with his welcome, and the apparent enthusiasm went far to deceive him as to the real feelings of the people, multitudes of whom wept or scowled in their hearts while smiles covered their faces.

The next day the Parliament assembled, the members marching in grand procession in company with his majesty up High street, through the outer door of the high Tolbooth, the king entering first and sitting down upon his tribunal, and lords and bishops following. The king had already laid his plans to secure if possible unopposed assent to his measures. Ten Englishmen, Laud among them, were introduced into the privy council. The Lords of the Articles embraced those most subservient to the king. The Parliament, by its first act, granted Charles the largest subsidy ever yet given to a Scottish king. And then was introduced "An act anent his majesty's royal prerogative and apparel of churchmen"—a bit of kingcraft combining the two, so as to compel assent to or rejection of both. The Assembly was only too willing to allow anything in the way of prerogative, but to swallow the whole wardrobe of prelatic millinery was a little too much. The earl of Rothes called for a division of the act, and expressed his readiness to vote for the prerogative clause. The aged Lord Melville exclaimed, "I have sworn with your father and the whole kingdom to the Confession of Faith, in which the innovations intended in these articles were abjured." Charles, taken by surprise, retired for a while, and, returning, ordered the members to vote without debate. Rothes attempting, however, to show that the second clause was opposed to the liberties of the Church, the king silenced him, and drawing forth a list he exclaimed:

"I have your names all here, and I shall know to-day who will not do me service."

The question was then put, and Rothes voted "not content." His manly example was followed by fifteen earls and lords, several barons and forty-four commissioners of counties and burghs, constituting a decided majority. This the king must have known, for he held the list in his hand and marked the votes himself. But the sycophantic clerk, seeing an opportunity of buying royal favour at the cheap price of a falsehood, affirmed that the motion was carried, and the king, with the regard for veracity and honesty that characterized the Stuart race, confirmed the report of the clerk. Rothes affirmed the contrary, but the king declared that the vote must stand unless Rothes would accuse the clerk of falsifying the record, which was a capital offence, and subjected the accuser to the penalty of death if he failed to make good the charge. Rothes declined the perilous duty. Thus, through falsehood, in league with despotism, the act became a law.

The enthusiasm with which the Scotch had hailed the king's arrival now gave place to scowls and murmurs. Even the king did not fail to perceive the change, which drew from Bishop Leslie the comforting remark:

"The Scots are like the Jews—they cry 'Hosanna!' one day and 'Crucify him!' the next.

The lords, disgusted at the treatment they had

undergone, drew up a supplication to the king, explaining their conduct and remonstrating against the way in which their deliberations had been overawed. But the king refused to look at it, but proved afterward that he neither forgot nor forgave their manliness.

The oppressed ministers also came together at Edinburgh to consult upon a proposition to petition the king and Parliament for a redress of grievances. A petition was accordingly drawn, entitled "Grievances and petition concerning the disordered state of the Reformed Church within the realm of Scotland." This petition the clerk-register, a fierce prelatist, with quiet insolence put in his pocket. Another was then drawn, in which the former was alluded to, and Mr. Thomas Hogg presented it in person to the king. He looked over it, and let it pass without farther notice. Deeply wounded by such treatment, the ministers waited on the members of Parliament, and found many of the influential members quite ready to listen to them. The king's conduct now became the subject of general and angry discussion, and the public mind began to heave with half-stifled indignation. Hounded on by the prelates, his majesty not only took no pains to conceal his dislike of the lords who had voted against his measure in Parliament, but, by his disdainful treatment, made them for ever his enemies. Among other bits of royal courtliness, when Rothes and others had gathered two thousand horsemen splendidly equipped to greet the king along his proposed line of advance through the country, Charles kept them waiting for hours, and then contemptuously avoided them by taking a byway.

At length, having succeeded during his stay in Scotland in filling the great body of the nobles and people with aversion, he went back to England to encounter the scowls with which his arbitrary temper and tyrannical schemes had clothed the brows of his English subjects.

As if to make sure that his Scottish subjects should not forget his insulting conduct, he determined to set up a monument to keep it in their remembrance. Accordingly, he erected Edinburgh into a separate bishopric; and William Forbes, full of prelatic hauteur, was honoured with the mitre. A new broom sweeps clean, and this broom, new or old, would leave no Presbyterian dust within sight of his palace. The king had honoured him, and he would gratify the king, and at once he laid every minister within reach of his power, who could be cowed to submission, on the Procrustean bed of the Perth articles, and elongated or amputated him to suit its dimensions. And, in the weakness of poor human nature, many submitted, but in the strength of Christ many resisted; and not only resisted, but boldly, in the name of God, warned the proud prelate of the divine wrath for thus crushing the conscience of the saints. Nor was the warning groundless, for, ere he had time by persecution to rebuke his rebukers, after flaunting his robes about ten weeks in the face of the people, he was called to exchange them for his shroud.

And now, as if the fire of indignation kindled in Scotland during his inauspicious visit was in danger of dying out Charles managed to heap fresh fuel on the flame by one of those acts in which the Stuarts were so skilled. Lord Balmarino had procured a copy of the petition and remonstrance presented to the king on the matter of his treatment of Parliament in the passage of the "Prerogative and Apparel Act," and retained it in possession, hoping by softening some of its expressions yet to make it productive of relief. For this purpose he entrusted it to a legal friend to examine it and suggest modifications, under pledge to allow no eye but his own to see it. This friend showed it to Hay of Naughton under like promise of secresy. Hay stole a copy and hastened with it to Spotswood; and Spotswood, full of unholy zeal, mounted his horse on Sunday morning and flew post-haste with it to London, announcing the fearful tidings that the lords were yet bent on the crime of petitioning; and the king, to Spotswood's joy, at once resolved on wreaking vengeance upon Balmarino. The zeal of Spotswood in this matter is explained by the fact that Balmarino's estates consisted largely of lands once the property of the Church, and could the latter be condemned for seditious practices, the archbishop's purse might be replenished. There was a law in Scotland making it a capital offence to sow dissension between the king and the government, or even to know, without disclosing the fact, the author of any such seditious matter. Under this law Spotswood and Charles determined that Balmarino should lose his head. To the earl of Traquair, lord treasurer, an able man and an eloquent speaker, and unhindered by any excessive tenderness of conscience, the management of the trial was entrusted. To make the matter sure, this unscrupulous contriver managed to secure such a jury as he thought he could trust, and besides this got appointed as assessors to the justice-general several of the personal foes of the accused. Balmarino pleaded his own cause, telling the whole story about the petition. While the verdict was under consideration, Gordon of Buckie, a very aged man, who in earlier days had displayed daring ferocity of character, rose and said:

"This is a matter of blood, and would lie heavy on them as long as they lived. 'I in my youth was drawn in to shed blood, for which I obtained the king's pardon, but it cost me much more to obtain that of God. It has given me many sorrowful hours, both by night and day.'

"The tears, as he spoke, rolled down his furrowed cheeks, and for a time the chill of sympathetic horror held the guilty conclave silent." At length, after much discussion, seven of the jury voted for acquittal and seven for condemnation. Traquair gave the casting vote of guilty, and the sentence of death immediately followed, its execution being delayed till the pleasure of the king could be known.

An intense interest was excited in the public mind by this iniquitous trial, and when the result was known a storm of indignation burst from the lips of men. Secret meetings were held, at which it was resolved either to force the prison and set the condemned man at liberty, or, if this failed, to revenge his death by taking the lives of the judges and jurors who condemned him, and to set fire to their houses. The wretch Traquair, perceiving the danger, hastened like a coward to the king and declared that though Balmarino deserved death, yet his execution, in the present state of Scotland, would be replete with danger, and begged for his pardon; and the king, having in England as much on his hands as he could well manage, reluctantly withdrew his hand from the throat of his victim, and granted him a pardon.

But the mischief had already been wrought. The people had been certified beyond all room for doubt of the tyrannical arbitrariness of the king, who could brook not even the opposition that took the form of humble supplication; and they had been compelled to see that his majesty could be satisfied with nothing but the subjection of the realm to English Prelacy. Even the lords who abominated the rigid moralities of Presbyterian rule were compelled to acknowledge to themselves that even this was infinitely preferable to the dominion of those who, while they easily tolerated all moral iniquities in others, were themselves the malignant foes of all freedom, civil and religious.

To the ever-growing indignation of nobles and people, however, the prelates were judicially blinded. Reluctantly releasing Balmarino, they now set themselves to procure a book of canons for the government of the Church, and a liturgy for its form of worship. From such a step Spotswood and the more cautious prelates shrunk with well-grounded fear. But, encouraged by Laud, the more reckless carried the day. Some wished to transfer the English system bodily to Scotland, but yielding to the suggestion that the simple fact that the scheme came from England would increase the probabilities of resistance, they agreed that a framework should be shaped in Scotland and transmitted to England for revision under the eye of Laud and his coadjutors. In the mean time, Spotswood, on the death of the former chancellor, secured his own appointment to that office, while Maxwell, bishop of Ross, was made lord treasurer, and nine prelates were made members of the privy council.

Mistaking the sullen gloom of calm, deep-lying discontent and indignation for brokenness of spirit and hopeless submission, the prelates carried matters with a high hand and an outstretched arm. Inquisitorial courts, subordinate to the High Commission, were erected. By one of these courts Alexander Gordon, of Earlston, was fined and banished because he opposed the settlement of a minister repudiated by the parish; and because Robert Glendinning, seventy-nine years old, would neither conform to the wishes of the persecuting party nor admit an innovator into his pulpit, and because the magistrates would hear and would not incarcerate their beloved pastor, both magistrates and pastor were sent to prison. And feeling themselves firm in the saddle, with haughty superciliousness the prelates rode sneeringly over "dissenters," lay and clerical.

In April of 1635 a convocation of prelates met in Edinburgh to give shape to that important engine of oppression, the Book of Canons. It was high time that Presbyterianism be removed, root and branch, for, till this was done, Charles could not sleep with a quiet conscience, the prelates could not exult in a complete triumph, nor could either king or prelate be quite easy from the fear of evil. Bishops Ross, Galloway, Dunblane and Aberdeen having done their best upon the book, Maxwell posted with it to London, that it might receive what finishing touches it needed at the hands of Laud and two other English prelates; and then brought back the treasure, accompanied with an order from the prerogative royal issued under the great seal, bearing date 23d of May, 1635, enjoining its strict observance on all the dignitaries and presbyteries of the Church of Scotland. This book subverted the whole constitution of the Church. It excommunicated all who denied the king's supremacy in matters ecclesiastical, and who should say that the Book of Common Prayer, which somebody was going some day to write, was contrary to Scripture, and all who should assert that Prelacy was unscriptural. It enjoined all ministers to adhere to the liturgy *yet to be written*, on pain of deposition. It decreed that no General Assembly should meet but by order of the king; no ecclesiastical matter discussed but in the prelatic courts; no private meetings, conventicles, presbyteries or sessions held for expounding Scripture, and that on no public occasion should a minister pray but from the book! Minute arrangements were also decreed respecting forms and ceremonies, fonts and altars and ornaments, and whatever "other fooleries Laud's busy brain could devise or fantastic Rome suggest;" and, to cap the climax, all this was said to be compiled from former acts of the General Assembly!

Verily, now Scotchmen and Scotch Presbyterianism must have become something other than what they had been in the days of Knox and the Melvilles, or this book will make a stir among them! And indeed it was indignantly condemned in terms the most unsparing, while many of the nobles secretly exulted at its glaring offensiveness, knowing as they did that the Scottish neck could never be made to bow to such a yoke. The mass of the people looked upon it as popish in its nature and as the entering wedge of Popery itself. But the general hostility, instead of at once breaking forth in popular tumult, only fed itself upon the fuel and stored up force for the hour of need.

The year following the publication of the Book of Canons was spent by the prelates in possessing themselves of every possible instrument of civil and ecclesiastical power, and by their persecuted victims in pleading at the throne of grace, and teaching the people the condition of things and the nature of the present and impending conflict. In the scramble for official position and emolument the prelatists began to snarl at and bite each other. Traquair, who, by his casting vote, in heart had murdered Balmarino, and Maxwell, the new-fledged prelatic zealot, quarrelled over the office of lord high treasurer, and thenceforward became bitter and irreconcilable foes. While these contests went on the Book of Canons was in a measure lost sight of, but anti-presbyterian zeal soon revived, and ere long the liturgy which Charles had, in advance, enjoined upon the Church was framed by Ross and Dunblane, on the model of the English Prayer-book, and of course transmitted to Laud for revision. Having made it as nearly popish as he thought Scotland would bear, he remitted it to his faithful imitators across the border. A royal proclamation also followed, commanding all faithful subjects to receive with reverence and conform themselves to the public form of religious service therein contained.

The keystone was now let into the arch. The various arbitrary acts of the king, warmly carried out by the prelates, crowned by the Book of Canons, had remodelled the government of the Church, and the liturgy had done the same for its form of worship; and now, at last, the labour of two reigns was completed, and the Scottish Church was lying submissive under the heels of Charles and Laud! NOT YET!

THE IMPENDING CRISIS.

If a strange seed is put into the hand, the recipient must possess a strange power of insight, or be master of a marvellous process of analysis, if he can determine what contents lie close-folded in its little bosom. And the crisis now impending in Scotland was a seed destined to evolve a marvellous vegetation—a tree from whose prolific boughs the whole world was to gather a delicious and healthful fruitage. To comprehend the contents of this seed we must take into view the political situation into which Charles I., helped on by wily, unscrupulous coadjutors, had thrust himself.

Charles had inherited to the full the despotic spirit and principles of James. This spirit had been inflamed and these principles urged to high development both by the character of contemporaneous governments and the mad zeal of sycophantic advisers, and, above all, by the inflated notions of divine royal right instilled into his mind by his prelatic adulators.

At this time the government of France was in the hands of Cardinal Richelieu. On his accession to power, this able and unscrupulous ecclesiastic had formed the purpose to make the crown thoroughly, absolutely despotic. In pursuance of this scheme, he seized, tortured, threw into prison or put to death all who ventured in any way to withstand him, and at length climbed to complete success, and delivered the nation, bound hand and foot, into the hands of the king.

Upon this millennial condition of affairs in France Charles looked with envious eye, and longed for the hour when the Anglican spirit should be constrained to bow to the despotic rigours of Gallic rule. It vexed his royal soul beyond endurance that he should be hampered and hindered in the execution of his own august will, while his brother in France was revelling in a power worthy of the name. Impertinent Parliaments and a stubborn people were always in his way. The English people unfortunately had been born and bred in the air of constitutional freedom, and what was bred in the bone it was hard to get out of the flesh. But a consummation so desirable surely could not be impossible. But to reach it he must have money, and little or no money could he lay hands on, except as it was voted to him by a free Parliament, and this Parliament was too shrewd to volunteer, and too bold to be overawed, and too powerful to be coerced into a vote for fetters to bind its own limbs. Thus, finding that Richelieuism was impossible in England, except in spite of Parliament, he resolved to dispense with that awkward institution. He accordingly dissolved it, and proceeded to levy taxes by his own royal authority. But the cow proving very restive, and yielding milk very reluctantly and in very small quantities, he was constrained to try another Parliament, and finding it more intractable than the former, he dissolved it, and by violence and arbitrary imprisonment proceeded to levy new taxes. He billeted soldiers on the people, and substituted here and there martial law for regular legal jurisprudence. Again, under stress of necessity, he convoked Parliament, and finding it proof alike against threats and bribes, he put his constitutional dissimulation into exercise and made liberal promises, and bound himself, even by law, under his own signature, to raise no more money without the consent of the houses, to imprison no more but under process of law and to refrain from coercion by courts-martial. Parliament was filled with joy; but in three weeks, his duplicity becoming manifest, Parliament remonstrated and was again angrily dissolved; and now, for the first time in English history, and so far also in the worst time for the monarch, Charles set himself systematically to make himself a thorough despot, and from 1629 to 1640 no Parliament was called. The king had covenanted with himself to become lord and master in Church and State.

Louis of France had one Richelieu; Charles of England had two—Laud and Wentworth.

Thomas Wentworth afterward earl of Strafford, was now about forty years of age. Of infirm health, he was petulant and irascible. Unscrupulous and merciless, of great abilities, commanding eloquence and of undaunted courage, he was peculiarly fitted to do well the work the king desired at his hands. Having been also a distinguished leader of the opposition, "he perfectly understood the feelings, the resources and the policy of the party to which he had lately belonged, and he had formed a vast and deeply meditated scheme which very nearly confounded even the able tactics of the statesmen by whom the House of Commons had been directed. To this scheme, in his confidential correspondence, he gave the expressive name of *Thorough.* His object was to do in England all and more than all that Richelieu was doing in France—to make Charles a monarch as absolute as any on the continent; to put the estates and personal liberty of the whole people at the disposal of the Crown; to deprive the courts of law of all independent authority, even in ordinary questions of civil rights between man and man, and to punish with merciless rigour all who murmured at the acts of the government, or who applied, even in the most decent manner, to any tribunal for relief against those acts. This was his aim; and in Ireland, where he was viceroy, he actually succeeded in establishing a military despotism, and was able to boast that in that island the king was as absolute as any prince in the whole world could be."

The other member of the English triumvirate was William Laud, archbishop of Canterbury, a little, choleric, unscrupulous man, who hesitated at no measures, however unjust and cruel, that promised realization of his schemes. When, in Scotland with the king, the magistrates of Perth presented him with the freedom of the burgh, and, as usual on such occasions, tendered him the oath of adherence to the Protestant religion, with characteristic superciliousness he replied:

"It is my part to exact an oath for religion from you, rather than yours to exact one from me." And when once the Reformation was mentioned, he replied:

"Reformation! Better say Deformation!"

He was a great dreamer. In his diary he wrote: "Sunday night I did dream that the lord keeper was dead; that I passed one of his men that was about a monument for him; that I heard him say that his lower lip was infinitely swelled and fallen. This dream did not trouble me." Again he dreamed that he was reconciled to the Church of Rome.

He was a most zealous persecutor, and under him Dr. Alexander Leighton, father of Archbishop Leighton, was condemned in the Star Chamber to have his nose slit, his ears cut off, and to be whipped from Newgate to Aldgate and thence to Tyburn, and kept eleven years in prison. Respecting him, Macaulay writes:

"Of all the prelates of the Anglican Church, Laud had departed farthest from the principles of the Reformation and drawn nearest to Rome. His passion for ceremonies, his reverence for holidays, vigils and sacred places, his ill-concealed dislike of the marriage of ecclesiastics, the ardent and not altogether disinterested zeal with which he asserted the claims of the clergy to the reverence of the laity, would have made him an object of aversion to the Puritans, even if he had used only legal and gentle means for the attainment of his ends. But his understanding was narrow and his commerce with the world had been small. He mistook his own peevish and malignant moods for emotions of pious zeal. Under his direction every corner of the realm was subjected to a constant and minute inspection. Every little congregation of separatists was tracked out and broken up. Even the devotion of private families could not escape the vigilance of his spies. Such fear did his rigour inspire that the deadly hatred of the Church, which festered in innumerable bosoms, was disguised under an outward show of conformity. The bishops of several extensive dioceses were able to report to him that not a single dissenter was to be found within their jurisdiction."

Thus in Ireland and England the system of "thorough" was pretty thoroughly realized. Church and State lay handcuffed before the throne. "The judges of the common law, holding their situations during the pleasure of the king, were scandalously obsequious."

The two great additional instruments of oppression were the Star Chamber for political and the High Commission for religious inquisition. Through them the government was able "to fine, imprison, pillory and mutilate without restraint." A council at York under Wentworth "was armed, in defiance of law by a pure act of prerogative, with almost boundless power over the northern counties. All these tribunals insulted and defied the authority of Westminster Hall. There was hardly a man of note in the realm who had not personal experience of the harshness and greediness of the Star Chamber, and the tyranny of the council of York had made the Great Charter a dead letter to the north of the Trent."

With so firm and terrible a grasp did Charles now hold his subjects down. They were, indeed, sufficiently restive under the yoke. Irritation inflamed the public mind, but "men had become accustomed to the pursuits of peaceful industry, and, exasperated as they were, they hesitated long before they drew the sword."

"This was the conjuncture at which the liberties of our country were in the greatest peril. The opponents of the government began to despair of the destinies of their country, and many looked to the American wilderness as the only asylum in which they could enjoy civil and religious freedom."

All that was now wanted to seal the destiny of freedom in Europe for many (and who can say how many?) a long day, was simply time—time to consolidate the despotism—time to familiarize the minds of the people with its sway, with the new methods in which Charles was becoming rapidly skilled of securing revenue—time, above all, to establish a standing army, which careful economy and avoidance of foreign wars would soon enable the king to support. Every passing day was hurrying the English Richelieu toward his goal. Indeed, even now the king could look almost without envy toward his brother despots on the Continent.

There was, however, one—insignificant to be sure, but still one—Mordecai sitting in the king's gate, who must be humbled, and that was Scotch Presbyterianism, or the little that was left of it. It was not to be tolerated that, with England and Ireland crouching at the foot of the throne, this northern bull of Bashan should toss his head defiantly and refuse to submit to the yoke. But the Book of Canons and the Liturgy, now to be made the law of Scotland, would supply all that was lacking to complete success; then farewell, freedom—then all hail, despotism!

But will this Presbyterianism submit? More than once during the reign of Elizabeth, when continental alliances in league with deep-laid conspiracy among the English Papists had prepared the way for the overthrow of the Reformation, the whole scheme had been thwarted by this same Scotch Presbyterianism. More than once naught had been wanting for the return of the Papacy to her old dominion in England but a highway for invasion through Scotland; but Presbyterianism forbade, and the billows recoiled to break themselves in impotant wrath upon the shores whence they were first precipitated. And now the time has come for another trial of her strength and spirit. It was now to be seen whether, weakened and broken as she seemed to be by protracted and cruel persecution, she would meekly submit, or whether she would rise in her might and fling Prayer-book and Canons, king and prelate into the sea, and, as she had in other times saved the Reformation, now save the liberties of the world! With Charles and Laud the suggestion of serious resistance was preposterous. Of course Scotland will submit! "Where," exclaimed the English Rabshakeh, "where are the gods of those who have opposed us? I have removed the bounds of the people, and have robbed their treasures and put down their inhabitants, and there was none that moved the wing, or opened the mouth, or peeped. As my hand hath found England and Ireland, so shall my hand find Scotland also."

And so indeed it seemed. The two books had been proclaimed and published as the law of church government and worship, and what opposition was shown had expended itself in impotent murmurs and frowns. Instead of violent outbreak, there was naught but apparent meek-spirited submission.

THE EXPLOSION.

The advance of the king toward "Thorough" in the Church of Scotland had been continuous and sufficiently rapid. Taking up the work where his father had left it, he had pressed, in every possible way, subscription to the Perth Articles—had laid his plans for the revocation of the Church lands to secure thereby a revenue with which to reward and support his faithful creatures, the prelates—had largely remodelled the government, displacing from public office all who loved liberty and the national religion, and filling their places with men eager to carry his plans into execution—had established a Scottish Star Chamber and High Commission—had visited Scotland and ridden roughshod over all who had shown any symptoms of opposition—had issued the Book of Canons, and had now proceeded to the final act of the drama in the proclamation of the Liturgy.

The mere proclamation, however, of this offensive instrument of tyranny had been followed by no outburst of popular indignation, for the Liturgy had not yet been printed off for distribution. And the apparent apathy of the people served to deepen the conviction in the minds of Laud and Charles that opposition was over and submission complete. Some of the more wary prelates, however, being nearer the scene of action and more familiar with the temper of the Scottish mind, were unable to blind themselves to the signs of a gathering tempest. They knew too well that among that people apparent hesitancy might indicate, instead of submission, a quiet, resolute gathering up of the powers for a tiger-leap into the midst of the prelatic camp. Among a people largely imbued with Anglo-Saxon spirit great national upheavings do not begin in a day. Such a people is neither unthinking nor impulsive. Of all styles of human character it is patient and enduring. It scans great measures long and well ere it issues the decree for change. With amazing patience it weighs great principles in the balance of meditation, and endures the lack or lopping off of minutes if only fundamental principles are left to germinate and bear fruit in coming better days. But though an ox to bear, once aroused it is like a lion coming up from the swellings of Jordan. And when once, the cause manifestly adequate and the necessity resistlessly urgent, it has girded on the harness, it will rarely put off that harness again until satisfied that an end has been reached worthy of the sacrifice wrung from it in the execution of its purpose. A Greek or Gallic community will burst into revolution one day, and then undo all their work the next; but a people such as that of which we speak, like the mills of the gods, if it grinds slowly is pretty sure to grind fine.

And the grindings of this mill were already heard by the Scottish Prelacy. In May a few copies of the Liturgy quietly stole out to the light, and found way into hands that set its provisions between the New Testament on the one hand and the ancient system of Scottish worship on the other, and the result was anything but favorable to the Liturgy. And now, to forestall opposition by intimidating possible opposers, an order of privy council appeared empowering the prelates to "raise letters" of outlawry against ministers who should show reluctance to receive this Liturgy, and commanding them to procure two copies for use in each parish within fifteen days after the order came to hand, on pain of being held and treated as rebels against the king and the law. Over this order even the council quarrelled, the only two lay members present against eight bishops refusing to vote, on the sufficient ground that they had not even seen the book. The book, in the mean time, was keenly scrutinized and ably criticised both in and out of the pulpit, and the people saw that it was the popish mass under a so-called Protestant imprimatur.

But now, for some reason, a strange delay in the action of the persecutors intervened. The day on which the new book was to have been introduced into the pulpits was allowed to pass by. Where is "Thorough?" What is the matter with the zealots? The truth was that there was division in the camp, not unaccompanied by fear in the bosoms of the captains. This delay was diligently employed by the Presbyterians for the further enlightenment of the public mind on the nature and significance of the crisis. Some of the leaders met at Edinburgh to arrange plans of procedure in the exigency.

But what courage could not do covetousness could, and lust of gold precipitated the explosion.

Spotswood was scheming to pocket the whole of the tithes of the abbey of St. Andrew's, and thus greatly augment his own income by diminishing that of others, and especially that of the duke of Lennox and the earl of Traquair, the treasurer. Traquair, who had not forgotten the efforts of the proud prelates to drive him from office, now saw with fresh indignation their scheme to afflict his purse, and by exerting all his influence at court he secured an order from the king to stay, at least for a time, this procedure of the archbishop. Accordingly, Spotswood, accompanied by his brother in chagrin, Lindsay, the archbishop of Glasgow, resolved to hasten to London for redress at the hands of the king. But what plea would be most likely to win the royal ear? They must not fail, else Traquair would triumph, and, what was not to be endured, they would lose the purse at which they grasped. If then, they said, we can only tell the king that the Liturgy is enthroned in Scotland, that "Thorough" is inaugurated, that the Scottish masses are meekly saying Amen in the house of God to prayers read to them by prelates and prelatic ministers, Laud will be on our side and the king cannot resist. Thus while wisdom hesitated and courage hesitated, covetousness drew up and issued the decree that on the following Sabbath notice should be given that one week from that day—viz., July 23, 1637—the Liturgy would be introduced into all the churches.

During the intervening week the long-continued silence was broken. The city was agitated by a swelling commotion that reached to every hearthstone and to every faithful heart. Pamphlets were passed from hand to hand, discussions were heard, condemning the Liturgy as a piece of papistry, and the prelates for foisting it upon the people without sanction from either Parliament or Assembly. Numerous meetings for consultation and prayer were held throughout the realm. Cries of ardent supplication went up to heaven in many a closet, in many a family circle, for help in this solemn and trying hour, "and the low murmur of indignant Scotland's voice began to be heard like the awakening thunder on far distant hills or the deep sound of the advancing tide."

The day came—big with the fate of Scotch Presbyterianism. Submission now would fix the yoke securely upon its neck for many a long day to come. In Edinburgh the public eye was chiefly fixed upon the cathedral church of St. Giles. Thither swarmed the crowds on that memorable Sabbath, packing the church in every part. A profound, melancholy solemnity brooded over the assembly. The dean of Edinburgh entered the pulpit book in hand and surplice on his person. The book was opened, the dean began and Jenny Geddes responded. Her stool flew through the air. The tempest broke—the long-gathering, long-smothered tempest—and it stormed and hailed outcries and missiles, and St. Giles became a bedlam. The prelates fled, pursued by the long-insulted, shamefully-oppressed people.

Through the next day the commotions continued, drawing from the privy council a proclamation prohibiting all tumultuous assemblages under pain of death, and enjoining magistrates to use their utmost diligence to apprehend those engaged in the riot of the preceding day. Edinburgh was laid under episcopal interdict. Neither preaching nor public praying was allowed upon week-days, and all public worship was suspended on the Sabbath.

Scottish Presbyterian writers, with a solicitous loyalty, strive to make out that this riot was a mere unpremeditated outburst of popular wrath, confined to the populace. And no doubt this was not just the way which grave divines would have chosen for the utterance of their dissent. No doubt they withheld their hands from flinging church-stools and their lips from coarse and vulgar vociferations. But just as little is it to be doubted that all of them rejoiced in the evidence thus afforded of the stern, unbending opposition of the masses to the Liturgy, and also that the wisest and gravest of them were sworn in their own souls to resist its imposition unto death. While the prelates were either cowering in fear or engaged in mutual recriminations, tidings of the Edinburgh outburst flew like wildfire through the realm, giving the welcome signal for universal revolt. The people saw in it "the cloud like a man's hand rising out of the sea, soon to cover all the skies and descend in showers of new life and energy. The thrilling fervour of the people told their long-oppressed ministers that the day of deliverance was drawing near, and that they had now but to guide that strong national feeling which was rising in its might to burst through every barrier. Nor were *they* wanting in their duty to the people, to themselves and to the Church of their fathers in this momentous crisis."

Everywhere the imposition of the Liturgy was resisted. Alexander Henderson—a name ever thence venerated among Presbyterians—hastened to Edinburgh to petition for release from the odious mandate, and there met commissioners from various interior presbyteries sent up upon the same errand. On the 22d of August their petitions were presented, accompanied with letters from noblemen and gentlemen from all parts of the country, urging attention to the petitions. The council, now aware of the actual feeling of the people, answered them respectfully, though falsely, that the charges respecting the book extended no farther than to the buying of it—as if the king, Laud and other prelates had only meant to become a great publishing firm and had taken this mode of vending the stock on hand. The council then wrote to the king, informing him of the unwelcome fact that the attempt to enforce the Liturgy scheme was too full of peril to be further pressed, and leaving it to his royal wisdom to determine how the present storm might be allayed. But the king was not one of the temporizing kind. He bade his hirelings onward. The Presbyterians flocked from all parts of the country to Edinburgh, and in three days twenty-four noblemen, many barons, a hundred ministers, commissioners from sixty-six parishes and from many of the chief burghs, and many gentry, were there, girded with true Scottish resolution to defend the national religion. The whole kingdom was aroused, and the gathered hosts united in one formidable petition for redress. This petition was presented to the council and sent to the king.

Other papers were drawn up expressing the opinions and sentiments of united Scotland. Opposition on the part of the city provost provoked further popular commotions in Edinburgh, in which all classes joined. While awaiting the king's response various meetings were held, and, as the numbers were now too great to meet in one place, they separated into four divisions—noblemen, gentry, burgesses and ministers. Each meeting was opened with prayer, and then each member answered in the affirmative to the question, "Do you disapprove of the Service-book?" But instead of favourable answer from the king, there came thunders of condemnation. The Presbyterians now assumed the offensive, and laid two complaints before the privy council, accusing the prelates of being the cause of all the troubles that disturbed the nation, and denouncing the Canon and Prayer-books as superstitious, idolatrous and heretical; demanding redress of grievances and the right to worship according to the principles and doctrines of the Reformation. These papers were signed by great numbers of the nobility and gentry, and by nearly all the ministers in the realm. Opposition provoked other popular outbursts. The Presbyterians now proceeded to more thorough organization for the conflict, by forming a general commission to represent the whole Church and concentrate its revived energies. This commission consisted of all nobles willing to act, two gentlemen from each county, one minister from each presbytery and one burgess from each burgh. The commission was to assemble on extraordinary occasions, and it appointed a sub-commission to reside in Edinburgh, keep careful watch of events and communicate with the general body; the sub-commission consisting of four noblemen, four gentlemen, four ministers and four burgesses, and being styled *The Four Tables.* Besides this, one from each of the tables formed a Chief Table of Last Resort. Thus was organized an instrument of incomparable vigilance, promptness and efficiency. And now, at every turn, the persecutors found a sternly-determined Presbyterianism standing athwart its path. Traquair, with all his zeal, could not find a horse fleet enough to bear him to the place where he might issue his proclamation consigning the Four Tables to the dishonour and penalties of treason, without finding the Church in advance of him with its solemn protest. Then came the solemn renewal of the COVENANT. The 25th of February, 1638, found Gray Friars' Church, Edinburgh, packed within and encompassed without by dense masses of the faithful, listening with awe while the Covenant was read. A deep silence followed, which was broken by the stepping forward of the venerable earl of Sutherland, who, reverently bowing his head, put his name to the bond. When all within the church had signed, it was taken out and laid on a gravestone, and there, above the ashes of dead saints, multitudes put down their names amid sobs and tears; some adding the words, "till death!" and others opening a vein in the arm and signing the deed in their own warm blood! The Scottish lion had waked from his slumbers!

And at last, wrung from his cruel, despotic heart, came a decree from the king *forbidding* the enforcement of the Book of Canons, the Book of the Liturgy and the Five Articles of Perth; and then, on the 21st of November, 1638, after a dark parenthesis of thirty-six years, a *Free General Assembly!* It met at Glasgow, made Alexander Henderson moderator, and at once proceeded to the cleansing of the Augean stable. The corrupt Assemblies which had introduced Prelacy, were annulled—the Perth Articles, the Canons, Liturgy and Book of Ordination were abjured, and with them all Episcopacy excepting that of a pastor over a particular congregation. Eight of the prelates were deposed and excommunicated; four more were deposed—kirk sessions, presbyteries, synods and General Assemblies restored according to the Book of Discipline; and then, having completed the Second Reformation, and having appointed another to meet the next year in Edinburgh, the moderator dissolved the Assembly, adding these words: "*We have now cast down the walls of Jericho; let him that rebuildeth them beware of the curse of Hiel the Beth-elite!*"

Thus the insignificant—almost ludicrous—missile from the hand of Jenny Geddes dealt a blow at the head of Prelacy in Scotland from which it never recovered, nor did it leave the head of civil despotism unscarred!

Tidings of the outbreak at St. Giles and the events immediately subsequent filled Wentworth with chagrin. Could Laud, the proud priest, and Charles, the—if possible—prouder king, but have kept their souls a while in patience, until "Thorough" had been well consolidated in England and Ireland

and quietly stolen in upon Scotland, all had been well. But instead of driving the steed with moderation and reason, they had goaded the poor horse to death. They had killed the bird that was laying for them the golden egg. All was now thrown into confusion, and what had been already gained was now in jeopardy. Still, Wentworth was not the man to put his hand to the plough and then look back. The Scotch must and shall submit! But for this the king must have an army, and for this he must have money, and for this he must have a Parliament. Accordingly, a Parliament was called, and, beginning to talk of grievances, was dissolved. But the king must have an army. Hence soldiers were enlisted and money exacted by force, and even by torture. His troops set out. The Scots invaded England. Murmurs broke out on all sides in the king's army, and the king was compelled to call another Parliament; and before it adjourned Wentworth and Laud were impeached and executed, and the headless trunk of Charles cast into a dishonoured grave. Thus fared it with this proud, imperious triumvirate! But the liberty of the world was saved. It fared with despotism as with the usurper Abimelech. As it was warring against Presbyterianism and went hard unto the door of the tower to burn it, a certain woman cast not a piece of a millstone, but a church-stool, upon its head, and all to brake its skull. (Judges ix. 50–54.)

As to the actual political results of that outbreak at St. Giles there is no disagreement among intelligent historians. Macaulay writes: "To this step"—that is, the effort to impose the Liturgy upon Scotland—"taken in the mere wantonness of tyranny"—a wantonness, however, which he acknowledges to have been part and parcel of the "Thorough" scheme—taken "in criminal ignorance or more criminal contempt of public freedom, OUR COUNTRY OWES ITS FREEDOM! The first performance of the foreign ceremonies produced a riot. The riot rapidly became a revolution. Ambition"—for this let us read solemn purpose to forbid King Cæsar to supplant King Jesus in his own blood-bought Church—"patriotism, fanaticism"—for this read Presbyterian loyalty—"were mingled in one headlong torrent."

Hallam writes: "What were the consequences of this unhappy innovation, attempted with that ignorance of mankind which kings and priests, when left to their own guidance, usually display, it is here needless to mention. IN ITS ULTIMATE RESULTS IT PRESERVED THE LIBERTIES AND OVER-

THREW THE MONARCHY OF ENGLAND. In its more immediate effects it gave rise to the National Covenant of Scotland, a solemn pledge of unity and perseverance in a great public cause, long since devised when the Spanish Armada threatened the liberties and religion of all Britain, and now directed against the DOMESTIC ENEMIES OF BOTH."

The able but eccentric Carlyle, in his Lectures on Heroes, writes: "A tumult in the High Church at Edinburgh spread into a universal battle and struggle over all these realms; there came out, after fifty years' struggling, what we call *the glorious revolution, a habeas corpus act*, free parliaments and much else."

We have now sketched an outline of church government as indicated in the sacred records, and shown its proper relation to that of the State. We have followed Presbyterianism in Scotland through a portion of its history in conflict with despotism, during which it won a great victory for, and earned, what it never has received, the admiration and gratitude of mankind. We have seen it moulding the Romish masses of Scotland, moving in their degradation and ignorance at the priest's beck "like dumb driven cattle," into A PEOPLE—a people instructed in their religious nature and privileges, and thus incapacitated from fawning subserviency to despotic men. We have seen how Presbyterianism could burn at the martyr's stake in the persons of its Patrick Hamiltons, George Wisharts and others, and how, in its Knoxes and Melvilles and their compeers, it could rebuke tyranny to its face, whether it came in the guise of a beautiful Queen of Scots or a wretched pedantic despot James VI., or a proud, obstinate Charles I., telling them that Jesus was King of Scotland's Kirk, and calling them "God's silly vassals." We have seen it shaping "Confessions of Faith" and "Books of Discipline," that, speaking from God's word, to-day, find loving echo in millions of hearts. We have seen it forming covenants amid prayers and tears, and signing them with warm blood from freshly-opened veins; and we have seen it, as full of patriotism as of piety, always ready to sound the alarm trumpet whenever the national liberties were threatened, goading to action the indolent if not treacherous king, and flying to arms to shed its own blood in the cause. And last, but not least, we have seen it, when the chains of despotism were forged by the English triumvirate, Charles, Laud and Wentworth, and fastened upon the limbs of prostrate England and

Ireland, bursting those bonds asunder, flinging them into the sea, and sending the world on toward enlightened freedom—"the habeas corpus act, free parliaments and much else." And now we say, God be praised for our venerable, noble New Testament Presbyterianism, and let all the people say AMEN!

APPENDIX.

"CANONS OF DISCIPLINE," *page* 84.

No less than their brethren on the Continent, the Scotch Reformers adopted the same principle, and in the "First Book of Discipline," drawn up by John Knox, Spottswood, Douglass and others, in the year 1560, and then "subscribed by the Kirk and the lords," we find these words: "It appertaineth to the people and to every several congregation to elect their minister. Altogether this is to be avoided, that any man be violently intruded or thrust in on any congregation; but this liberty with all care must be reserved to every several church, to have their votes and suffrages in the election of their ministers."

The "Second Book of Discipline," which was agreed upon in the General Assemblies of 1577 and of 1578, which contains the present discipline of the Scotch Establishment, has the following maxims: "Election is the choosing out of a person or persons most habile—suited—to the office, which vaikes—is vacant—by the judgment of the eldership and consent of the congregation to whom the person or persons is to be appointed. The liberty of election of persons called to ecclesiastical functions, and observed without interruption so long as the Kirk was not corrupted by Antichrist, we desire to be restored and to be retained within this realm."—BAPTIST NOEL, *Church and State*, Harpers' ed., p. 145.

JOHN KNOX, *page* 223.

"THE change of times has brought with it the toleration which Knox denounced, and has established the compromises which Knox most feared and abhorred; and he has been described as a raving demagogue, an enemy of authority, a destroyer of holy things, a wild and furious bigot. But the Papists whom Knox grappled with and overthrew—the Papists of Philip II., and Mary Tudor, and Pius V.—were not the mild, forbearing innocents into which the success of the Reformation has transformed the modern Catholics. When their power to kill was taken from them—when they learnt to disclaim the Inquisition—to apologize, to evade, to fling the responsibility of their past atrocities on the temper of other times, on the intrigues of kings and statesmen, or on the errors of their own leaders—then, indeed, their creed could be allowed to subside into a place among the *religiones licitæ* of the world. But the men who took from Popery its power to oppress alone made its presence again endurable, and only a sentimental ignorance or deliberate misrepresentation of the history of the sixteenth century can sustain the pretence that there was no true need of a harder and firmer hand.

"The reaction, when the work was done—a romantic sympathy with the Stuarts and the shallow liberalism which calls itself historical philosophy—has painted over the true Knox with the figure of a maniac. Even his very bones have been flung out of their resting-place, or none can tell where they are laid; and yet, but for him, Mary Stuart would have bent Scotland to her purpose, and Scotland would have been the lever with which France and Spain would have worked in England. But for Knox and Burghley—those two, but not one without the other—Elizabeth would have been flung from off her throne, or have gone back into the Egypt to which she was too often casting wistful eyes."—FROUDE, vol. x. p. 458.

DEMOLITION OF SACRED EDIFICES, *page* 237.

"SCARCELY anything in the Scottish Reformation has been more frequently or more loudly condemned than the demolition of those edifices upon which superstition had lavished all the ornaments of the chisel and the pencil. To the Roman Catholics, who anathematized all who were engaged in this work of inexpiable sacrilege, and represented it as involving the complete overthrow of religion, have succeeded another race of writers, who, although they do not in general make high pretensions to devotion, have not scrupled at times to borrow the language of their predecessors, and have bewailed the wreck of these precious monuments in as bitter strains as ever idolater did the loss of his gods. These are the warm admirers of Gothic architecture and other relics of ancient art. Writers of this stamp depict the ravages and devastations which marked the progress of the Reformation in colours as dark as were ever employed by the historian in describing the overthrow of ancient learning by the irruption of the barbarous Huns and Vandals.

"But I am satisfied that the charges usually brought

against our Reformers on this head are highly exaggerated, and, in some instances, altogether groundless. The demolition of the monasteries is, in fact, the only thing of which they can be fairly accused. Cathedral and parochial churches, and in several places the chapels attached to monasteries, were appropriated to Protestant worship, and in the orders issued for stripping them of images, idolatrous pictures and superstitious furniture, particular directions were given to avoid whatever might injure the buildings or deface any of their ordinary decorations. It is true that some churches suffered from popular violence during the ferment of the Reformation, and that others were dilapidated in consequence of their most valuable materials being sold to defray the expenses of the war in which the Protestants were involved; but the former will not be a matter of surprise to those who have attended to the conduct of other nations in similar circumstances, and the latter will be censured by such persons only as are incapable of entering into the feelings of a people who were engaged in a struggle for their lives, their liberties and their religion. Of all the charges thrown out against our Reformers, the most ridiculous is that, in their zeal against popery, they waged war against literature by destroying the valuable books and records which had been deposited in the monasteries. The state of learning among the monks at the era of the Reformation was wretched and their libraries poor; the only persons who patronized and cultivated literature in Scotland were Protestants; and, so far from sweeping away any literary monuments which remained, the Reformers were disposed to search for them among the rubbish and to preserve them with the utmost care. In this respect we have no reason to deprecate a comparison between our Reformation and that of England."—McCRIE'S *Life of Knox.*